"This excellent book is comprehensive, original and above all, authentic. Her scope includes The Worlds of Creation, The Sacred Centres, The Funerary Cities, Temples, and the Creation Cycle. I warmly recommend this book."

—Lady Olivia Robertson, Co-Founder of the Fellowship of Isis, Clonegal Castle, Enniscorthy, Irish Republic

About the Author

Rosemary Clark (Virginia) founded Temple Harakhte in 1976, a forum devoted to retrieving the religious teachings and practices of Old Kingdom Egypt. She is the author of *The Sacred Tradition of Ancient Egypt,* and guides groups to Egypt and other sacred places.

To Write to the Author

If you wish to contact the author or would like more information about this book, please write to the author in care of Llewellyn Worldwide and we will forward your request. Both the author and publisher appreciate hearing from you and learning of your enjoyment of this book and how it has helped you. Llewellyn Worldwide cannot guarantee that every letter written to the author can be answered, but all will be forwarded. Please write to:

Rosemary Clark
℅ Llewellyn Worldwide
P.O. Box 64383, Dept. 1-56718-130-9
St. Paul, MN 55164-0383, U.S.A.

Please enclose a self-addressed stamped envelope for reply,
or $1.00 to cover costs. If outside U.S.A., enclose
international postal reply coupon.

Many of Llewellyn's authors have websites with additional information and resources. For more information, please visit our website at
http://www.llewellyn.com

THE
SACRED MAGIC
OF
ANCIENT EGYPT

THE SPIRITUAL PRACTICE RESTORED

ROSEMARY CLARK

2003
Llewellyn Publications
St. Paul, Minnesota 55164-0383, U.S.A.

First Edition
First Printing, 2003

Book design based on design by Tom Lewis
Cover art © 2003 Corel
Cover design by Gavin Dayton Duffy

All photographs by the author.

Library of Congress Cataloging-in-Publication Data
Clark, Rosemary, 1948–
    The sacred magic of ancient Egypt : the spiritual practice restored / Rosemary Clark.—1st ed.
      p.   cm.
    Includes bibliographical references and index.
    ISBN 1-56718-130-9
     1. Magic, Egyptian. I. Title.

BF1591.C52 2003
133.4'3'09932—dc22   2003054622

Llewellyn Publications
A Division of Llewellyn Worldwide, Ltd.
P.O. Box 64383, Dept. 1-56718-130-9
St. Paul, MN 55164-0383, U.S.A.
www.llewellyn.com

 Printed in the United States of America on recycled paper

Other Books by Rosemary Clark

The Sacred Tradition in Ancient Egypt: The Esoteric Wisdom Revealed
(Llewellyn, 2000)

To
Bentreshyt

"Harp of gladness"

For a life well remembered

Hymn to Harakhte

Hail Harakhte, lord of the two horizons,
In your beauty, in your splendor,
On your thrones, in your radiance!

Great One, whose greatness cannot be comprehended,
Lord of the throne, who keeps secret what is hidden.
High One, whose circuit is unknown.

Greatest of powers, foremost one of the East:
How mysterious are your forms,
Though you reveal yourself in heaven each day.

I raise my arms in praise of your Ka,
You have gladdened my heart with your beauty,
All rejoice when you are seen!

You are ancestor of the living,
Guardian of those in the Duat,
You are enduring in time.

You are possessor of the royal crowns,
Custodian of the sceptres,
Keeper of all offerings in the Western land.

Sole watchman, who loathes slumber:
You shine upon the millions
With your beautiful face.

Grant that I may cross the sky with you,
And complete the task of yesterday each day.

Photo 1—Harakhte: the Great Sphinx at Giza.

CONTENTS

Chapter One, The Legacy of Ancient Egypt 1

Egypt's sacred tradition and its relevance to modern spirituality. Ancient cosmogony, beliefs of the powers inherent in nature, humanity, and spiritual beings. Sacred Science and its component disciplines: esoteric architecture, cosmic resonance, and theurgy.

Chapter Two, Esoteric Architecture 25

Sacred geography, construction, and functions of the ancient temple. Planning the modern temple with cosmic orientation, symbolic furnishings, and art. The spiritual constitution of the temple through ritual: dedication of the cardinal quarters, invocation of the elemental forces.

Chapter Three, Cosmic Resonance 83

The sacred astronomy of the ancient temple with a delineation of the Lunar, Solar, and Stellar calendars. Ceremonial events following the rhythms of the New and Full Moons, the Solar Ingresses, and cosmic tides. The dekanoi and sacred hours, understanding the "seasons" of the Neteru.

Chapter Four, Theurgy 139

Egyptian spiritual practice in the temple setting—theurgy and the sacraments. The daily ritual, ceremonies following the sacred calendars, and special rites. Ancient initiation and the fabrication of the light body.

Chapter Five, Liturgy 185

The components of ancient Egyptian ceremony and a complete Solar liturgy of twelve monthly observances, honoring the twelve Neteru of the Heliopolitan cosmogony.

Chapter Six, Ceremony 237

Twelve Hebu (festivals) that convey the benefit and special powers of the twelve Neteru in the Solar cosmogony. Healing, divination, coming of age, marriage, funerary, and offering services for the modern temple.

Chapter Seven, Transformation 313

The function of high ritual in divination, protection, and execration. The transformative ceremony of the Opening of the Mouth for animating sacred space, healing, and funerary observance. A daily practice that fulfills the initiatory tradition of ancient times.

ILLUSTRATIONS

Figures

Chapter Three

Chapter Four

Chapter Five

Chapter Six

Chapter Seven

Tables

Chapter One

Chapter Two

Photographs

ACKNOWLEDGMENTS

An individual's spiritual practice is rarely isolated, and this quest to recover the knowledge and practice of Egypt's Sacred Science and put it into tangible form has been assisted by a number of supporters and colleagues. They not only possess their own specialized knowledge in the vast realm of egyptology and ancient science, but a profound understanding of their value to the modern world.

I would like to thank Michael St. John, the man of "dekans and digits" who, like many egyptophiles around the world, possesses a special knowledge of ancient art and science, and a love for sharing it that is rarely met in academic settings.

Bernadette Brady of Astro Logos in South Australia is another specialist who combines unique astrological insights with a great depth of astronomical knowledge and practical application. She came to my aid quite generously on matters celestial. Marianne Luban served as an expert guide through the maze of ancient linguistics and history. Her imaginative skills in resurrecting the personalities and events in Egyptian chronology are a marvel and considerable resource to spiritual time travelers. And Denise Koehler of Deniart Systems in Toronto has once more made it possible to render the ancient words with the sublime artistry and accuracy of her hieroglyphic fonts.

I am grateful to Frank and Lyn Taliaferro and Lynn Gray as steadfast supporters of my work. And along the way, Arthur H. Blackwell thoughtfully gave me the keys to a sacred astronomy that opened the door to my temple and made his name live.

PREFACE

Over the centuries, much has been alluded to concerning the powers and wisdom possessed by the ancient Egyptians, in a civilization that never fails to evoke our contemplation and awe. And though some of the groundwork for understanding its profound body of knowledge has been circumscribed over time both academically and metaphysically, the realization of all its mystic promise has been for the most part an elusive goal.

The decipherment of the hieroglyphs in the nineteenth century of our era opened up a world of ancient literature that articulated Egypt's religious doctrines, moral code, and customs. From this, facets of a wisdom tradition that melded science and metaphysics unfolded through the translation of literary collections such as *The Book of Going Forth by Day, The Pyramid Texts, The Coffin Texts,* and the many detailed works on medicine, astronomy, and cosmology that gradually came to light.

These texts disclose a world view that recognized an indivisible unity among three lifestreams—the *Neteru* (gods or divine principles), the *akhiu* (spirits in nature, including the elevated souls of the deceased), and the *ankhiu* (living human beings). And by virtue of this unity, they also outline a process by which the human soul may assume divine status and know all the powers in nature, and the realms in which they exist.

Since most of these writings were discovered in tombs and funerary monuments, it was initially believed that they were intended for the dead, and that the

Egyptians held elevation of the soul to these experiences in the afterlife as the supreme accomplishment. But it soon became apparent that these writings were intended for the living as well, since many were found in the same form and style on the walls and chambers of the ancient temples. And within the literature itself are found explicit instructions to the living on reciting the spells and hymns, observing the sacred times, and performing the rites for attaining divine status while on Earth.

The praxis that is herein presented fulfills that aim. It contains all the essential elements required to comprise an effective spiritual technology—objectives, doctrines, rituals, and organization—as expressed by the Egyptians themselves.

The objectives are as real today as they were thousands of years ago—discovering the origin of our existence and realizing the full dimensions of the soul and its workings. The doctrines for accomplishing this have been articulated in the cosmogonies of the ancient temples, and preserved in the legends of the gods and their divine acts. These ideas were articulated in themes of order, continuity, and harmony—for both the mundane and the spiritual worlds in which we exist.

And while the rituals are preserved in monumental and literary form, it was the organization of the temple in ancient times that made all these elements coherent and living. We know much of their history and organization, but other forces replaced the temple as catalyst for our spiritual objectives over time—new theologies, philosophies, and governments. Despite this, the temple tradition evokes our highest aspirations and longings, as we recall the beauty and dignity of the ancient ceremonies every time Egypt is contemplated.

One might ask why the apparent remnants of an ancient religion should be of value to anyone today. Does the symbolism and world view of a past civilization have any relevance to a person living in modern times?

The answers to these objections are quite obvious. Although today we have tremendous success in the material sphere, the acquisition of spiritual wisdom is not a striving deemed important. The result is that one's personal power—the type that provides true dignity and self-mastery to an individual—is not really understood in context with the powers in nature and the universe. This, combined with the spiritually sterile atmosphere of the modern age and the unrealistic demands on our time and attention, has created a genuine yearning in many of us for the serenity reflected by the past. And so it is no wonder that many individuals involve themselves in imaginative ways with creative or contemplative endeavors—through art, historical reenactment, and the re-creation of cultural rites and religious ceremonies.

The ancient Egyptians recognized this sense, and found meaningful ways to channel it through everyday life. Temple ritual, drama, and ceremonial events employed nearly all the talents of the culture's artisans, teachers, tradesmen, and intellectuals. Without a strict division between secular and spiritual life, there were few limits on the involvement of all members of society with some aspect of the religious domain. As a result, the ancient temples became spiritual theaters, where creation was reenacted and the subsequent rhythms of nature—procreation, birth, and death—were commemorated. These events took place each year at the gods' great feasts, and each month at the ancestral tombs. And on an hourly basis, the circuit of Solar and Stellar light through the sky was marked by the hour priests to ensure the orderly passage of divine vitality. Thus, the powerful forces evoked by natural and divine acts were solemnized continuously in the temple, either through public festivals or priestly seclusion in the sanctuaries.

Many of the details of Egyptian spirituality were explored in the predecessor to this work, *The Sacred Tradition in Ancient Egypt: The Esoteric Wisdom Revealed.* But a sacred tradition must be lived to realize the benefit and vital power it possesses. This book is a guide to living that tradition in the Egyptian spirit.

Blessed is the day of homecoming,
When the doors of the Great House are open once more.

INTRODUCTION

Though no complete guide to Egyptian religious practice has come down to us in modern times, much can be discerned from the multitude of sacred texts inscribed on papyri, in temple and pyramid chambers, and on tomb walls. From these considerable remnants and the reports of ancient chroniclers, a fairly wide view of ancient spirituality and its observances is known.

At first glance these remnants reflect an approach to life that appears to represent the material concerns of all individuals—health, prosperity, and mortality. But Egypt also addresses the unspoken imperative that transcends our material needs, and this legacy is truly relevant to our spiritual life today. With an elaborate canon of religious and philosophical wisdom that is conveyed through hymns, legends, and instructions, Egypt offers an approach that inspires our appreciation for the value of existence on Earth, its purpose, and its rewards.

Whether this approach was passed down from an unknown, prehistorical source or was developed over time is not our concern here. However, it was believed by the Egyptians that their sacred tradition descended from ancient time, a beginning called *sep tepi,* "the first occasion," when all life existed consciously, harmoniously, and undivided. The return to this moment, in temple and tomb, formed the core of all ritual acts. In doing this, the experience of unity, order, and limitless perception could be regained by the soul.

The primary sources that reflect this process include the sacred texts of *The Ritual of the Divine Cult, The Opening of the Mouth,* and *The Liturgy of Funerary Offerings.*

I have referred to the hieroglyphic renditions of these texts transcribed in modern times by Ernest A. Wallis Budge. From these were derived the ceremonial elements that comprise the liturgy presented here, adapted by my own translations.

In addition, a number of hymns from the familiar *Book of Going Forth by Day* restate ceremonial passages inscribed in temples from an extensive range of historical periods; my reconstructions of this material were gleaned from Thomas George Allen's translation, *The Book of the Dead or Going Forth by Day*. For the older sacred literature, I consulted the hieroglyphic supplement to R. O. Faulkner's *The Ancient Egyptian Pyramid Texts* along with the hieroglyphic plates and translations in Alexandre Piankoff's *The Pyramid of Unas*, and Faulkner's translations of *The Ancient Egyptian Coffin Texts*.

I am also pleased to provide a restoration of two ancient rituals. *The Book of Breathings* is derived from a translation by Mark Smith, published in 1993 by the Griffith Institute, and *The Book of Hours* is adapted from a monograph by R. O. Faulkner, published by the *Journal of Egyptian Archeology* in 1954.

The ancient Egyptians called their writing *medu neter*, "divine words." Unfortunately, little is known of the pronunciation of ancient Egyptian, and in this realm we are truly limited. Hieroglyphic language is consonantal, the vowels not being known with certainty. Words that were transliterated 100 years ago by the early egyptologists have been considerably refined with more sophisticated linguistic techniques, such as comparing the sounds of existing languages related to or derived from ancient Egyptian and assigning those sounds to the hieroglyphs. However, the newer transliterations can be confusing to the layperson; i.e., the letter *j* designates the sound of "ee," formerly indicated by *y*. And so to provide a workable use of the ancient idiom, I have rendered Egyptian words in a manner that will allow the practitioner a viable re-creation of the spells and invocations.

An analytical treatment of Egypt's beliefs and practices can not convey their full meaning and power. To those who do seek the deeper realization of Egypt's legacy, this work is a blueprint for that pursuit in all of its dimensions. It is a guide to living the history of a culture that believed its sacred tradition was timeless and could lead to the spiritual awakening they regarded as *mekh neter*, "divine knowledge."

SACRED NAMES

The power of the spoken word, especially the names of the gods, was regarded as the ultimate knowledge of the theurgist in ancient Egypt. In a collection of Theban religious poems from the time of Rameses II, the secret name of Amun is described:

One falls down with terror if his ineffable name is spoken.
Not even another god can call him by it,
He whose name is hidden.
Because of this he is a mystery.
—Papyrus Leiden I: 350

In deference to this tradition, the Egyptian names, rather than the Hellenised names of the *Neteru* (male and female divine principles) are used throughout this work. To the ancients, the sacred names, words of power, and original appellations of spiritual figures convey, both in their writing and enunciation, the spirit that they engender.

Egyptian	*Greek*
Amun	Ammon, Zeus
Amunhotep (Son of Hapu)	Amenothes
Anher	Onuris
Anpu	Annubis

Egyptian	*Greek*
Anqet	Anukis
Apep	Apophis
Apuat	Ophois
Asar	Osiris
Asar Hapi	Serapis
Auset	Isis
Bakha	Buchis
Djehuti	Thoth
Hap	Apis
Harakhte[1]	Harmakhis
also: Her em Akhet	
Her em Anpu	Hermanubis
Herishef	Harsaphes
Heru Behutet[2]	Harendotes
Heru em Aakhuti[3]	Harmakhis
Heru pa khart[4]	Harpocrates
Heru Ur[5]	Haoeris
Heru[6]	Harsiesis
Het-Her	Hathor
Ihy	Harsomtus
Imhotep	Imouthes
Imset	Mestha
Khnum	Khnoumis
Maat	Mayet
Min	Chemmis, Pan

1. Horus (dweller) in the Horizon.

2. Horus of the Winged Disc.

3. Horus of the Two Horizons: the Sphinx at Giza.

4. Horus the Child.

5. Horus the Elder.

6. Horus the Younger.

Egyptian	*Greek*
Montu	Buchis
Nebt-Het	Nepthys
Nefertum	Iphtimis
Neit	Athene
Nekhebet	Eileithyia
Nem Ur	Mnevis
Pakhet	Artemis
Ptah	Hephaestos
Sah	Orion
Sekhmet-Bast	Sakhmis
Selqit	Selkis
Sept, Sopdet	Sothis, Sirius
Set	Sutekh, Typho
Shu	Sos
Sobekh	Suchos
Sokar	Sokaris
Taurt	Thoeris
Tefnut	Thphenis
Un Nefer	Onnophris
Wadjet	Buto, Edjo

PROLOGUE

The royal prince Khaemwas could ask for anything he desired, but among all the sons and daughters of Pharaoh, he sought things that few believed even existed, let alone could be among the unlimited indulgences Rameses II provided for his many children. From the sleek, sable-hued horses in the royal stables to the finely wrought vessels from the *Per Nub,* the House of Goldsmiths, every rare and beautiful object in the Two Lands of Egypt could be his for the asking.

But Khaemwas did not think of such things, because from his youth he sought the scholar's life. For as long as he could remember history was his passion, and the ancient legacy of Egypt filled him with awe. As he matured, many studious hours were spent at the palace libraries and temple scriptoriums, learning the annals of former monarchs and the wisdom of the sages.

Rameses indulged his son, encouraging him to pursue his interest without cessation. He called the *Kher Heb* priests of Amun's great house to bring the rare papyri in leather rolls and copper chests to the palace for examination, and reveal to Khaemwas all that was known of former times. But this was only the beginning of the young prince's quest. He embarked on a journey to visit all the glorious temples in Egypt to see what literary treasures they possessed, to meet with the priests and learn the secrets of every sanctuary.

The devotion of Khaemwas to these things impressed all that he met. He earnestly entered each temple and completed his study as a scribal student, going on to acquire initiation through all the grades of the Divine House. He learned the enigmatic tradition of the sanctuaries, the words that brought the god into his shrine and the acts that protected the sacred precinct.

Eventually, the prince withdrew from palace life altogether. After marrying his childhood companion Mehusekha and begetting handsome children by her, he found a home in the formidable school of Ptah at Memphis, where he was invested as high priest to oversee of all the scriptoriums in the Lower Kingdom. Here he could certainly indulge his passion, spending hours inspecting the ancient scrolls, ordering eager young scribes to copy the rare books, and strolling through the vast necropolis of the city to read the wondrous inscriptions on the great ancestral monuments.

It was during one of those casual walks one afternoon in the city of the dead that Khaemwas encountered an old sorcerer, one infrequently seen among the crumbling tombs in the dusk hours. Though he seemed to avoid the company of others who went about their business in this place, on this occasion the sorcerer approached Khaemwas and spoke unpretentiously to him.

"Venerable prince, I am told that you seek the great secrets of our ancestors and that you walk among these old tombs in the hope of finding such treasures."

"Well, what do you know of these things?" Khaemwas responded, rather surprised at the encounter. He waved his flywisk in the air to dispel the dust and scrutinized the wizened old man.

"Ah," he said knowingly. "I know much of these things. In fact, I know of a tome that you have never seen, a book written by the hand of Djehuti himself. It exists right under your nose, you know."

Khaemwas ceased waving the flywisk and looked at the man intently. "Your speech is sacrilege," he said, "The noble book you speak of has been returned to the gods because men have made poor use of it. No one knows its whereabouts."

Indeed, the book of Djehuti, divine scribe to the gods, was fabled for centuries to contain the formula for charming the wind, the spirits of the mountains and waters, and knowing the language of birds and beasts. It was also said to endow its owner with the power to see the spirits in shadow worlds, and to see Ra in the sky with his retinue of attendant divinities. These secrets were no longer known to the living, because the book was protected by Djehuti himself.

But the old sorcerer did seem to know the whereabouts of the book. He led his scholarly companion to a simple tomb, down timeworn steps hidden by a broken lintel, and through an unsealed door that looked like a solid wall. There he saw the legendary book, wrapped with the swathings of its former owner. It was so powerful that its light illuminated the whole of the chamber.

Khaemwas was overwhelmed by the discovery. Without compunction he seized the prize and clutched it in excitement, nearly overcome with a mixture of awe and joy. But as quickly as he had taken possession of the book, a ghost appeared in the shadows, warning him against his deed.

"I paid for knowing the secrets of Djehuti's book with my life, and the lives of my wife and son," the apparition declared, "You must not take it, ever!"

Khaemwas was not unnerved by the appearance of the specter, being an accomplished magician. From his occult studies and temple training, he understood that spirits could do no permanent harm to the living, though they could certainly bring havoc.

"Indeed, I shall take this book," he responded with courage. "I am a scholar and high priest, and I possess the authority to examine this artifact."

The ghost moved closer to him, but failed to deter his visitor. "Well then," he said, "You may prove yourself worthy to take it if you play a game of draughts with me and win it thereby." He pointed to a worn set of hounds and jackals on a table.

Khaemwas sat sagaciously at the gaming board, assured that he would succeed at the ghost's challenge. It was actually amusing, he thought, that a mere shade, confined to this little chamber, would try to frighten him with this bluff.

But after two losses to the ghost, he realized that the third and last play could jeopardize his conviction. He sent the sorcerer to bid one of his scribes to bring the books of magic in his library and, for good measure, the amulets of protection against nefarious powers. With the assistance of these things, he did triumph at the gaming board, and liberated the prize from its moldering cache. As he moved toward the exit of the funerary vault, the light of the book went with him, leaving the chamber in darkness.

"You will return the book!" the ghost admonished from the shadows.

But Khaemwas hurried out of the tomb, up the worn steps, and into the shadows of the twilight. Satisfied that he had acquired the prize honorably, he did not even turn to heed the words.

"You will bring it back, with a forked stick in your hand and a lighted brazier on your head!" the ghost sounded into the night.

Khaemwas was giddy with success. He immediately went to his reading chamber, lit the lamps and set to reading the aged papyrus, contemplating the divine words that were inscribed on it, reflecting on their power. It was indeed a sacred text, disclosing the knowledge of ancient times. He recited the words and charmed the wind, the spirits of the mountains and waters, and understood the language of the birds and beasts around him. Moreover, he acquired the power to see the spirits in the shadow worlds and Ra in the sky with his retinue of attendant divinities. It was marvelous.

After several days, Khaemwas went to the temple of Ptah to thank his patron for the wonderful discovery. On the steps of the pillared forecourt, he saw a procession of handsomely dressed escorts, surrounding a beautiful young woman. He moved closer, never having seen such a spectacle. Then he held his breath.

She was the most stunning female he had ever encountered. Her limbs were like gold, and her eyes reflected the light of the heavens. Around her slender waist hung a jeweled girdle that swayed with each graceful step, and her exquisite face wore the alluring smile of a goddess. Khaemwas stood mute, wondering what he could do to know this woman. Surely it was fate that brought him here today, to see her beauty and discover its promise.

He summoned one of the attendants to his side, and spoke as one senseless. "Listen to me," he said. "I have been cast of a spell by your mistress. I must know her, I must meet with her. Is there any amount of gold she is in need of, is there any wrong I might settle for her? Go quickly and tell her I will spare nothing to spend time with her."

The attendant obeyed, and in short time he returned with an answer. "My mistress is the lady Tabubu, an honorable person of priestly rank," he explained. "She asks that you go to her house at the temple in Bubastis. Only there will she consent to meet with you."

Khaemwas was overjoyed. He quickly booked passage on a boat to go north from Memphis and arrived at twilight the next day in Bubastis, full of expectation. There he entered the house of the lady Tabubu, and marveled at its great hall, with inlaid floors of turquoise and lapis lazuli. As time passed, servants brought him wine to drink and oil was rubbed on his tired shoulders. Incense filled the air and the sound of harps soothed his distraught nerves. Still later, the object of his passion finally appeared.

"I have waited long enough to accomplish what I came here for," he said in great distress. "And I will give you whatever you ask for it."

But Tabubu waved him aside. "I am an honorable person of priestly rank," she declared. "I can do nothing until you commit to me a compensation for my value, and that would be all the goods that you have title to."

"Send for the scribe. I will do so and put my seal upon it," Khaemwas answered without hesitation. Nothing would stand in the way of consummating his desire! Soon enough, a deed was made for what Tabubu asked, and he implored her to fulfill his wish.

"Now," he said, "I long to accomplish what I came here for."

Once again she held her ground. "Because I am an honorable person, I must ask that you assure me I will indeed have title to all you possess," she insisted. "To do that, you must have your children removed, so that no future claim on the property you gave me can be made by them."

"This is an abomination," her suitor opined, "but if it must be done, let it be so. Then I will have accomplished what I came here for." With that, the order was sent out to dispatch the children of Khaemwas, and he felt no blame for the deed.

Tabubu led the anxious suitor to her private chamber, where he lay on an ivory couch in expectation. He closed his eyes, feeling the waves of passion bathe his heated head, hardly believing he had arrived at this stage of fiery abandon to all he once deemed important to him. The goddess whom his lady served would reward him for his sacrifice, he assured himself.

But a terrible howl forced his eyes back open, and when he gazed again at his beloved, she dissolved in the evening light. He sat up in great alarm, looking about in confusion. His clothes were gone, the ivory couch had disappeared, and he was in a different chamber altogether. He stood in bewilderment, seized a curtain from the window to cover himself, and ran out into the hallway. There, he realized that he was in the golden palace of his father, Rameses. Pharaoh's sentries saw his anguish, and informed their master of his condition.

"Khaemwas, what state are you in?" came the voice of Pharaoh, who quickly responded to the scene.

His son poured out the saga, from finding the book of Djehuti in the old tomb in the city of the dead to becoming besotted with Tabubu and his journey to Bubastis to have her. "And now," he mourned, "I have given over the lives of my dear children for this folly and will be cursed for all time because of it."

Rameses sighed in exasperation at what he heard, but laid his hand reassuringly on the head of his son.

"Listen, Khaemwas. Your children are alive in Memphis, and no harm has come to them. I advise you to return that book to the tomb where you found it, and do so with a forked stick in your hand and a lighted brazier on your head."

The young priest blinked in realization, and quickly put on the clothes that the palace servants brought him. "I will do as you say," he said to Pharaoh, and arranged for immediate passage on a boat back to Memphis.

Khaemwas did as his father advised him, and returned to the ancient tomb in the city of the dead. With a forked stick he made his way down the worn steps, and with a lighted brazier on his head he found his way back into the dark chamber. Unwrapping the book from his carrying cloth, it gradually illumined the vault in the same manner as when he had first seen it. Thus returned, he backed out of the old tomb and returned to his library in the house of Ptah, thankful that the ordeal had cost him only his pride.

Now it is said that Khaemwas had recorded on a papyrus the formula of the book for charming the wind, the spirits of the mountains and waters, of knowing the language of birds and beasts, and of acquiring the power to see the spirits in the shadow worlds and Ra in the sky with his retinue of attendant divinities. But after he returned the book of Djehuti, he burned this papyrus, dissolved the ashes into a vessel of beer, and drank it. In this manner, he believed that no one would ever again know the secrets he had once possessed.

Chapter One

THE LEGACY OF ANCIENT EGYPT

We shall omit from our history the stories invented by Herodotus and certain other writers on the affairs of Egypt, who deliberately prefer fables to facts, and who spin yarns merely for the purpose of amusement. We shall, however, set forth the things written by the priests of Egypt in their sacred records, which we have examined diligently and minutely.
—Diodorus Siculus: *Bibliotheca Historica*, Book I: 69

The story of Khaemwas, though written of events more than 3,000 years ago, still evokes our fascination with the mystic legacy of Egypt. It speaks of an arcane doctrine believed to be lost, of mysteries buried by time. We know that in ancient times, despite hardships we can only imagine, the established spiritual traditions endowed people with the guidance and skills needed to understand the powers of their environment and live in harmony with them. But we seem not to be so equipped in the modern age, despite the advances of science and industry. This is undoubtedly why we look to past cultures like Egypt for the elusive powers and insights we miss. We are in many ways the same as Khaemwas—we desire to know our sacred heritage, to understand the secrets that everyday life conceals from us, and to discover the source of all wisdom. For these reasons, Egypt's mystic legacy continues to summon our interest.

1

What is this legacy of which so many ancients spoke? The Egyptians freely passed their legends on to travelers, as the Greek historian Diodorus Siculus (60 B.C.E.) noted. And similar narratives were consistently repeated in the literature and monumental writing of the temples and tombs. The legends pertained to their gods, royal persons, sages, and adventurers—beings who embodied the natural and supernatural forces of the world around them. Most were chronicles of metaphysical events, handed down from antiquity. But they differed from the myths of other cultures, including the Greeks, who viewed this heritage as symbolic or metaphorical imagery of natural phenomena and the universe, not factual events. The ancient Egyptians were not so philosophically rigid; they made no distinctions between legend and myth. The chronicles they inherited from antiquity were believed to be real occurrences, taking place either at an historical time when their gods inhabited the Earth or in a dimension they called "timeless time," when divine powers are directly accessible by human beings. By virtue of this, their legends were both vital and practical, because they infused past, present, and future with meaning and purpose.

Moreover, Egypt's narrative legacy embraces far more than the exploits of the gods and the acts they performed to create the manifest world. Within them are contained the canons of their art, architecture, language, and ritual—the foundations of a tradition that sustained their cultural existence for thousands of years.[1] This is probably the most powerful dimension of Egypt's legacy, because it appears to have defined the overall goals and mandates of her society—from the farm worker and fisherman to the scribe and temple priestess, and ultimately, to the seat of all temporal power, the Royal House. In all these realms, spirituality and science coalesced to produce a body of metaphysical knowledge that formed the underpinnings of Egyptian civilization.

Is it possible to retrieve this wisdom? Many have posed this question over the ages, and some of the answers have been discovered in the literary heritage of the Egyptians. Firstly, the ancient Egyptians did not see a rift between the workings of the divine and mundane spheres. The sacred encompassed the secular in their world view; the physical world—including natural phenomena and the plant and animal kingdoms—was seen as a reflection of the divine world, and everything in it possessed a divine nature. The gods manifested through the visible—human beings, trees, stars, wind and storm, even though these living things possessed an identity of their own as well. If we could express the essence of

---

1. See Appendix 1: Chronology of Ancient Egypt.

Egyptian philosophy over the thousands of years it existed, it would indisputably reflect this doctrine. A sacred text from the time of Rameses II describes this immanence of divinity in nature:

> *The soul of Shu is the air, the soul of Neheh is the rain,*
> *The soul of Ra is the primeval ocean.*
> *The soul of Asar is the ram of Mendes,*
> *The soul of Sobekh is the crocodile.*
> *The soul of every god resides in serpents,*
> *The soul of Ra is found throughout the land.*
> —The Book of the Celestial Cow, Dynasty 19

Secondly, the unity of the lifestreams, drawn together by divine vitality, is also described in many of the sacred texts at temples, tombs, and on ancient papyri—and they disclose more than a glimpse of this doctrine. Unification of the soul with the gods and natural life was a vital approach to one's spiritual identity. An early funerary inscription delineates these associations succinctly:

> *If I live or pass on, I am Asar.*
> *I enter you and appear through you,*
> *I decay in you, I spring forth from you,*
> *I descend in you, I repose on my side.*
> *The gods are living in me,*
> *As I live and grow in the emmer that sustains the exalted ones.*
> —Coffin Text #330

These beliefs were fundamental in their world view, but the mandate that arose from them was just as essential. Maintenance of the unity created by these relationships occupied the time and resources of all members of Egyptian society in a form that we most associate with Egypt—sacred ritual. This activity was performed in a clearly prescribed canon on all levels of society, and generally unaltered over the course of thousands of years of recorded history. Its consistency and continuity was based on another important belief—that their rituals were recreations of the acts of divine beings when life arose in the beginning of time. And the performance of rites was regarded not only as a high calling, but a spiritual exchange that offered countless benefits to the participant:

To the prophets, divine fathers, priests, and lectors
And all who enter Amun's temple of Ipet Sout:
By performing the rites and making the offerings,
By doing the service of the month priest,
The great god will give you life.
You will be flawless in his presence,
You will be fortified with his blessings.
　　　　　　　　—Inscription on the statue of Harwa, Dynasty 25

The Worlds of Creation

In Egyptian cosmology, the forces of creation are mirrored in nature—they are both transcendent and cyclic. In this view, all of the lifestreams, including human beings, nature, and the gods, partake of a process that ordains a return to the creative source and a reappearance in the phenomenal world, in a perpetual cycle of renewal, called *Neheh* ("forever," "eternity").

Returning to the world of creation was a theme continually emphasized in the liturgies of the temple and tomb. The powers that brought the deity into the temple were believed to originate even beyond the sway of divine beings, yet they could be harnessed to bring human beings into the realm of the gods. This return was not only possible, but an inevitability of mortal existence because humans, natural forces, and even the gods were subject to the cyclic forces that operate in the creative realms.

In the temple, the worlds of creation were ever present. On approaching the holy precinct, a *temenos* wall emulated the primeval ocean, from which life arose in the beginning of time. Passing through the portals to the house of the god, entry into the sphere of creative powers was indicated by forests of soaring columns that mirrored the initial appearance of life in the form of aquatic plants. And on entering the temple proper, the foundation of the material world was depicted in artistic representations of divine beings manifesting their nature through acts of creation in the physical world—the birth of royal persons, the initiation of natural laws and cycles, and the establishment of order in society.

Photo 2—The colonnade of the Temple of Auset in Philae, emulating the primeval marshes of creation (Graeco-Roman ca. 250 B.C.E.).

In the tomb, the deceased returned to the creative powers in nature and the universe with scenes of hunting in the primeval marsh, where life proliferates and renews the soul. But this new phase of existence was not limited to those who passed from mortal life to new life in the immortal worlds. The living were bonded and renewed by these powers as well, and were welcomed into the field of creation by participating in the same ritual processes that inaugurated the new existence for their departed ones.

In the Egyptian universe, the cosmogenesis was not defined by one episode. Rather, it was seen as a cyclic process in rhythmic phases, where four dimensions exist, interpenetrate, and interact through time and space.

South • Water

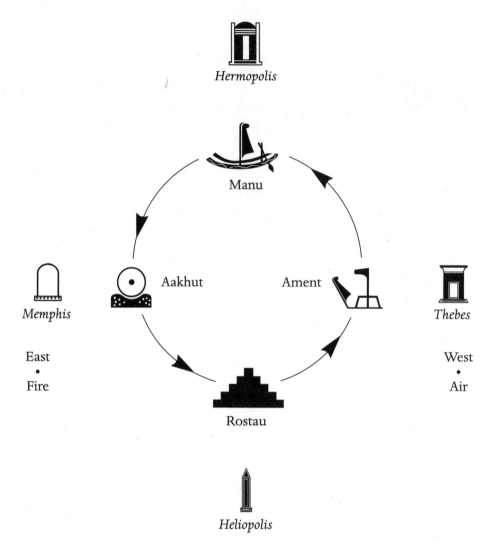

Hermopolis

Manu

Aakhut   Ament

Memphis   *Thebes*

East   West
•   •
Fire   Air

Rostau

Heliopolis

North • Earth

Figure 1—The Creation Cycle

In the first phase, the world of *Manu* ("horizon of waters") comes into being as the macrocosm or celestial sphere, from which the elements of creation emerge. Its image is a watery mass of undefined powers, where all possibilities are articulated, but not manifest.

In the second phase, the world of *Aakhut* ("luminous horizon") appears, in the fiery form of light that illuminates the primeval waters and impels patterns or forms to come into being.

In the third phase, the world of *Rostau* ("horizon of spirits") comes into being, symbolized as a mound upon which the forces of the upper worlds come to rest. This phase expresses the containment of the sacred fire in matter, the genesis of material life in microcosmic form.

The last phase of creation, the world of *Ament* ("horizon of the west") represents the phenomenal world that we experience, where cyclic forces govern the conditions of existence—birth and death. Here, the return to the upper worlds becomes possible, as this realm expresses the fulfillment of the creative forces as well as their predestination for cyclic renewal. This world also possesses the mechanisms for the mutation of the physical form, which make possible the conscious experience of moving through several phases of existence.

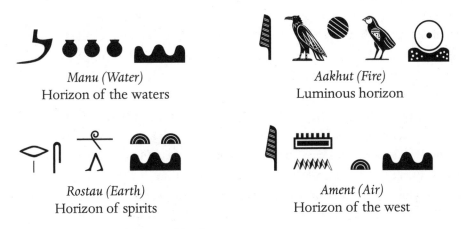

Manu (Water)
Horizon of the waters

Aakhut (Fire)
Luminous horizon

Rostau (Earth)
Horizon of spirits

Ament (Air)
Horizon of the west

Figure 2—The Names of the Worlds of Creation

The four creative realms embody the elemental forms of the ancient universe: Water (Manu), Fire (Aakhut), Earth (Rostau), and Air (Ament). As such, they do not represent conflicting or alternate themes of the cosmogenesis, but stages of manifest reality that exist interdependently. Each world possesses a creator who proliferates particular functions that interact with the others, and each has an equally significant influence on the world of human life.

In these four worlds of creation, the Egyptians saw certain universal functions come into being as divinities, the *Neteru* ("gods" or "divine principles," the *Neter* being the individual deity of a place or action).[2] The Neteru represent universal forces that organize and maintain the life of creation. They also perform specific functions both in their natural realms and in the world that we experience. Hence, families of gods are depicted who govern processes in nature, in the human body, and in the phenomena of the sky—much of which brought confusion to many observers of Egyptian culture in ancient times. But each group of divinities conveys a comprehensive view of a reality that has both cosmological and mundane wisdom.

The principles that each creative family represents were articulated in distinctive philosophical schools that possessed unique imagery and temple traditions in ancient Egypt. The cosmogony of Hermopolis in Middle Egypt was one of the earliest, expressing the creative powers in the world of Manu as an *ogdoad,* or group of eight divinities (Nun and Naunet, Huh and Hauhet, Kuk and Kauket, Maat and Djehuti) who bring the elemental forms of life into being. Here, the creator is Nun, the primeval waters, who brings forth life from the darkness by stirring and speaking the creative utterance. Another group of divine powers, the Solar Triad (Ra, Khepri, and Sopdet), stems from archaic times. It is associated with the world of Manu by its imagery of creative beings in barques that cross the primeval ocean cyclically. These powers circulate the elemental forms of life through the universal landscape in epochs of time. In this family, the creator is Ra, the Sun god, who precipitates life via light or illumination into the dark waters of Nun.

The world of Aakhut is represented by the triad of Memphis (Ptah, Sekhmet-Bast, and Nefertum) where the creator is Ptah, the artificer who fabricates life forms through thought. In this world also operates the triad of Esna (Khnum, Neit, and Heka), who fuse the light of creation to these thought forms, evoking

---

2. The *t* in the word is pronounced as a soft "tch."

the patterns of life that come into being in the material world. The creatrix of this family is Neit, the androgynous "mother-father" of the gods who infuses elemental substance with vitality. Of Khnum, he is depicted as the "fashioner" of the material form, and his powers extend from the immaterial world of fire into the visible realms:

He fashioned mankind and engendered the gods,
All live by that which emanates from him.
. . . his manifestations are hidden among people,
They constitute all beings, since the time of the gods.
　　　　　　　　—Temple of Khnum, Ptolemaic Dynasty

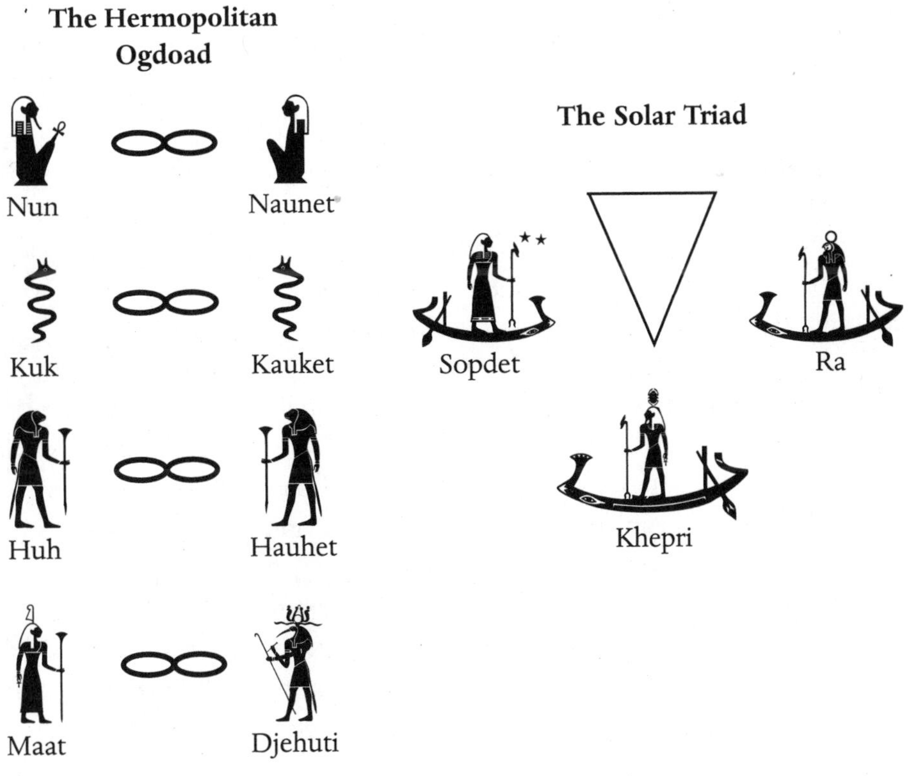

The Hermopolitan Ogdoad

The Solar Triad

Nun　　　　　Naunet

Kuk　　　　　Kauket

Sopdet　　　　　　　　Ra

Huh　　　　　Hauhet

Khepri

Maat　　　　　Djehuti

Figure 3—The World of Manu

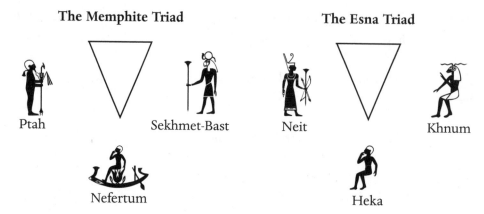

Figure 4—The World of Aakhut

The world of Rostau represents the organic world of creation, where the *ennead* (group of nine) of Heliopolis govern the processes of physical manifestation (Atum, Shu and Tefnut, Nut and Geb, Asar and Auset, Set and Nebt-Het). Atum is the creator who proliferates by spitting or ejaculating to bring forth his divine progeny. They are followed by the triad of Dendera, which rouses the creative powers within the manifest form (Het-Her, Heru, and Ihy). They are completed by the Funerary Quaternary (Imset, Daumutef, Qebsenuf, and Haapi), which transmits the creative impulse from one form to another.

And in the world of Ament, the triad of Thebes governs the processes that mature and complete physical life (Amun, Mut, and Khons). The head in this realm is Amun, the invisible breath of creation. They share their functions with the Initiatory Triad (Heru Ur, Sokar, and Anpu), who refine the cosmic elements in the corporeal body, and the Cyclic Triad (Taurt, Hapi, and Apep), which brings completion to periodic processes and renewal in new realms.

Altogether, the four worlds of creation are constituted by ten families of Neteru, who represent the principles of creative manifestation and embody the functions of the phenomenal world. Forty-two divinities inhabit this landscape, and express the mystic forces of Egypt's religious pantheon.

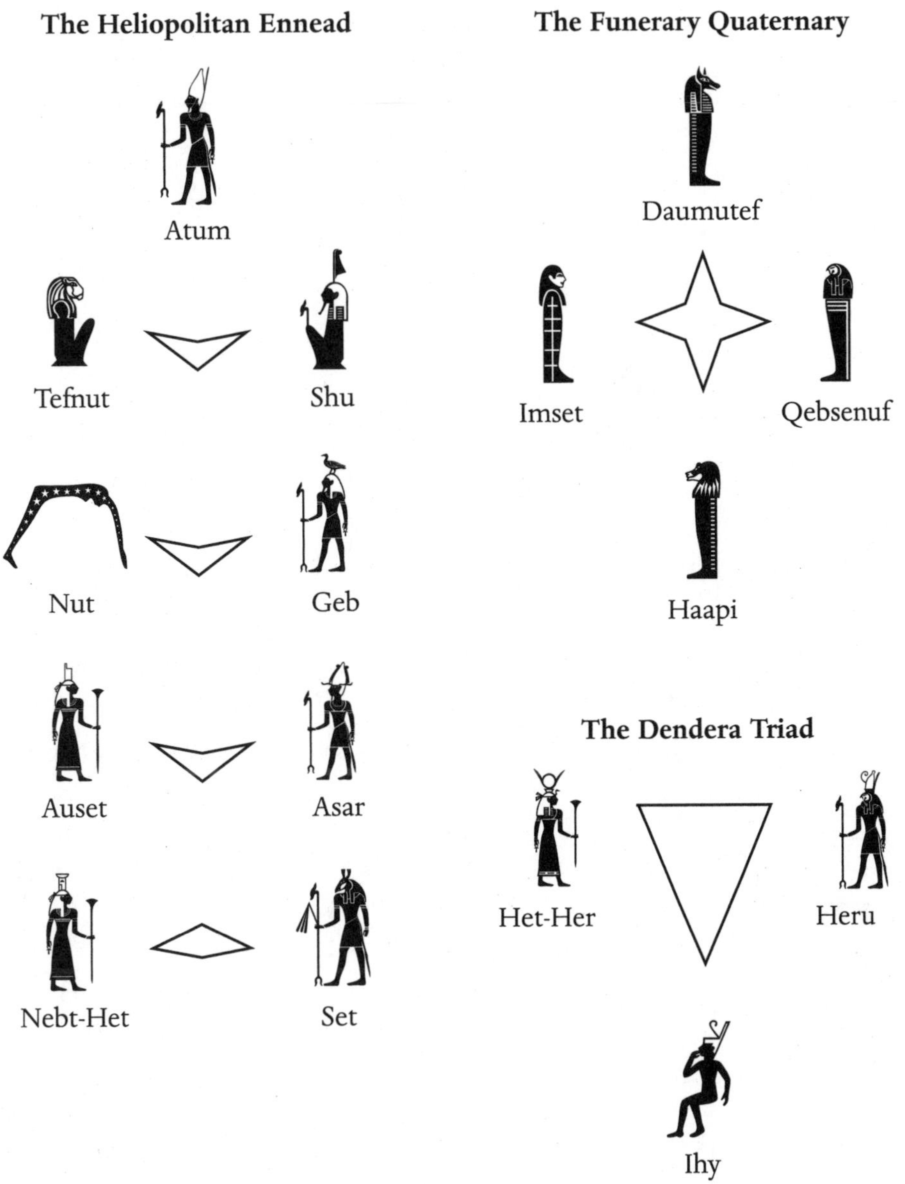

The Heliopolitan Ennead

The Funerary Quaternary

Atum

Tefnut   Shu

Nut   Geb

Auset   Asar

Nebt-Het   Set

Daumutef

Imset   Qebsenuf

Haapi

The Dendera Triad

Het-Her   Heru

Ihy

Figure 5—The World of Rostau

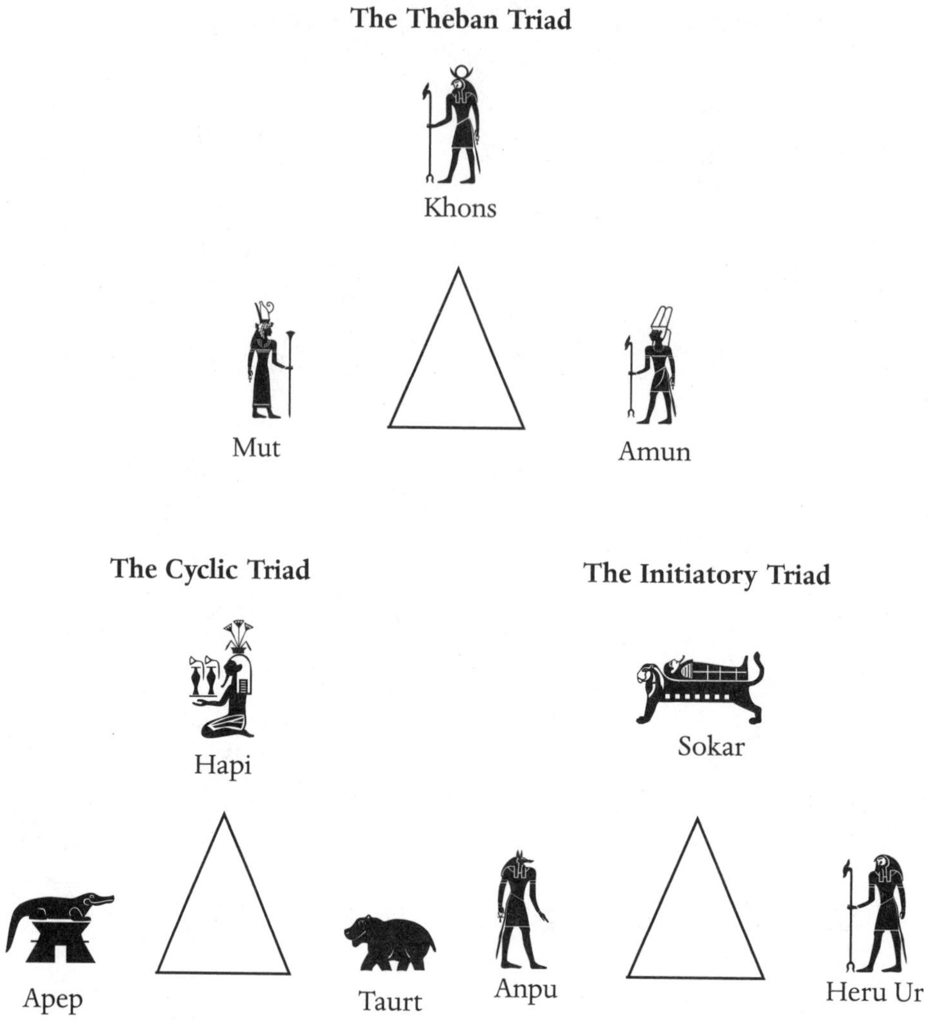

The Theban Triad

Khons

Mut

Amun

The Cyclic Triad

The Initiatory Triad

Hapi

Sokar

Apep

Taurt

Anpu

Heru Ur

Figure 6—The World of Ament

World		Family	Neter	Principle	Function
Manu	I.	Hermopolis Ogdoad	Nun	Genesis	Motion
			Naunet	Substance	Matter
			Huh	Expansion	Space
			Hauhet	Contraction	Time
			Kuk	Quiescence	Darkness
			Kauket	Mutation	Light
			Djehuti	Resonance	Communication
			Maat	Order	Structure
	II.	Solar Triad	Sopdet	Presentience	Precession
			Ra	Circulation	Rotation
			Khepri	Metamorphosis	Revolution
Aakhut	III.	Memphis Triad	Ptah	Animation	Fabrication
			Sekhmet-Bast	Purification	Purgation
			Nefertum	Precipitation	Desire
	IV.	Esna Triad	Khnum	Distillation	Embodiment
			Neit	Fusion	Healing
			Heka	Transformation	Ritual
Rostau	V.	Heliopolis Ennead	Atum	Unity	Consciousness
			Shu	Inhalation	Breath
			Tefnut	Diffusion	Sensation
			Nut	Augmentation	Gestation
			Geb	Creation	Vegetation
			Asar	Renewal	Germination
			Auset	Fruition	Birth
			Set	Fixation	Corruption
			Nebt-Het	Secretion	Sustenance
	VI.	Dendera Triad	Het-Her	Fertilization	Conception
			Younger Heru	Ascension	Mastery
			Ihy	Insemination	Procreation
	VII.	Funerary Quaternary	Imset	Coagulation	Liver
			Haapi	Circulation	Lungs
			Daumutef	Decomposition	Stomach
			Qebsenuf	Assimilation	Intestines

Table 1—Principles and Functions of the Forty-Two Neteru

World		Family	Neter	Principle	Function
	VIII.	Theban	Amun	Completion	Maturation
		Triad	Mut	Incubation	Protection
			Khons	Enumeration	Periodicity
Ament	IX.	Initiatory	Heru Ur	Exaltation	Initiation
		Triad	Anpu	Transmutation	Digestion
			Sokar	Latency	Inertia
	X.	Cyclic	Taurt	Multiplication	Partuition
		Triad	Hapi	Continuity	Inundation
			Apep	Repetition	Metempsychosis

Table 1—Principles and Functions of the Forty-Two Neteru

Within this cosmological scheme is found the mandate of Egyptian spirituality—the unity of life in interpenetrating worlds and its inevitable renewal. And while it was understood that these processes were natural events, the means of achieving these aims consciously and progressively comprised the legendary wisdom that has been sought through the ages.

The Powers of Creation

Daily life in ancient Egypt encompassed far more than attendance to personal need or social duty. It was an existence intertwined with the perception of and a deep regard for divine life, and a desire to communicate with its powers. We know this from a vast body of writings and illustrated texts that the Egyptians left the world to study through the centuries. The gods, nature, and the conscience of human beings were viewed as equally decisive in shaping the future, and the conscious participation with these forces was viewed as the supreme accomplishment. This was possible not only because of their proximity to nature and the powers it brought, but also because they recognized certain forces within human life that emanate directly from the worlds of creation.

The rhythms of the primeval genesis, where water, light, the patterns of life, and land came into being, established the foundations for the world of life in Egyptian cosmology. As these elements were born, certain forces or powers of consciousness also became manifest, each of them occurring from the creator's articulation of its nature. Besides embodying the powers of the creator, these forces also assumed the identities of divine beings, and came to represent important religious concepts in the symbolism and art of ancient Egypt. Of these, some take precedence in the spiritual endeavors that the Egyptians employed to further their imperative to consciously participate in the creative process of the universe.

In the world of Manu, the appearance of the four divine pairs coalesced in an elemental balance called *Maat* (also the name of the goddess in the ogdoad who represents the culmination of this creative phase). This force permeates all the worlds of creation and dictates the processes found in the natural world. Abstractly, Maat represents divine order, and in the phenomenal world it is the force that ensures the harmonious balance of life despite the conflicts brought by competing powers. In the life of human beings, Maat represents the source of truth and righteousness, and the action of adhering to natural law.

The ancient Egyptians regarded Maat as the supreme guide to harmony with nature and the gods. Depictions in temples of royal persons offering icons of the goddess Maat symbolize a restatement by the monarch to manage the burden of power according to the canon established by the gods. And in the tombs, individuals offer Maat in the form of the deity as evidence of a truthful life and proof of admission into the region of the gods. In these instances, Maat is seen not only as a universal force, but as an individual power that can be dedicated to the harmony of the whole.

When the Solar Triad came into being in the world of Manu, a set of secondary forces emanated from this creative outpouring. Five senses, or cognitive powers, appeared when Ra, the Sun god, assumed consciousness upon proceeding with his creative impulse. The first of these powers is *Heka* ("magic"), which essentially represents the generative force in the universe when it initially formulated into the elemental substances that constituted the gods. Heka was the first manifestation of Ra, regarded as his *Ba* ("soul") or visible appearance. But this power is not restricted to him—all of his creations possess some degree of Heka, and it moved into other creative realms as a Neter, the offspring of Khnum and Neit in the triad of Esna.

Heka was regarded as an innate sense in human beings and operates in the human sphere through magical acts. It was viewed by the Egyptians as a natural

Figure 7—The Maati Goddesses: Maat, the Neter of cosmic harmony, manifests in forty-two aspects, each embodying the ideals of Egyptian morality and balance with nature and the gods.

function, like eating and breathing. Heka may be concentrated, transmitted, and depleted in living forms, but it emanates unceasingly from the highest cosmic regions. The concept of Heka in action is embedded in Egypt's tradition of high magic. It is expressed continuously in funerary literature, where the living must employ Heka to avoid the dangers of the unseen worlds, and the dead must use it to journey through the unfamiliar regions of the afterlife in order to meet the gods.

In the temples, copious inscriptions detail every aspect of sacred work—from the physical purifications, the preparation of offerings, the singing of hymns, and the performance of powerful rituals—all done for the benefit of the Neteru. In these instances, Heka is viewed as a natural expression for human beings, one that must be exercised to maintain the bonds between the living worlds and used to extend one's senses into those worlds.

In addition to the liturgical texts, certain types of knowledge were also used to exercise Heka appropriately and commune with the gods. Scent, sound (chant and music), ritual gesture (including dance), and the observation of celestial phenomena were choreographed with the use of sacred literature to evoke the divine presence into the human sphere. This was seen as an emulation of the cosmogenesis, and could invite the forces of creation to enter the temple. In an Old Kingdom royal text, the monarch is informed of some of the innate powers that the creator-god endowed to the human race in order to deal with supernatural events:

He made heka for them,
To use as a weapon for warding off occurrences.
And he made them dreams for the night,
To see the things of the day.
——Instruction for King Merikara, Dynasty 10

Four universal functions or senses followed the genesis of Heka—*Sia* (innate intelligence), *Hu* (utterance), *Maa* (sight), and *Sedjem* (hearing). They are in some instances depicted as passengers or "members of the crew of Ra" in the Solar barque over the sky, symbolizing the appearance of divine faculties that are reborn with the Sun each day. In other instances, they are a depicted as the *genii*, or helping spirits of Djehuti and Seshat, the divine chronocrator and measurer, respectively, in the world of Manu.

Sia embodies the qualities of conscious intelligence—understanding, perception, recognition, and foresight. The Egyptians believed that this function is innate in the living, and endows human beings with the knowledge of their origins and destiny. Sia appears as a bearded man in the Solar barque of Ra, and in some instances with Djehuti and Seshat as one of the "souls of Hermopolis."

Hu is another personification of the Sun god's conscious emanations—he is the authoritative utterance that gives life to the creative urge. In human life, Hu provides the sense of taste, and in the temple he provides one of the divine offerings that feed the gods, *djefau*. Maa (sometimes referred to as *Iri*, "seeing") represents the function of sight, which in the Sun god was fulfilled with one all-seeing eye. Here he emphasizes the significance of attention and observation in the creative process. Lastly, Sedjem personifies the power of hearing, appearing in the Solar barque at times to serve as the "hearer." The powers of the Egyptian gods were often invoked through a chamber in the temple called "the chapel of the ear," where specific requests were made for healing or relief from suffering. This faculty was especially regarded for approaching the deity through hymns, prayers, and the recitation of its mystic names and being heard.

In the world of Ament, the legend relates that Atum, the creative head of the realm, brought forth the first divine pair, Shu and Tefnut, functions of cosmic wind and moisture, respectively. In doing so, he emanated the initial force that bonded his creations to himself and all that followed—*Sa,* a cohesive energy that

Maa

Sight, intuition, clairvoyance

Hu

Taste, authoritative utterance

Sedjem

Hearing, to harken

Sia

Perception, understanding

Heka

Magic, creative impulse

Maat

Order, harmony, balance

Sa

Universal force, spiritual substance

Figure 8—The Names of the Seven Cosmic Powers

encompasses the living universe. Known to the ancient Greeks as the *aether*,[3] Sa binds creator and the created together, ensuring unity and affinity throughout the phenomenal worlds. But Sa is not only the creative emanation, it also represents the process itself, the outpouring (the same word has the meaning of "son" and "daughter").

In hieroglyphic representation, Sa represents divine protection, and its image is derived from the floating device used on Nile vessels to protect boatmen from drowning. It is used in the context of "constituting" or "establishing" an action or a place, and in representations of the sky, the Sa is often shown at the center of the pole, to represent the "mooring post" or place of stability in the heavens.

To the ancients, the landscape that these powers embodied requires the participation of human beings for its maintenance and continuity. The seven cosmic powers emanated by the worlds of creation were understood to be powers resident in human life; the awakening and use of these forces constituted the essential spiritual goals of both temple and tomb.

Maat, the principle of order and harmony, provides pattern and definition to all acts, religious and secular. Heka, the creative force, is imbued in all living beings and was viewed as the means to maintaining and enhancing the divine order. Furthermore, the Egyptians knew that one dimension of human consciousness is descended from and eternally connected to the cosmic dimension of the creation, and this power is transmitted through Sia, the innate intelligence possessed by all sentient life.

Through the power of authoritative utterance, Hu allows the will of the soul to communicate with universal principles. With this, Maa provides the power of observation and knowledge of the unseen worlds, while Sedjem furnishes cognizance of these realms through sound. And ultimately, Sa enables thought to constitute both the will of the individual soul and the will of the creative source, binding them together with what is and will be created.

In all, these powers were recognized as components of the human psyche as well as the created worlds. They convey to the living the same creative impulses as the demiurge and the gods that followed, providing the means to recapitulate the moment of genesis and perpetuate the forces that came into being with it.

---

3. In Western metaphysics, aether is the psychic substance (etheric force) that constitutes all physical life.

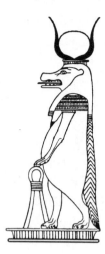

Figure 9—The Neter Taurt Anchors the Polestar with the Sa Marker

Sacred Science

We possess remnants of the Egyptian legacy in a diverse range of systems in use today—timekeeping, astronomy, medicine, and chemistry, to name a few. But some of the ancient disciplines stood out as far more significant, at least to the Egyptians. These were employed in the construction of the temples, tombs, and pyramids; they occupied the time and talents of learned specialists, and they infused nearly all literary endeavors with the spiritual objective communicated by the creation legends—realizing and maintaining the harmony among gods, nature, and human beings.

The means to accomplishing this interaction between the lifestreams was a time-honored, spiritual technology that was believed to have been given to the human race by divine beings. It included the application of language, art, science, and theology in a manner that even in the ancient world was regarded as enigmatic and sublime. Through the ages, it has been regarded as a Sacred Science, a methodology that intertwined all of Egypt's high disciplines to support the legacy alluded to by the creation legends, that a purpose exists for the living—the acquisition and integration of the full measure of divine life in steps or stages, a conscious realization of the primeval unity.

	Universal Power	Principle	Human Power
	Maat	Order	Definition
	Heka	Magic	Creativity
	Sia	Intelligence	Knowledge
	Hu	Utterance	Will
	Maa	Sight	Observation
	Sedjem	Sound	Cognizance
	Sa	Constitution	Affinity

Table 2—The Seven Cosmic Powers

From this tradition, many ancient cultures—such as the Persian, Greek, and Roman—developed similar systems that have come down to us in the Western magical tradition. Many introduced practices that were standard in Egypt, including sacred drama, the reserved teachings known as the "ineffable mysteries," and initiation rites designed to alter and enhance the recipient's perceptions or powers. But the Egyptian form is arguably the most ancient, and in the view of its surrounding societies, was probably the most effective in achieving its spiritual goal—maintaining the bonds between the human, divine, and natural worlds.

Evidence of Egypt's Sacred Science is abundant—in the design and construction of monuments that cannot be duplicated today, in an elaborate practice of mummification that eludes our understanding, in the record of a superior skill in medicine mingled with magic—to name a few. But even though we can, for instance, intellectually discern examples of advanced geometry in the construction of Egyptian pyramids, or account for the success of their healing art by virtue of the placebo effect, the meaning and objective of these endeavors is quite often eluded. How can we fully apprehend the information that we have? And if we could, what destination does it lead to? To discover those answers, we will be looking at the legacy that conventional scholars have circumvented mostly to avoid the religious and philosophical implications that challenge the status quo of modern spirituality.

One of the implications of this spiritual technology—Sacred Science—was the transformation of the human form into a vehicle for higher functions. In the words of the Egyptians, it was a process of "making gods." This profound goal is reflected in the knowledge that was employed to further its process. We know of three essential components that comprised this goal: esoteric architecture, cosmic resonance, and theurgy. And within these three components were several metaphysical disciplines.

Esoteric Architecture

The encryption of sacred principles in monumental building based on models in nature. The Egyptians employed numerology, sacred geometry, measures found in natural forms, and mathematical models based on celestial motion. An intricate approach to constructing their temples, tombs, and pyramids also included the use of symbolic art and unique building materials. For example, certain stones and metals were viewed as emanations of divine qualities, such as light and permanence. These were incorporated into the construction of sanctuaries and other sacred structures to embody and maintain divine forces.

More importantly, the layout of every shrine was an emulation of the landscape of creation. The house of the god was a mirror image of its domain in celestial regions, and the chambers, halls, and passages represented functions of the deity in rest, active manifestation, and procreation.

Cosmic Resonance

The science of invoking and communicating with divine forces via celestial timing. In the Egyptian world view, nature is neither random nor obtuse, but organized and intelligent. Some schools of modern physics and cosmology may allude to this, but they fall short of representing the universe the way the ancient people did—as conscious and immanent.

The Egyptians practiced a sacred astronomy—that is, they observed celestial events in context with their connection to and influence on terrestrial life. This stems from their belief that divine forces reside in all natural phenomena—the

Sun, Moon, planets, stars—and that their rhythmic appearances mark significant events for other living beings. From this body of knowledge arose most of our contemporary systems of prophecy, divination, astrology, and geomancy.

Theurgy

The performance of "divine work." Heka—the creative impulse—is both a sensory function and a divinely regulated action that forms the underpinnings of Egyptian spiritual practice. We know that in the ancient culture, spiritual practice was sensate and expressed through sacramental forms of ritual. All the conscious faculties were employed toward this end, including sight, sound, scent, taste, and feeling. In addition, special knowledge was transmitted through the physical vehicles of the religion—the art and architecture of the temples—and through symbols, color, spatial harmonics, and carefully selected materials for dress and ceremony. In turn, all of these elements were designed for use in episodes dictated by cosmic timing—in cycles determined by the day, month, and year.

The purpose of this elaborate system was aimed to synchronize the senses of mortals with the phenomena of the natural landscape, both visible and invisible. It was believed that in this manner, the unity between the three lifestreams could be experienced and, most importantly, maintained.

It was not until much later in Egypt's history, during the Graeco-Roman period (332 B.C.E. to 395 C.E.), that the cognitive approach, emphasizing intellectual learning and the use of logic rather than symbolic thinking and the use of intuition, took precedence in religious practice. This remains the dominant approach in Western religion today. Thus, though much of Egypt's spirituality can be studied from its texts and monuments, the experiential form of the temple tradition must be restored in order to apprehend its full purpose and power.

The choreography of these three disciplines—esoteric architecture, cosmic resonance, and theurgy—comprised the practice of Sacred Science. With this, the Egyptians believed that they were fulfilling the spiritual goals of creation:

- Maintaining the interface between the three words—the divine, the human, and nature;

- Realizing the ultimate accomplishment of human life—transformation into divine existence, consciously and progressively.

This is the sacred tradition of ancient Egypt. And this is what many conventional scholars have failed to discern, despite the overwhelming proliferation of clues. Egypt's religion, government, arts, and industries were deeply rooted in this Sacred Science. We see examples of esoteric architecture, cosmic resonance, and theurgy whenever we look at the artifacts of Egypt. Scholars may examine the minutiae of the temples, tombs, and pyramids and from their data constitute the cognitive face of ancient times. Yet they fail to discern the purpose that shines through these enigmatic monuments. That purpose is expressed consistently in those monuments and Egypt's sacred literature—the Pyramid and Coffin Texts, the Books of the Dead, and the later philosophy of Hermetism. It is from these sources that we may re-create the contemplative face of Egyptian esotericism and retrieve those "ineffable mysteries" that are our true legacy.

Chapter Two

ESOTERIC ARCHITECTURE

I will create a work, a great house
For my father Atum.
I will make it broad, as broad as what he has caused me to conquer.
I will place offerings upon his Earthly altars,
Beauty shall be commemorated in His house,
Eternity is the excellent thing I have built.
　　　　—Senusert I (Dynasty 12)
　　　　　　Building inscription for the temple of Heliopolis

I f anything could be said to have unequivocally determined the scope of Egyptian spirituality, it is the terrestrial landscape of the Nile Valley. Divided geographically into two distinct regions, the country is melded by the life-giving river that flows from south (the Upper Kingdom) to north (the Lower Kingdom). The southern region, comprised of a deeply cut valley hewn over time by the river's cyclic inundation, features a narrow strip of land bordered in places by high limestone cliffs and arid desert. The northern region, a marshy delta once divided by seven branches of the river that emptied into the Mediterranean, features lush fields of reeds and waterfowl that contrast markedly with the inhospitable knolls of endless sand, rock, and scrub brush in the south.

Ta Mehu (North)   *Ta Shemau (South)*

	Kemet, "Black Land"		*Deshret,* "Red Land"	
District		Delta		Valley
Plant		Papyrus		Lotus
Pharaonic Emblem		Bee		Sedge Plant
Royal Crown		Red (*Deshret*)		White (*Hedjet*)
Sceptre		Flail (*Nekheka*)		Crook (*Heka*)
Archaic Neter		Wadjet of Buto		Nekhebet of El Kab
Metal		Gold (*Nub*)		Silver (*Het*)
Temple Tradition		Solar		Lunar
Neter		Heru		Set
Predynastic Center		Pe-Dep		Nekhen
Capitol		Buto		Hierokonpolis
Ancient Necropolis		Saqqara		Abydos
Sacred Astronomy		Equinoctial		Solstitial
Economy		Agriculture		Husbandry

Table 3—Symbols of the Two Lands

This landscape set the stage thousands of years ago for an environmental duality that was consistently mirrored in Egyptian art, architecture, and spiritual practice. The "Two Lands," as Egypt was regarded by its inhabitants, embodied the extremes of mortal existence and cosmic activity—fertility (the marshes) and sterility (the desert), the proliferation of life (the black land) and the isolation of death (the red land). These concepts were incorporated in images that arose from predynastic times, images that came to represent the contrasting powers of the Two Lands and their union under the aegis of the gods and the Royal House.

The Nile's efflux was believed to nourish the lands of the south and north from two unique sanctuaries, where nilometers gauged the height of the river at inundation. Kebeh Set ("sanctuary of Set") was located on the island of Elephantine, close to the southern border of Egypt and Kebeh Hor ("sanctuary of Heru") was situated near Heliopolis, near the Delta's geographic apex. As the names imply, each site housed a shrine that represented the vital powers of the two antagonistic gods who represent both the division and the fusion of Egypt.

The peculiar cycle of the river itself also played prominently into the mythological motifs of Egypt. The Nile is fed upstream by the waters generated by the spring rains of Ethiopia's highlands, which pour down into the Blue and White Niles that join in the Sudan, arriving in Egypt by mid-July. Once in the Nile Valley, the floodwaters spread a thick layer of rich silt that is deposited when the waters recede in late October. In prehistoric times, the people of the Nile Valley exploited this phenomenon by instituting a highly productive agricultural agenda that contributed significantly to the miracle of their civilization.

Profound spiritual themes arose from the Nile's annual rise and fall. In concert with the astronomical rhythms that fused with and came to predict the river's periodic changes, an understanding of both the transitory and the eternal qualities of nature became embedded in Egypt's cultural consciousness. The gods were believed to appear and retreat in time to celestial conditions that signaled their connection to mortal life, yet at the same time their resolute and dependable return could be expected—qualities of transcendent and timeless existence. These divine attributes were incorporated in Egyptian art and architecture, with the expectation that the gods in nature and the sky would embody places that emulated their supernatural origins.

Figure 10—Heru and Set, Governors of the Two Lands

With the completion of a series of dams in southern Egypt in the twentieth century, the Nile ceased to flood the valley annually and the silt deposits no longer fertilize the land. Despite this, the rhythm of nature can still be discerned in the stellar landscape and the seasonal flux. The gods are no longer drawn into their familiar territory in modern times, but their appearances are nevertheless apparent. They require only a seat upon which their powers may become manifest and be honored.

Orientation

In modern times, we consult maps to orient our position, looking at the four cardinal points of the compass—north, south, east, and west. In ancient Egypt, orientation was gauged by the natural landscape, and primarily by one's position in relation to the Nile. The cardinal points were well understood from astronomical observation of the Sun's path during the day and the passage of stars overhead at night, but these were the guideposts for divine forces; those on Earth stood essentially in relation to the river and its natural course.

The source of the Nile was the prime geodetic marker for orientation. The Nile is not only the longest river in the world, it flows in a nearly vertical line from the south (upstream) due north (downstream). For these unique reasons, the beginning and origins of all life were regarded to exist in the southern regions. Facing south, the territory of primeval creation—the watery world of Manu—was believed to flow from that direction. The place of rising for the Sun and stars would appear to the left of the viewer in the fiery world of Aakhut, and the place of sunset and the disappearance of the asterisms would be on the right, the airy world of Ament. And ultimately, the place of stability and unmoving forces would be identified with the north, the position of the observer. Here, the mound of creation in the Earthly world of Rostau would come to rest.

The Egyptians associated the right side with the darkness of sunset on the western bank, and the left side with the brightness of sunrise on the eastern bank. Hence, "going to the western land" was a metaphor for leaving mortal life and in a similar vein, going south "upstream" was a euphemism for returning to the source of life and renewal.

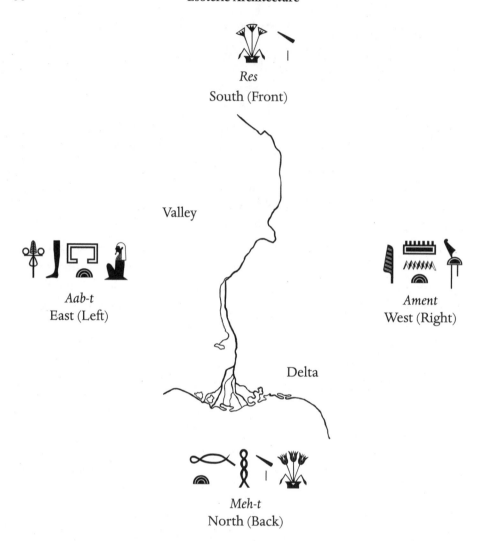

Res
South (Front)

Valley

Aab-t
East (Left)

Ament
West (Right)

Delta

Meh-t
North (Back)

Figure 11—The Directions (Looking South)

Notable Temples

Although the sacred places of the gods were manifold in ancient times and were periodically relocated or rebuilt in response to alterations in the monarchy and the motion of celestial bodies, certain locations remained intrinsically tied to the powers of specific deities and their traditions. Of these, the four centers that propounded the four creation rhythms are included, as well as those that promulgated the mysteries of exalted divine beings over extended periods of time.

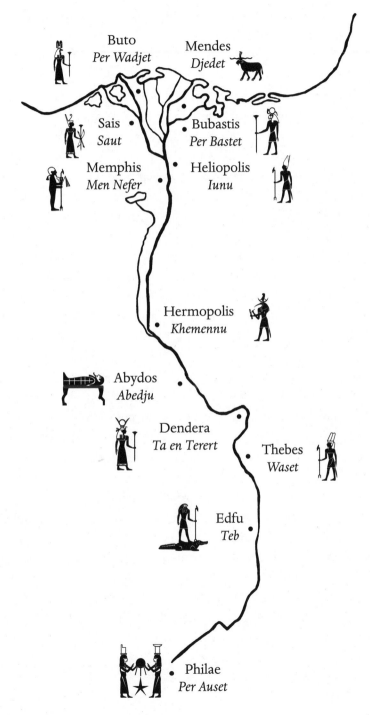

Figure 12—The Sacred Centers

The ancient northern and southern sanctuaries of the Two Lands, known as Pe and Nekhen,[1] were established in prehistory and remained seats of the powerful throne goddesses throughout time. In the north at Buto *(Per Wadjet)*, a most archaic site honored Wadjet, Neter of the Royal House, in her image as protective cobra. This ancient deity presided over the Red Crown, one of the pharaonic insignia that was bestowed at each royal investiture. Wadjet, and her sister-goddess Nekhebet in the form of a vulture and the White Crown, endow the diadems of Egypt that awaken in the royal person the spiritual functions of dominance and protection, respectively. In the crowning ceremonies of the Royal House, priestesses assumed the forms of the two deities, and presented the royal insignia as a gesture that all the gods of Egypt accepted the monarch as a member of their company.

The imagery of the serpent in Egypt is complex and profound. There are many indigenous types, from the poisonous hooded cobra (Asp) that Kleopatra VII used to take her life to the horned viper—both similarly dangerous. But the serpent also protects the Solar gods, and they themselves often assume serpentine form to defend the territory of Egypt and shield their followers from harm. In the afterlife, an elaborate set of journeys is undertaken by the soul on approaching and entering the realm of the gods; numerous reptilian deities guard the secret entries or give protection to those armed with their powerful names.

East of Buto is the sanctuary of *Ba Neb Djedu* ("soul of the pillar"), the ram-headed deity of Mendes *(Djedet)*, associated in later times with Set and, as a result, with pagan sorcery. This city, along with Alexandria to the west, was a launching point in late history for Egypt's influence throughout the Mediterranean. After the Crusades, when Europeans gained knowledge of the ancient temple traditions, Ba Neb Djedu became transposed to the medieval Baphomet, the alleged patron of the Templars.

The ram was associated with a number of powerful deities, including Amun of Thebes and Khnum of Esna. Its hieroglyphic sign *(Ba)* is also the ideogram for the human soul *(Ba)*, and in the ancient language, also possesses the meaning of "appearance" or "visible aspect." As such, the Ram of Mendes embodies the soul of the creator in the Solar rhythm of the cosmogenesis.

---

1. For the Greek and modern equivalent sites, see Appendix 2: Place Names of Ancient Egypt.

Photo 3—Nekhebet and Wadjet present the crowns of Egypt to the third Ptolemy, Euergetes II (170–116 B.C.E.) at Edfu.

Sais *(Saut)* is the seat of the creatrix Neit, the active principle in the Esna Triad. One of the most visited ancient sites, this city was reported by Herodotus to have featured an annual festival of lamps in honor of the goddess, who governed the sacred fire of the temple. This became the prototype for the oracular Vestals of Rome. Neit is co-creator of the *Ka* (vital body or "double" of human life), fashioned in premortal existence by her consort, Khnum. Together these deities infuse the vital body with life force and the imprint of its future physical form. In temples that depict the divine genesis of the royal person, they are seen fabricating the royal Ka, which often takes seven or more forms.

To the east of Sais is another ancient sanctuary, Hebyt, near modern Benbeit el Hagar. This is the oldest shrine city dedicated wholly to Auset, and though her temples here—from Old Kingdom to Roman times—are in ruins today, it demonstrates the extent of her power to devoted followers through the ages.

Continuing eastward is Bubastis *(Per Bastet),* the city of the cat goddess, which even today yields to archeologists countless artifacts from several temples, shrines, and cat cemeteries dedicated to Bastet. As the benevolent face of Sekhmet-Bast in the triad of Memphis, Bastet was regarded as a protective deity for both temple and home. Our erstwhile ancient traveler Herodotus also reported the utter devotion of her followers, from shaving their eyebrows at the death of a cat to imposing capital punishment on a Roman soldier for accidentally dispatching a feline in one of the city streets.

Ba
The soul, divine appearance,
visible aspect

Ka
The Double, astral body, vitality

Figure 13—The Ba and the Ka

Traveling southward to the apex of the Nile Delta are the two most important—and oldest—cities of the Lower Kingdom. Heliopolis *(Iunu)* on the east bank of the Nile was regarded as the "city of the Sun," where the Solar cosmogony was propounded through the ages in the House of Life at the ancestral temple of the early pharaohs. The wisdom tradition of this center was known from antiquity; Plato, Pythagoras, and Solon were said to have consulted the priests of Heliopolis on their mathematical and historical knowledge.[2]

Heliopolis is the seat of the Ennead, the nine deities who formed the well-defined cosmology of divine descent that began with the creator Atum, passed to the god-kings Asar and his son Heru; from thence to the pharaonic line of the Royal House. The Westcar papyrus, an historical document of the Old Kingdom, tells of a priestess of the temple who was visited by the Sun god Ra and con-

---

2. Diodorus Siculus: *Bibliotheca Historica,* Book I: 69, C. H. Oldfather, trans. (Cambridge, Mass.: Loeb Classical Library, Harvard University Press, 1933).

ceived three sons. The result of the divine coupling was the birth of the Fifth Dynasty monarchs, Userkaf, Sahura, and Neferirkara, who built pyramid complexes on the west bank of the Nile and adopted the epithet "son of the Sun." For centuries

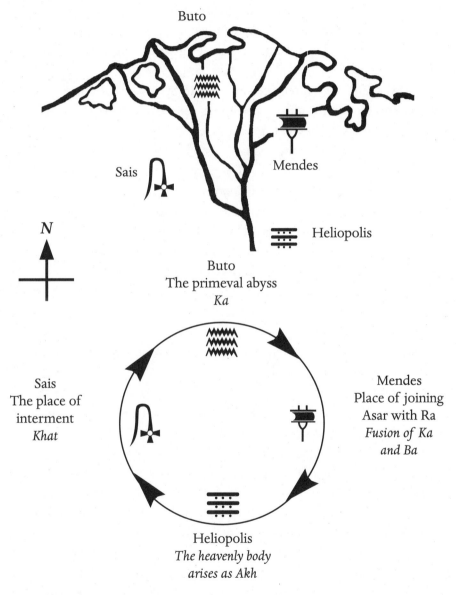

Figure 14—The Funerary Cities

afterward, the Heliopolitan priests were the custodians of the royal wands and sceptres, insignia of the powers given by the gods to the human race.

The cities of Buto, Mendes, Sais, and Heliopolis altogether form a quaternary of sacred territories that represented the ascent of the Lower Kingdom's royal dead to the worlds of creation. In a dramatic funerary cortege that emulated the archaic journey of deceased monarchs to their ancestral origins, these four cities formed the cardinal points of a journey that restored vital spiritual functions at each station.

The royal funerary cortege commences in Sais where the *Khat* (corporeal body) is interred with the ancestral spirits in the west. It then proceeds north to Buto where the *Ka* is liberated from the body and is renewed in the primeval ocean. The sacred journey then moves east to Mendes, where the renewed Ka fuses with the Ba to become a fully conscious being in the celestial worlds. The cortege concludes in the south at Heliopolis, where the restored functions move into the *Akh* (light body) and join the celestial beings in the sky.

This metaphysical journey was adapted to the last rites for common burials in later times, but its original intent was to initiate the royal soul into the realm of celestial life that is its origin and its destination. The clockwise procession of the royal funerary cortege was the last journey of the Earthly entity, but it stood as a timeless metaphor for all natural forces that participate in creation and re-creation in Egyptian cosmology.

Situated just below the Delta apex, Memphis *(Men Nefer)* grew from a geodetic center established in archaic times as *Ankh Taui*, "the life of the Two Lands," to a metropolis of vast proportions. Here the divine artisan Ptah governed temples that once provided a full range of education for ancient times— from medicine and theology to engineering and warfare.

From the west bank of the Nile, Memphis also held sway over the extensive necropolis of Saqqara—a name derived from Sokar, Neter of hibernation and the deity who represents the powers of this locale. Here, several pyramid fields intersect with temple complexes that honor the dead, from deified monarchs of the Old Kingdom to cult animals of Graeco-Roman times. This was the spiritual destination of the reposing soul in the Lower Kingdom; the gateway to eternal life. The monuments here span a 5,000-year period at the very least, each reflecting the awesome skills of the ancient engineers and the wisdom of the temple masters.

During several short historical periods, Middle Egypt governed the Two Lands, but the distinctive identities of the north and south inevitably dictated separate capitals that joined under unifying dynasties. One center remained neutral from the occasional divisions and came to be regarded as the repository of Egypt's mystical past—the theological school of Hermopolis *(Khemenu)*. Here was housed the Earthly seat of Djehuti, the Neter of divine measure, in a city of shrines and temples that honored the deity in his manifest forms—as recorder of divine speech, god of writing, inventor of number, and master of divinations. The legend arose that his sacred book, containing the secrets of antiquity that had once been endowed to the human race by the gods (enabling them to master nature and the supernatural worlds), was hidden in the repository of Djehuti's great temple.

Moving upstream to Abydos *(Abedju)*, we enter the chief sanctuary of Asar, the time-honored deity who represents the ancestral past of Egypt and the inevitable denouement of mortal life. Established even before remembered time in the ancient world, Abydos was the ultimate pilgrimage for both the living and the dead, the place where Egypt's funerary tradition was faithfully preserved through the ages. But here the renewal of physical existence was also honored, in an elaborate cycle of annual ceremonies that reenacted the vigil of the slain god, the restoration of his broken body, and his reinstatement as governor of the natural world.

A vast plain on the outskirts of the ancient city called Omm el Qa'ab, "the mother of pots," has yielded fascinating artifacts from Egypt's past, as the name implies. A complex of forts, funerary monuments, and the remnants of ancient cities continues to reveal the face of a civilization whose origins are truly archaic and may never be discerned. The great mythos that was honored here speaks of a time when Asar was the benevolent ruler of the human race, and one of the last demigods to live on Earth.

At Dendera *(Ta en Terert)*, the great temple of Het-Her depicts the vast sky realm of the deity who is said to "travel in the barque of her father, Ra." Her association with birth, death, and regenerated existence is commemorated on three levels in her Divine House—a labyrinth of halls and chambers dedicated to her cult activities, a series of mystical crypts inscribed with celestial images, and a set of roof chapels that honor the restoration of Asar by his sister goddesses.

Inscriptions here and at the Edfu *(Teb)* describe a distinctive set of ceremonies performed at each temple, honoring the deities of each that are united in an annual marriage festival of the gods. The priesthoods and citizens of several districts participated in this event, following the barque of the goddess, whose form was carried from her temple to that of her consort.

The city of Thebes *(Waset)* was known throughout the ancient world for its glorious temples, gardens, caravan stops, and spacious quays where ships from as far away as Lebanon moored. As the capital of Egypt in several episodes for hundreds of years at a time, most of the country's wealth was centered here, and much of it was stored in the great house of the Theban gods we know today as Karnak. Comprised of hundreds of sanctuaries, chapels, sacred lakes, and pillared festival halls, it remains today the largest religious monument in the world.

In the north, the precinct of Mont housed the temple of the regional gods and the military quarter, while Amun's vast temple occupied the central plain of the city. The unique architecture of Amun's sanctuary reveals a metaphysical plan to embody the temple with cosmic life. Inscriptions on this temple's pylons and chambers reveal the Egyptian belief that the Royal House transmitted the sacred blood of Egypt's divine ancestors through the pharaonic initiations that took place here amidst great ceremony.

This "city of sanctuaries" encompasses a multitude of spiritual traditions, each with its own priesthood and ceremonies. Among the splendid monuments found here is the temple of Khons, god of divination, and the the temple of Ptah, which also honors the lioness Sekhmet-Bast in her aspect as healer and patroness of physicians.

On the west bank, several monumental funerary complexes built by the Theban monarchs reveal a society that was guided by a belief in the divinity of the royal person and lifelong service by her subjects to its maintenance. The Ramesseum, Hatchepsut's terraced temple, and the Valleys of the Kings and Queens remain as glorious testimony to this tradition.

Deeper into the Nile Valley at Edfu, a series of unique inscriptions in the temple of the hawk-headed god depict the most ancient mystery play known. Dedicated to the victory of Heru over his adversary Set, the drama represents the initiation of Pharoah as vanquisher of chaos and darkness, and his ascension as son of the gods and light bringer. The ceremonies of this temple reprise a series of battles between the two gods before they made peace, and the tradition of endowing the royal person with the maintenance of Maat.

Although the present temple was rebuilt in the Graeco-Roman period, its foundation in remote antiquity is recorded on the west enclosure wall. The deified Old Kingdom sage Imhotep is depicted as the temple's founder and record-keeper, retelling the saga of Set's military defeat by the *Heru Shemsu* ("followers of Heru") in predynastic times.

Just north of Edfu in the ancient city of El Kab, Wadjet's sister-deity bestowed the powers of the White Crown for the Royal House. Here, the seat of the vulture goddess Nekhebet is also the site of one of the earliest predynastic settlements in Egypt, emphasizing the great antiquity of the two goddesses who spiritually protected the monarchy.

Like the cobra, the Egyptian vulture represents a number of symbolic powers possessed by the archaic goddesses. Fiercely protective and devoted to her young, the female vulture will face any danger to safeguard the nest, and this is the essence of spiritual protection endowed to the royal person by the gods at coronation. At the same time, this power—along with the dominion bestowed by the uraeus image—is wielded by the monarch to protect the people and territory of the nation she governs.

At the southern border of Egypt, a serene island houses the tranquil sanctuary of the supreme goddess in ancient times. Philae *(Per Auset)* was an enduring stronghold of the pagan religion into our modern era; the last hieroglyphic inscriptions were carved here in 394 C.E. Auset's powers are inseparable from those of her consort Asar, and the priests of her graceful temple complex also honored her husband on the neighboring island to the west, Biga. There, the god was believed to repose in the swirling waters that emanated from the deepest region of the Nile, where the river's legendary source existed. She, "the most powerful one," established her seat in the holiest place on the river to bring forth from it all life that originated from celestial regions and descended into the world through the waters of the Nile.

In addition to the major temples, each locality possessed a shrine dedicated to an indigenous deity, one who embodied the character of the terrain and the cultural consciousness of the region. Egypt was divided into these regions in the mists of antiquity, and they acquired their distinctive qualities long before the unification of the North and South in predynastic times. Upper Egypt was divided into twenty-two regions, designated as nomes[3] by the Greeks, while Lower Egypt was divided into twenty nomes. Each was governed by the local official *(nomarch),* and in many

---

3. The word *nome* comes from the Greek *nomos,* "region," similar to our modern counties.

Nome Spirits—Lower Egypt

Nome	Name	Nome Standard	Nome Spirit	Greek Capital
1	Ineb Hedj	White Palace	Herybakef	Memphis
2	Khenshu Aa	Ox Foreleg	Kherty	Letopolis
3	Ament	West	Hap	Naukratis
4	Sapi Meh	Southern Shield	Wadjet	Sais
5	Sapi Res	Northern Shield	Djebauti	Buto
6	Khasut	Mountain Bull	Sakha	Xois
7	Nefer Ament	Western Harpoon	Hu	Metelis
8	Nefer Abt	Eastern Harpoon	Heret Kau	Succoth
9	Per Asar	Two Pillars	Andjety	Busiris
10	Kam Ur	Black Ox	Khentekhtai	Athribis
11	Ka Heseb	Heseb Bull	Mahes	Leontopolis
12	Theb Ka	Divine Calf	Anher	Sebennytus
13	Heq At	Prospering Sceptre	Iusaas	Heliopolis
14	Khent Abt	Foremost of the East	Wadj Wer	Pelusium
15	Djehut Unnu	Ibis	Sefkhet Abwy	Hermopolis Parva
16	Kha	Dolphin	Hatmehit	Mendes
17	Behdet	Place of the Throne	Behdety	Diospolis
18	Am Khent	Southern Royal Child	Horhekenu	Bubastis
19	Am Pehu	Northern Royal Child	Khonshu Neferhotep	Tanis
20	Sopdu	Plumed Falcon	Sopdu	Pharbaithos

Table 4—The Nomes of Ancient Egypt

Nome Spirits—Upper Egypt

Nome	Name	Nome Standard	Nome Spirit	Greek Capital
1	Ta Sety	Land of the Bow	Satis, Anuqet	Elephantine
2	Thes Hertu	Throne of Heru	Behdety	Apollonopolis Magna
3	Ten	Shrine	Nekheny	Hierakonpolis
4	Iuny	Plumed Sceptre	Mont	Thebes
5	Herui	Two Falcons	Heqet	Apollinopolis Parva
6	Aa-Ta	Crocodile	Hesat	Tentyris
7	Seshesh	Sistrum	Bat	Diospolis Parva
8	Ta Ur	Ancient Land	Khentiamenti	Abydos
9	Amsu	Min	Kaumutef	Panopolis
10	Uadjet	Cobra	Antiu	Antaeopolis
11	Set	Set	Sobekh	Hypselis
12	Tu-ef	Viper Mountain	Anti	Antaepolis
13	Atef Khent	Upper Nedjfet Tree	Ap Uat	Lycopolis
14	Atef Pehut	Lower Nedjfet Tree	(A form of Het-Her)	Cusae
15	Un	Hare	Wennut	Hermopolis Magna
16	Meh Mahedj	White Oryx	Pakhet	Hipponon
17	Iunyt	Black Jackal	Ap Uat	Cynopolis
18	Sepa	Falcon	Nemty	Ankhyrononpolis
19	Uabut	Two Sceptres	(A form of Set)	Oxyrhynchus
20	Nart Khent	Upper Sycamore	Herishef	Herakleopolis Magna
21	Nart Pehut	Lower Sycamore	Sobekh	Crocodilopolis
22	Matenu	Flint Knife	Renutet	Aphroditopolis

nomes the laws varied, often stemming from local religious custom. For example, the eating of the Lates fish was forbidden in the Seventeenth Nome of Upper Egypt, where at the temple of Esna it was a form of Khnum and sacred to his cult.

In the Egyptian world view, Earth and sky are intrinsically bonded, and each mirrors the other in the metaphysical dimension. In view of this belief, the forty-two nomes were believed to reflect the powers of the sky, also divided into regions governed by the forty-two Neteru. In this scheme, entry into celestial regions becomes possible through the nome spirits, who embody the cosmic functions of the gods in terrestrial form. Those powers were seen to descend into the region and accumulate in the nome standards, which were deposited in the local shrines. Whether brought into the precinct of the great temples or carried into battle, the nome standards were viewed as powerful fetishes containing the vital forces of the Egypt's Earth gods.

In addition to the nomes, other potent influences were recognized at work in the land. In the Osirian mythos, the god's dismemberment by Set resulted in the scattering of his members along the Nile; they were reassembled and reconstituted in the mystic rites of his restoration. Yet each member was commemorated through time at a shrine where it was discovered in legend by his sister Auset and her supporters. For instance, at Abydos the nome fetish was fashioned in the image of a shrine that preserved his head. In the metaphysical sense, the members of Asar that were preserved along the Nile shrines are also metaphors of the active cosmic functions that are stationed in the region. Returning to Abydos, the spiritual function of identity, reflected in the visage of the face and the senses of seeing, hearing, and speaking, were constituted here by the powers of the temple, known to the ancients as "the shrine of the head." The reassembly of Asar's body is thus a metaphor for the reconstitution of the identity and functions of the individual on the spiritual plane.

Though the temple was regarded in ancient times as the residence of the god, it also served a multiplicity of purposes that extended beyond its religious character. The Egyptian temples were cultural repositories, political and judicial hubs, and social plexes. Education was its most important mundane function, but spiritually, the *Per Neter* ("divine house") allowed the creative powers of the Neteru to become ritually accessible to the environment, and this is the primary objective in the practice of Sacred Science.

	Body Relic	Location		Protective Funerary Amulet	Cosmic Function
1	left leg	Biga Island		Haapi (Lungs)	Distinction
2	head	Abydos		Ahat	Identity
3	heart	Athribis		Kephri	Memory
4	feet	Herakleopolis		Imset (Liver)	Mobility
5	arm	Memphis		Qebsenuf (Intestines)	Authority
6	chest	Dendera		Menat	Emotion
7	thigh	Koptos		Shuti	Authority
8	eye	Heliopolis		Uadjat	Well Being
9	fist	Diospolis		Shenu	Strength
10	finger	Sais		Wadj	Fecundity
11	backbone	Busiris		Djed	Stability
12	ears	Hermopolis		Ursh	Communication
13	shin bones	Elephantine		Daumutef (Stomach)	Endurance
14	phallus	Letopolis		Thet	Propagation

Table 5—The Fourteen Shrines of Asar: Throughout dynastic history, many Osirian sanctuaries in Egypt claimed to possess relics of the god. These honors were apparently transferred as time passed, and in some instances the relics were duplicated at different sites.

Per Neter
Divine House, temple of the god

Per Ankh
House of Life, temple college

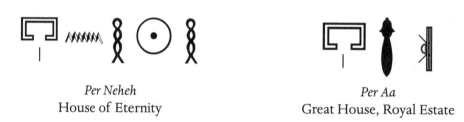

Per Neheh
House of Eternity

Per Aa
Great House, Royal Estate

Figure 15—The Temple Names

The realms of spiritual responsibility served by the ancient temples encompassed all dimensions of life in ancient Egypt. The three faces of human experience—creation, procreation, and renewal—were embodied in both the cosmic and practical functions of the *Per Neter*. And so it is not surprising to see that the activity of the temple took place through a network of religious centers that were dedicated to interpreting and transmitting the spiritual basis of those experiences.

In the *Per Ankh* (House of Life), the repository of Egypt's wisdom was maintained in scriptoria, teaching colleges, historical archives, and education for the professions. And because of the vast extent of that knowledge in ancient times, the Per Ankh was often city-like in proportions, with its own river quays, manufacturing districts, and lands for producing food supplies. An example of a foremost Per Ankh is the great house of Amun at Karnak, which encompassed hundreds of temples, schools, and subsidiary buildings.

Another tradition was taught and practiced that aimed at maintaining the bonds between the inner and after lives of both the living and the dead. This was accomplished through the function of the *Per Aa* ("Great House"). Though once believed by scholars to fulfill only the funerary observances of Egypt, the Per Aa was concerned with the entire natural cycle of the land—the inundation of the soil, the planting of seed, and the harvest. It also served to distribute the benefit of the Royal House to the region, with the consequent elevation of the royal person in a personal cult. Sacred drama and festivals, with members of the Royal House assuming the powers of the gods in these ceremonies, embodied the manifestation of divine life in the physical world and allowed the populace to participate in the Mysteries.

The Per Aa also provided essential services to the populace that included legal resolution, burial services, and employment. An example of the Per Aa is the Ramesseum on the western bank of Thebes, which once housed and employed thousands of laborers, artisans, and part-time priests from the region. Dedicated to maintaining the Ka ("vital spirit") of Rameses II, the temple functioned for hundreds of years after the monarch's passing yet maintained its spiritual agenda. Other temples in this tradition include the twin sanctuaries of Dendera and Edfu, and the great temple of Asar at Abydos.

In the enigmatic pyramid complexes—featuring extensive causeways, chapels, temples, and pyramids—another temple dispensation appears. The *Per Neheh* ("House of Eternity"), more frequently called *Per Heh,* was initially viewed as a reference to the tomb, but its name use at other places alludes to a very distinct type of function. The objective of the Per Heh was the fulfillment of the spiritual mandate of Sacred Science, exaltation to divine life. This was accomplished through an elaborate cycle of reserved festivals such as the Heb Sed, and involved a select category of clergy and participants—highly ranked members of the Royal House and the Divine House. The pyramid complexes at Saqqara, Abusir, Abu Gurab, and Giza were constructed to perform this transcendent function, and some enigmatic monuments such as the Osireion at Abydos served a similar purpose. In the waning days of Egyptian civilization, the sacred tradition of the Per Heh was disclosed to the Alexandrian sages of late antiquity and preserved in fragments of the Hermetic writings.

Throughout the history of Egypt, we find these three functions of the Per Neter consistently presented, irrespective of the cosmogony in use at the time or alterations made in the size or scope of the temple. Sometimes, religious and secular activities at the different centers were identical and priestly functions overlapped. This is wholly consistent with Egyptian religious practice, which was more inclusive than autonomous and emphasized practicality for the sake of society as well as the gods.

This triune scope of temple work can be expressed in the terms of Egypt's sacred astronomy, which best describes the nature of the cult agenda in each category as well as the type of clergy that fulfilled them. The temple emphasis in teaching, royal mortuary services, and reserved initiation rites that have been described to us by the ancients fall precisely into the roles of Solar (royal), Lunar (societal), and Stellar (initiatory) functions at the three types of temples. There are also physically distinguishing characteristics in the architecture and geographic locations of these three types of temples that reflect these categories.

While the Two Lands gave rise to the distinctive temple traditions of Egypt, they also reflect the psychic character of the two regions. From the cerebral, enigmatic pyramid complexes of the North and Lower Egypt to the celebratory, instinctive temple cities of the South and Upper Egypt, each region furnished a dimension of both cosmic and Earthly existence that was expressed through the sacred cult in numerous ways. Besides the daily ritual, the processions, sacred days, festivals, and ritual dramas offered boundless appearances of divine life that were reminders to the living of both their origin and destination. Those spiritual opportunities can certainly be accessed by modern initiates, but the physical structure must first come into being.

The Ancient Temple

The application of Sacred Science can be achieved in any environment, but the delineation of space dedicated solely to its execution is the traditional approach to commencing this work. In the ancient world, the construction of temples, sacred precincts, philosophic schools, healing centers, and memorials for royal persons all initially entailed selection of an environment where a divine principle could be implanted, maintained, and transmitted. These priorities should also guide the creation of the modern Per Neter, and alone serve to define the purpose of the sacred space. Considerations such as the size, the value of the property, or its outer appearance have no bearing on its ultimate merit. A garden gazebo, a walk-in closet, or an empty attic can serve as a conduit to spiritual life as well as an elaborate meeting hall or church.

No matter what the size or caliber of the accommodations, there are areas of temple work that have traditionally been segregated from others by virtue of their functions. For instance, the ancient temple was surrounded by a *temenos,* an outer wall that delineated the sacred precinct as a whole. Though some may assume that the wall served as protection in the same way that medieval fortifications surrounded castles, it more truly represents the boundary of the celestial regions contained within where they touch upon the outer, mundane world. On entering this sacred ground, the pilgrim enters the realm of the gods and shares in their divine life, without judgment of merit or status. It was often here that legal disputes were settled in ancient times. The temenos marks the boundary between human law and divine order. Passing into this region, both powers become accessible. In later times, the Christian churches adapted this tradition in the concept of sanctuary (protective asylum) within the sacred precinct.

One of the most complete temples of Egypt that provides a comprehensive view of the ancient sanctuary with its daily and cyclic activities is the temple of Heru at Edfu in Upper Egypt. Reconstructed over a period of several reigns by Ptolemaic monarchs, the temple was quite ancient when the restoration began in 237 B.C.E. under the third Ptolemy, Euergetes I. Inscriptions at the temple cite its founding and design by the Old Kingdom sage Imhotep, and evidence of older construction indicates that the temple existed on site for thousands of years.

The numerical design of features in the Per Neter was carefully executed. At Edfu, the presence of twelve columns in both the Pronaos ("before the sanctuary") and Great Hall of the temple allude to the Solar cycle of twelve months and the scheme of twelve constellations through which the Sun travels in Graeco-Roman cosmology and astrology. As this was the period during which the standing temple was last renovated, it embodies the philosophical basis of the Divine House in Egypt's waning years, a sanctuary of the Solar principle expressed in the numeration of a twelvefold cycle.

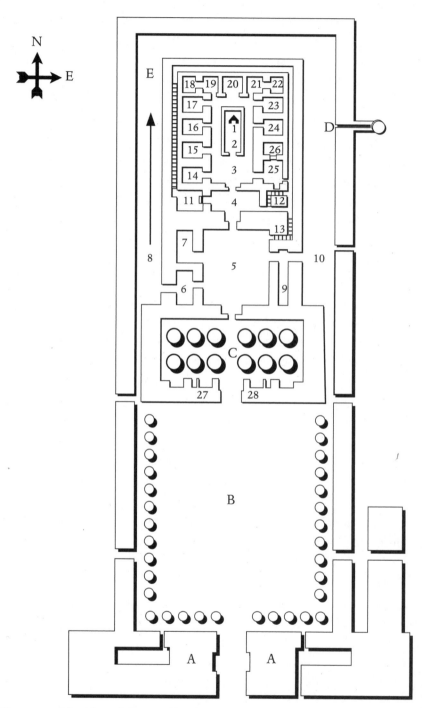

Figure 16—The Plan of the Temple of Heru at Edfu

Within the temenos at Edfu is a great gateway, the outer pylon (A) where processions began and ended in ancient times. This is the entry to the temple proper, and the two massive walls that usually formed the ancient pylon symbolize the two horizons *(akhet)* where the Sun rises and sets, coming into being and retiring each day. As temple life was regulated by these two celestial events, the pylons marked their perpetual return in the temple as well as the gateway through which the gods passed via the passage of light.

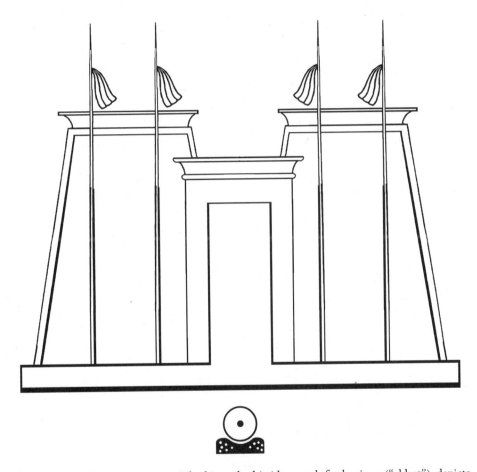

Figure 17—Akhet, the Horizon: The hieroglyphic ideograph for horizon ("akhet"), depicts the Sun positioned between two hills, depicting the reappearance of light at dawn. Similarly, the outer pylons of the temple mark the entry of divine light into the sacred territory. They emulate the spiritual horizon, where celestial forces reappear and enter through the temple axis into the sanctuary.

The pylon marks the threshold of public access and the entry to the god's exclusive domain. Beyond this, a number of guidelines for clothing, footwear, and criteria of physical hygiene were required before one could proceed further. After passing through, one enters an outer court (B), which once provided the forum for gatherings of both the public and the priesthood. This was where the great festivals of the god were celebrated, and offerings were brought to honor the deities within. In turn, spiritual benefits were dispensed to participants and observers in the form of oracles, oblations, and sacred dramas. The outer court is the "meeting place" between human and divine forces. At Edfu, a splendid colonnade of thirty-two pillars surrounds the open court.

In the temple proper, there are a successive number of inner courts, each representing regions of the spiritual world where the god moves and exists. The chambers narrow and the light becomes more selective while moving further into the interior of the god's house, symbolizing the mystic passage through the sacred region of the deity. In the Edfu temple, we first encounter the pronaos (C), which houses twelve monumental columns that symbolize the divine hours of day that Heru established by subjugating Set.

In this region of the temple is located a chamber called the House of the Morning (27) where daily ablutions were made for purification on entry into the god's house. Reliefs here show the king receiving purification by a *Setem* (provisioner) priest who wears the leopard skin of high ceremony; another shows the king being baptized by Djehuti and Heru. Sunrise was regarded as the time of renewal in the day, hence the name.

Opposite is situated the House of Books (28), or scriptorium, where a reader-priest was on duty "for the twelve hours of the day." A library that archived the records and wisdom of the temple tradition were kept here, and twenty-nine sacred books of the temple are enumerated; one of them is listed as "Formulae for Warding off the Evil Eye."

In the deepest part of the temple the ground is highest, where a black granite shrine once housed the golden image of the Neter (1) in the sanctuary (2) called "the high seat," representing the primeval mound of the deity's initial incarnation on Earth. The image and relics of the god reposed in this sanctum, where they were awakened each day and ritually fed, clothed, and honored with litanies and offerings of scent and music. This area is regarded as the living core of the temple, and is reserved for those who are knowledgeable in the maintenance and magical protection of the god's tabernacle.

Surrounding this holy of holies are subsidiary halls and chambers that maintain and support the life of the god; a most important area is the Hall of the Ennead (3). It includes the inner ambulatory, which encircles the sanctuary on the east, north, and west sides and is lit by apertures in the ceiling; the facade is inscribed with the morning litany, which is sung in the daily ritual.

The extensive corridors and rooms in this ancient temple bear testimony to the elaborate and meticulous care that was rendered in the god's house. The Hall of Offerings (4) was the place where the Neter's daily sustenance and gifts were presented; to the left (11) is an antechamber and landing from the straight stairway that descends from the roof, and to the right (12) is the winding stairway that ascends to the roof, where the night watch of the hour priests was observed.

The Great Hall (5) features twelve free-standing columns, another allusion to the Solar powers housed here. The eastern walls portray the symbolism of Upper Egypt, while the western portion symbolizes Lower Egypt. On the south wall, the foundation ceremony of the temple is depicted. The Chamber of the Nile is located in this area (6), where water was brought into the western entry to the left and consecrated for the offering ceremonies. Recipes for incenses and botanical elixirs are inscribed on the walls of the Laboratory at the northwest corner of the Great Hall (7); it is the domain of "the master of the laboratory." Also in this area of the temple is the western entry (8) to the temple, which accesses the west enclosure wall upon which is inscribed the sacred drama of the temple, the "Triumph of Heru." Opposite is the Chamber of the Treasury (9), used for storage of gold, silver, precious stones, and the amulets used for protection of the temple. At the eastern entry (10), daily offerings were brought from the outside of the temple, including water from the sacred well (D). Yet another stairway (13) ascends to the roof.

Liturgies and details of temple life are inscribed on the walls throughout the chambers of the inner ambulatory. The Chapel of Min (14) contains hymns dedicated to the Neter of virile power, while lists of the god's regalia are recorded in the Mansion of Raiment (15); the Throne of the Gods (16) kept images of the temple deities secluded. Chambers 17 through 19 are initiation rooms in the tradition of the Heliopolitan gods; Asar in his form as Sokar, Auset, and Nebt-Het preside in this region, where underground temple crypts are accessed.

The chamber directly behind the sanctuary (20) is alternately called the *Mesen* ("foundation") and Harpoon Room, a reference to the weapon used by Heru to slay his enemy Set. It contains the re-created barque of the temple, constructed for a reenactment by the English egyptologist Arthur Weigall, chief inspector of antiquities for Upper Egypt from 1905 to 1914.

Photo 4—Re-created sacred barque in the temple of Heru at Edfu (Graeco-Roman ca. 200 B.C.E.).

The double chamber (21–22), like that opposite (18–19), serves as a dual chapel, dedicated to Het-Her and Ra, respectively. Their images were kept in these rooms, where they were believed to retire in the dark hours and rise in the morning to join Heru, lord of the temple. Chamber 24 was known as *Behdet*, the name of the god's birthplace and the chamber of his regalia. An area outside of the covered temple (25) featured an altar, where offerings were presented to Nut in her chapel (26). Called the "Pure Place," it was the temple's gateway to the region of renewal.

The preservation of the Edfu temple allows modern eyes to view the extent of divine work that occupied thousands of Egyptians in the region over millennia. The daily service to Heru entailed an elaborate protocol of awakening, feeding, and maintaining the sacred environment, but the great festivals opened the powers of the god to society, and those events are carefully recorded on the temple's enclosure walls. On the outer ambulatory (E) walls are inscribed scenes from the legendary "Triumph of Heru," a mystery play that annually reenacted the victory of the god over Set. Rites also celebrated at the festival restated the powers of Pharaoh, who assumed the role of the god; the queen played the role of Auset, who guides her son in the play to come forward and slay his adversary.

The Modern Temple

In the modern temple, the entry area should be separate from the sanctuary, where ceremonies are conducted. It may simply be curtained or cordoned off from the temple area, to ensure separation from the sacred space. The entry is a place where the clothing and belongings of the mundane world are relinquished, and where the participant's outer identity is shed before approaching the god.

As in the ancient temple, a purification area should be defined, where a period of reflection prior to proceeding with divine work may be possible. Here also offerings may be prepared for ceremonies without distraction.

The sanctuary itself is the most reserved place in the temple; it is the physical house of the god and the place where its power emanates. As such, it must be protected from hostile influences and treated with reverence. The sanctuary may contain an altar for sacred work, and a *naos,* or shrine, for containing the sacred images.

In ancient times, the sanctuary was closed off from the mundane world for an important reason: it was in this chamber that creation was reenacted, and the powers that entered this sphere were regarded as powerful and chaotic. The Egyptians believed that to open the sanctuary to the outside world would unleash these forces, though sacred ritual would ensure that what was evoked would be directed to the mandate of the temple, rather than to ambiguous ends. This is an attitude that would be correct to maintain in the modern temple.

After ceremonies are completed, there should also be an area where participants may retire and reflect on the sacred work that has been performed. In ancient times, refreshment was considered to be an integral part of this process, as many tomb records denote. Even in the solemn funerary ceremonies in ancient Egypt, participants held a feast outside the tomb following burial, in part to be reminded that they were returning to the mundane world with nourishment that had been spiritually shared with the departed. And in the temples, food offerings were taken from the sanctuary "after the Neter was satisfied," and distributed to the clergy and their guests in the outer, open courts. It was believed that to partake of such offerings was to receive the highest blessing from the god. Lastly, the scriptorium should be a separate area in the temple space, where books may be stored and study can be performed leisurely, without interruption.

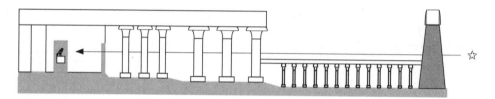

Figure 18—Elevation of the Temple of Heru at Edfu

The layout of the modern temple should accommodate these considerations as much as possible, but the most essential element is its location in relation to the cosmic environment. Orientation and alignment were of primary importance in the siting of the ancient temples, the former being the axis along which certain heavenly bodies pass. The construction of the great temples entailed an even finer precision with regard to celestial objects—alignment to the culmination of a particular star with which the temple's god was associated. In this manner, the sanctuary was targeted to the cosmic realm where the Neter resided, and was physically synchronized with its rhythm in the sky.

It may not be technically possible in most cases to site the modern temple to the culmination of a particular star, but its general orientation may be modified by simply moving a wall or doorway. For instance, the ancient Egyptians regarded the east-west axis as the path of vitality, or in modern parlance, electric. The visible circuit of the Sun and the planets was carefully observed, and it was noted that despite their descent into the west each day, the heavenly bodies infallibly returned in the east the next day. Thus, the cyclic return of vital forces was regarded as a critical phenomenon to which the ancient temple was oriented.

The cosmogeneses of the four great mythic traditions of Egypt—Hermopolis, Memphis, Heliopolis, and Thebes—represent one of the elemental rhythms of creation: Water, Fire, Earth, and Air, respectively. Each is an integral component in the scheme of spiritual work, though it should be noted here that the liturgy for spiritual practice provided in this work is based on the rhythm of Heliopolis.

Using Heliopolitan imagery, east is regarded as the place of renewal, and the quintessential Neter who embodies that principle is Asar. West is the place of passing into night and the entry to the shadow worlds where transformation becomes possible. Its power is relegated to Auset, consort of the renewing god and mistress of all magical operations.

Alternately, the north-south axis was regarded by the ancients as stable, static, and magnetic. North is the residence of the imperishable polestars and is the region of Set, whose inexorable powers are permanently fixed at the Earth's zenith, indicating that the temporal world is governed by forces that cannot be penetrated by other than the highest magic. South is the source of the Nile and the place where heavenly bodies emanate their powers as they culminate in the sky. It is also the quarter of protection and nourishment, the dominion of Nebt-Het.

The modern temple may be oriented to either of these axes and may open to any of the cardinal directions as the ancient temples were. No one direction was considered adverse, as each represents one of the four stations of creation. However, some consideration should be given to the location of the temple portal. East is highly energetic but is subject to constant movement and change with the rhythm of planetary and stellar bodies rising each day. West invites repose and introspection, as the heavenly asterisms retire to the western horizon, each in their turn. North is stable, but it deters change. South is fluid, but it requires continual adjustment. The temple work will, in general, invite these circumstances by its orientation.

The winged Solar disc is an emblem frequently encountered in the ancient temple, placed over the lintel of doorways or the opening to selected chambers. The symbol is derived from the legendary tale *Heru and the Winged Disc,* inscribed on the walls of the Edfu temple. In this saga, the young god as pharaoh battles

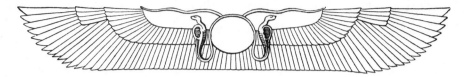

Figure 19—The Winged Solar Disc

his adversaries, and takes the form of the winged disc to dispel them. The two cobras on either side of the icon represent Auset and Nebt-Het, who accompany him on his quest and offer protection. Thus, the symbol is used for apotropaic effect as well as an indicator over chamber entries of the Solar axis in the temple.

Obelisks, or *Ben Ben* (Ben: "to rise," "ascend"), are used to mark either side of the sacred pathway into the portal of the temple. They may be erected when construction of the space is completed and the temple is dedicated with the ceremony of the Opening of the Mouth. Obelisks are icons of cosmic powers, and were incorporated in the "horizon" of every temple with their placement at the gateway of the Solar or Stellar axis of the Divine House.

The construction of Egypt's temples followed a design that mirrored the mythological origins of the first Divine House—the place where the Sun god rested on newly emerged land in the beginning of time. The four worlds of creation are represented—Manu, Aakhut, Rostau, and Ament—but in the temple, these four regions are also states of being, accessed at the cardinal quarters of the sacred territory. At the initial dedication, the Neter was believed to descend through these dimensions into the Divine House and rest upon its consecrated mound, as in primeval time. And those powers, stored in the repositories of the cardinal quarters, allow the temple to manifest its own creative nature through the rituals that will be celebrated there.

(Measuring from the first Digit to the full cubit)

Digits/*Djeba*	Deity/*Neter*	Nomes/*Sepet*	
1	Heh	Khasut	6
			(Lower Egypt)
2	Min	Sapi Res	5
3	Shepses	Sapi Meh	4
4	Herui	Ament	3
5	Anher	Khenshu Aa	2
6	Sah	Ineb Hedj	1
7	Sopdet (East)	Matenu	22
			(Upper Egypt)
8	Heka	Nart Pehut	21
9	Irinefdjesef	Nart Khent	20
10	Irimentef	Uabut	19
11	Irimaua	Sepa	18
12	Haqu	Iunyt	17
13	Dunawy (West)	Meh Mahedj	16
14	Djehuti	Un	15
15	Qebsenuf	Atef Pehut	14
16	Daumutef	Atef Khent	13
17	Haapi	Tu-ef	12
18	Imset	Set	11
19	Heru	Uadjet	10
20	Nebt-Het	Amsu	9
21	Set	Ta Ur	8
22	Auset	Seshesh	7
23	Asar	Aa-Ta	6
24	Nut	Herui	5
25	Geb	Iuny	4
26	Tefnut	Ten	3
27	Shu	Thes Hertu	2
28	Ra	Ta Sety	1

Table 6—The Cubit Gods

Art and Inscription

Metrology, the science of measurement, was developed early in Egyptian history and, like the other physical sciences, was based on natural phenomena. The cubit was the essential measuring device for surfaces, and a number of cubit measuring rods have been found in tombs and inscribed in temples. The curious discrepancies among them have led to speculation as to their practical and symbolic purpose, and it is understood that the differences apply to use in function and location. For instance, the cubit measure of land measurement differs from the cubit used in architecture.

The cubit *(Meh)* represents the length of an arm span. The version commonly found in tombs as a votive offering, the Royal Cubit *(Meh Nesut),* measures 20.6284 inches (.5236 meter). It is subdivided into the Palm *(Shesep)* of $\frac{1}{7}$ cubit and the Digit *(Djeba)* of $\frac{1}{4}$ palm or $\frac{1}{28}$ cubit.

Each division of the cubit is governed by a Neter. The cosmogony of Heliopolis is represented on the cubit rod, as well as the four genii and certain stellar asterisms. Besides the Neteru, each cubit division is also associated with one of the nomes. The twenty-two regions of Upper Egypt are represented, along with six of the nomes of Lower Egypt, to create a total of twenty-eight cubit divisions.

Balance, symmetry, and the ideal proportions of the human figure were sought in temple art, and this was fulfilled with an artistic canon that originated in early antiquity. Inscriptions that depicted the gods, humans, ceremonial regalia, and texts were all rendered in reference to this canon, believed to be divinely endowed to human beings. It is comprised of a squared grid that controls the height and width of all figures and scenes, and is based on the Royal Cubit measure, with one square being equal to one-sixth of the cubit. This ensures that not only will all figures be in symmetrical balance in the scene, but they will match the ideal scale of the human form. Ancient writings describing this work say that it was rendered "in truth" *(Maat),* and a cubit rod was written next to these statements to indicate the use of the divine canon.

27th unit

21st unit

13th unit

Figure 20—Ritual Scene from Abydos on Squared Grid

In the Old Kingdom, the canon for the human body divided the figure into 18 units from the ground to the hairline (19 to the top of the head). The body's navel is placed within the 11th unit, or $^{18}/_{11}$ (= 1.63636+). In the New Kingdom, the canon was revised to 21 units from the ground to the top of the eye (though Diodorus reports that it was comprised of 21¼ units). In this canon, the body's navel places at the 13th unit, or $^{21}/_{13}$ (= 1.61538+) This figure matches the phi proportion, related to the harmonious ratio known as the Golden Section, as defined by Leonardo da Vinci.

Texts were strictly arranged in the Per Neter to emulate the levels of spiritual reality in the universe and the circuit of natural forces. Inscriptions on the walls of temple chambers followed a clockwise arrangement. On entering the room, guidelines on the function of the chamber, ritual instructions, and contents that occupied the sacred space were carefully detailed, proceeding from the left and circumnavigating the chamber to the right. On outside walls, the same clockwise orientation was employed to record the festivals of the temple and its historical tradition.

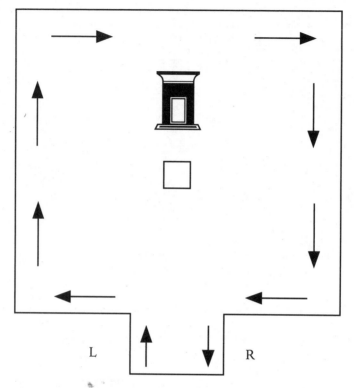

Figure 21—Arrangement of Texts in Space

The arrangement of inscriptions in levels also followed a time-honored canon. Horizontal registers within temple chambers depict information in a pattern that begins at the base with (1) the founding or primeval origins of the temple, representing the past; (2) the text and depictions of the daily ritual, representing the present; and (3) the unique celebrations and observances particular to the Neter of the temple, representing the future and the timeless realm of the Divine House. The theme of layered time in the celestial worlds is also mirrored in the spiritual practice of the temple, where the preliminary rites of a ceremony represent the ordering of the universe in the beginning of time (bathing, purification), followed by the daily rite of the Neter (the birth of the god and its feeding). And all was punctuated by the great feasts of the temple—re-creating the acts of the gods that endow the human race with their powers.

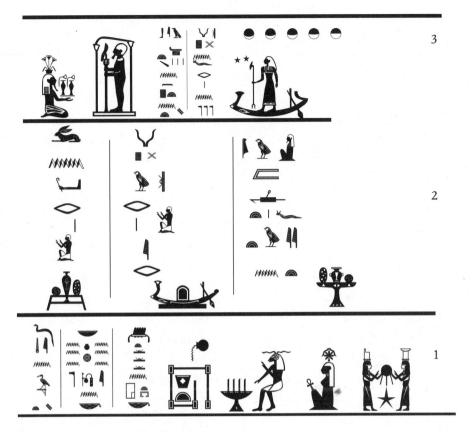

Figure 22—Arrangement of Texts in Time

The use of color in the temple also supported these metaphysical concepts of the divine descending through nature and into the temple for the benefit of human beings. Color had more than visual quality to the Egyptians; it represented cosmic substance, emanated by the gods themselves. Red *(Desher)*, the most vital color representing the essence of life (blood and the vital organs), was reserved for ceremonial objects that convey and maintain the powers of life. On occasion, the king is depicted with red skin in his role as subjugator of dark forces and the vital principle that awakens the life force of the temple. This color was also used to describe dangerous and violent gods, acts, and emotions; Set is described as the "red-eyed one." In consideration of these traditions, red is used sparingly in the temple environment.

Blue *(Irtiu)* is associated with cosmic phenomena and is used interchangeably with the precious stone lapis lazuli to describe physical qualities of the stellar gods: Nut, Amun, and ascended human beings. White *(Hedj),* the absence of color, is used to depict sacred beings and objects that have protective powers, especially winged beings: the vulture Nekhebet, the ibis Djehuti, and the Bennu (phoenix) of Heliopolis. And though black is regarded as a color of death and mourning in modern times, the ancient Egyptians equated the color with the black land of Egypt (Kem) after the waters of inundation receded and revealed the rich deposits left by the annual flood. This is also the color of Asar in his hibernating, passive aspect, until he is revived and assumes the color of natural life, green. From this ancient name and the transformation brought by the river, the Arabic name for Egypt, *Al Khemi,* has preserved the natural mystery of the land.

Many goddesses endowed human beings with goodness, growth, and prosperity, symbolized by the name for green, *Wadj.* Green malachite embodies the essence of this color. Yellow *(Khenet)* was used to color the skin of women, while men's bodies were shaded a russet brown. This convention was used in inscriptions and statuary, and symbolized the psychic associations of the sexes, Lunar/brown (male) and Solar/yellow (female). Inscribed hieroglyphs also have their associated colors, such as yellow for the quail chick *(w)* and blue for the water ripple *(n).*

Color themes are also associated with the great temple centers and their elemental forces: Heliopolis (Earth) is black, Memphis (Fire) is white, Hermopolis (Water) is blue, and Thebes (Air) is violet. Edfu and Dendera, being sanctuaries of Earth and Fire (Het-Her and Heru), is associated with red; Abydos is the locus of Earth and Water (Asar), and the color green.

Metals were regarded as emanations of divine principles. The temples of Egypt were well endowed with gold furnishings and decoration, as gold was viewed as the flesh of the gods. Conversely, silver was considered inferior because of its corrosive qualities, but it was mixed with gold to produce electrum—a highly valued metal used in statuary and obelisks. Copper is sacred to the female Neteru, and was used to make reflecting discs for mirrors, crowns, and divination. Lead was used extensively in the production of ritual objects and amulets, being valued for its weight and lasting quality. Meteoritic iron, though rare, was used for ceremonial objects in the highest magic and was regarded as divine substance, the "metal of heaven" *(bia en pet).*

Foundation of the Temple

The creation of a Divine House brought together all the specialists in ancient societies—engineers and construction laborers, spiritual advisors and technicians, and members of the Royal House who performed the dedication to the gods for all eternity. But for the Egyptians, the metaphysical construction of the temple was the supreme work, and a careful plan was followed for every Divine House that never deviated from tradition.

The *Mesen* ("foundation") ceremony was initiated by establishing the cardinal quarters of the temple (East-South-West-North) before the ground was broken. After determining these directions by astronomical and geodetic means, the four winds or four cultic gods of creation were magically summoned to each of the precinct's corners and invoked to appear and witness the founding of the Divine House.

At Dendera, an inscription at the temple of Het-Her records that the cosmic alignments of the building were first determined by a temple astronomer and priestess, followed by elaborate rites of ceremonial purification, dedication, and embodiment by an assembly of priestly specialists.

Then, Pharoah broke the ground and buried in the cardinal quarters brick amulets of the elemental forces that were expected to "grow" out of the ground and constitute the spiritual body of the temple.

In dedicating the tomb for the dead, the Ceremony of the Four Torches was similarly performed to establish the place of mystic transformation for the departing soul. Chapter 137 of *The Book of Going Forth by Day* denotes that four officiants, representing the sons of Heru (Imset, Daumutef, Qebsenuf, and Haapi), mark the cardinal places in the tomb with torches that evoke the celestial fire to enter the space and give it life. These deities, the "four genii," are essential for constituting every magical act, allowing it to take form in the four dimensions of creation with the four characteristics of physical substance.

In view of these ancient rites, the *Mesen Het Neter* (founding the Divine House) rite fixes the cardinal forces in the temple to establish the sacred precinct. Though in some traditions the founding rite is intended to protect the participants from disruptive forces on the outside, the Egyptian intention includes more transcendent purposes. Here, the rite is a reenactment of the creation and transforms the immediate environment into the primeval territory. The act of establishing the four quarters is the transposition of primordial chaos with order, as was done by the Neteru in the beginning of time when the universe came into being.

In ancient times it was the cosmogony of the temple that dictated the backdrop of the ritual as it was articulated by the genesis of its gods. For instance, the Memphite creation is recounted as fiery and volatile, with the creative source embodied by Ptah, the "fabricator." The Hermopolitan creation is watery and fluid, with the creative source being Nun, the "primordial ocean." Alternately, the Theban creation is airy and auric, depicting the breath of creation as reflected in the image of Amun, "the hidden." In this liturgy, the four cardinal powers are embodied by the four terrestrial Neteru of Heliopolis, who articulate how the physical world is maintained after coming into being from the first mound of earth that arose from the primeval waters after the mating of Nut and Geb. This was also envisioned as the erection of four pillars in the sky, which were held up by Shu, Neter of air and space.

The first quarter is in the east, the place of sunrise and beginnings. This is the station of Asar, whose function is germination. The next quarter is south, where all celestial bodies appear to culminate in the sky and emanate their powers. Here are stationed the powers of Nebt-Het, whose function is sustenance. Following that is the western quarter, where the Sun retires, and this is the seat of Auset, whose function is birth. The circuit is accomplished at the north, where darkness prevails. Here are stationed the powers of Set, whose function is corruption. Ritualists are familiar with this clockwise order, which represents the fundamental movement of life from the design of petals on flowers to the expanding Milky Way galaxy.

The quarters should be discerned using an accurate compass and marked prior to the foundation ceremony. In ancient times, a small rite known as the *Pedjeshes* (*pedj:* "to stretch," *shes:* "cord") was performed for this purpose. The night ritual called for two divine representatives—the royal person and a priestess representing Seshat, the measurer. A cord with an astronomical point already sited by the attendant priests was aligned, with the royal person gazing at the sky through the headdress of the priestess and marking out the axis of the temple by stretching the cord from that point. The corners of the temple were thus established, and a mallet held by the monarch tapped stakes of precious metal into the ground.

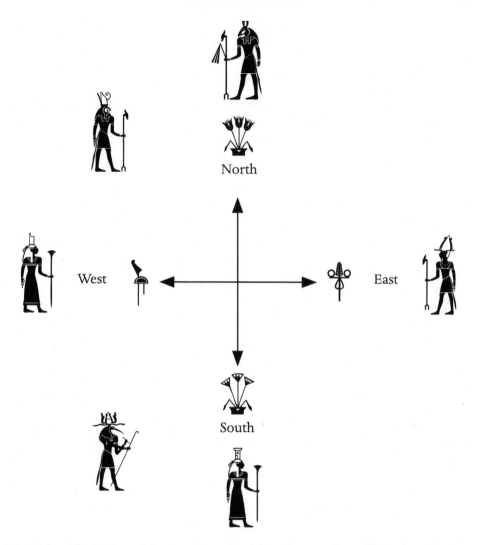

North

West

East

South

Figure 23—The Neteru of the Four Quarters: This scheme is derived from the Ptolemaic Papyrus Salt in the British Museum. Nebt-Het, mistress of water, is stationed in the south— the source of the Nile. Set's station is the northern heavens, the region of permanence. Auset takes her place as Mistress of the West, and Asar's region is "the East of the Holy Land," the place of renewal. In the papyrus, Heru is stationed at the northwest and Djehuti at the south-west. And in all sacred spaces, Geb governs the floor and Nut presides over the ceiling.

Another consideration of sacred space is to recall the protocol of the directions. In ancient Egypt, the right side was considered passive because of the geodetic orientation of the Nile. All directions were based on the observer looking south (the source of the river), with the back to the north. In this stance, the right side is on the west, the place of sunset and death, and the left side is on the east, the place of sunrise and renewal. Thus, the right side is considered dark, while the left is the place of light. That is why hymns and prayers recited at dusk were made facing south, to avoid the dark powers that drew the living toward the west. The symbolism should be employed in creating a temple that is exposed to light from certain directions. Obviously, the choice of a temple where sunrise floods the space with light is desirable, especially if it comes from the east or south.

It should be emphasized that contrary to European ceremonial traditions, the Egyptian rite of consecrating the Four Quarters is not performed at the beginning of every ceremony. Rather, it is a major rite whose intent is to create a new spiritual framework; it should be reserved for its own execution at a cosmically opportune time, such as the spring or autumnal equinox, when Earth forces are in balance and very potent. The Egyptians believed that once the Neteru were summoned to create the temple, their presence was established for as long as they were honored there and provided offerings. And the only certain way to banish their influences was to ritually and physically dismantle the temple, though it was believed that even the dust of the sacred precinct held powers that could survive through the ages.

Finally, the Divine House does not become a working temple until it is animated in the cosmic dimensions. This may not become possible until the dedicated space is furnished according to the basic features of the ancient temple, and a cosmically appropriate time is chosen (a Solar ingress, or New Moon). When it is viable, the last rite, the Ceremony of Opening the Mouth (given in chapter 7) is performed to give the Divine House its life in all dimensions.

In addition to temple space, the Mesen ceremony is recommended for consecration of the quarters in any temple member's home or private shrine. The Egyptians viewed such acts as equivalent to the planting of a seed, which would eventually flower to create a larger environment for the deity within.

The rite of establishing the Four Quarters may be repeated annually, just as the ancient Egyptians repeated pharaonic investitures and temple dedications annually. In these instances, repetition of the rite asserts the original intent of the participants, and invokes the divine beings to strengthen their bond with the sacred space.

While the Neteru of the Heliopolitan rhythm are incorporated in this rite, some practitioners may not feel comfortable establishing Set in the northern quarter, because of his association with hostile forces. The Neter Anpu is the alternative, as his presence ensures protection from the powers of the shadow worlds and his visage may appear more benign to participants.

Quarter	Sign	Period	Element	Neter
East	♈	Spring Equinox	Fire	Asar
South	♋	Summer Solstice	Water	Nebt-Het
West	♎	Autumnal Equinox	Air	Auset
North	♑	Winter Solstice	Earth	Set or Anpu

Table 7—Periods of the Four Quarters

Mesen Het Neter—Establishing the Divine House

Before the quarters are called into being in this ceremony, the divine parents Nut (sky) and Geb (Earth) are invoked to bring forth the sacred space. A procession then inaugurates the creation of the divine house. In ancient times, images of the temple gods were brought into the dedicated land and "settled" into the ground to denote their descent into the physical world as members of the living. Here, a statue or image of the temple's Neteru is carried into the space, and it goes forward with the ceremonialists in the circuit of invocations.

In the next phase, each quarter is established in two stages. In the first, the Neter of the quarter is formally summoned and the *hekau* (magical recitation) is spoken to invoke its presence. Following this, the Neter is greeted in its image as a cosmic rudder, to symbolically "steer" the temple through the cosmic region. Chapter 148 in *The Book of Going Forth* cites the operation of greeting the four rudders as the most ancient, esoteric rite of the temple, a secret that ensures the ritualist protection brought by the sky deities. In some papyri, the name of each rudder is accompanied by an *Uadjat* eye (the eye of Heru), as each was stationed at the four corners of the Solar barque in the heavens.

Mesen Het Neter
Founding the Divine House

Hemu Aakhu Heri Ab Het Ashemu en pet Abtet
Eastern Rudder

Hemu Nekhen Seshmu Taui Nefer en pet Amentet
Western Rudder

Hemu Sekhem Nefer en pet Mehtet
Northern Rudder

Hemu Khenti Herab Het Djesheru en pet Resi
Southern Rudder

Figure 24—The Names of the Four Rudders

A practice frequently cited for establishing the quarters was the recitation of the hekau four times *(djed medu)* at each station. This stems from the ancient belief that each corner of the temple or tomb had its equivalent in all four worlds of creation, and establishing those corners entailed a magical evocation for each and every dimension.

In the last phase, the elemental forces are invoked. It may not be possible to implant the traditional elemental bricks at each quarter in the temple ground if the edifice already exists, but in this phase the sigils of the directions or the hieroglyphic names of the rudders may be painted on the floor, or images of the cardinal deities may be hung on the walls. Another choice of marking the cardinal quarters of the temple is placing images of the four winds at the stations, especially if the temple is intended to be Solar in practice. These deities are regarded as the four Ba's of the Sun god Ra.

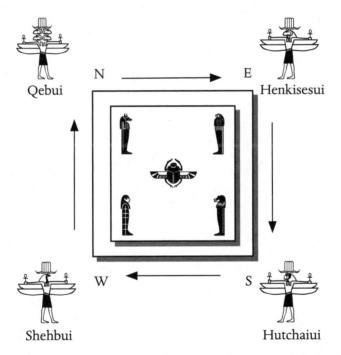

Figure 25—The Elements and the Four Winds: The four winds are aligned to the corners of the altar or sanctuary space. The four elemental genii, the "sons of Heru," are placed on altar inscriptions in the above order, with the scarabaeus in the center. This scheme may also be used to orient the altar of the temple with the cardinal axis in use at the temple.

When the Mesen ceremony is concluded, four poles or Djed columns, representing the pillars of Shu, may be erected at the four corners of the temple. Following this, the ceremony of the Opening of the Mouth will be performed at a cosmically appropriate time. This will mark the "birth" in time and space of the temple.

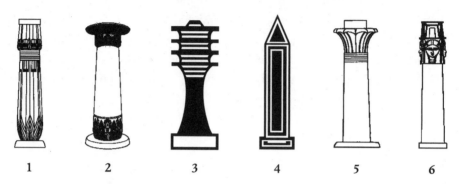

1   2   3   4   5   6

Figure 26—Forms of Temple Pillars: Egyptian temple columns embody cosmic principles as well as organic forces. The Lotus (1) represents the Water element and is found in the outer chambers of the Divine House. The Papyrus (2) is associated with the Air element and is placed in the archival regions of the temple. The Djed (3) embodies the Earth element, often placed before Osirian shrines and chambers of renewal. The Ben Ben (4) transmits the Fire element, marking the axis of Solar light in the temple and the embodiment of celestial forces in the Heliopolitan sanctuary. The fifth element—the Quintessence—is represented in the temple by the Palm (5). The branches of this tree are depicted on inscriptions as markers for endless time, and the leaves are used by the gods to inscribe the names of elevated human beings to ensure their perpetual existence. They are often found in dedicatory shrines and chambers. The column of Het-Her (6) is found in temples to the goddess and the shrines of Nut, where stellar events are observed and commemorated. The crotalum surmounting the head of the column elicits the cosmic rhythm that is transmitted from sky to Earth when celestial asterisms pass overhead.

Dramatis Personae

Since the temple may not be formally organized at the dedication of its space, there may not be the designated ritual players for the offices of *Kher Heb* (lector), *Setem* (steward) and *Urt Hekau* (temple magician). The Kher Heb fulfills the role of Djehuti, lord of measures, who was present at the founding of the ancient temples as divine architect. The Setem personifies the god Ptah, who constitutes divine patterns with physical powers. And the Urt Hekau embodies the goddess Seshat, land surveyor and divine astronomer. When the stations are established by this rite, she then enters that cosmic order, physically and consciously, to summon the Neteru and direct their energetic nature to the appropriate channels for embodying, protecting, and maintaining the temple.

Throughout this rite, the Setem presents the offerings and has charge of the ritual paraphernalia, such as images of the deities and the elemental substances. The Kher Heb recites the sacred texts, and the Urt Hekau pronounces the ancient formulas that constitute the ritual action.

Consecration of the Four Quarters

I. Processional

Kher Heb   The place of peace is established in Iunu,
Seshat draws the ground plan,
Khnum sets up its walls,
Anpu presides over the offerings,
Heru opens its mouth.
The divine sanctuary comes forth from the Earth-god.

Urt Hekau   *Khennu neter per em Aker.*

(The temple space is circumnavigated.)

II. Invocations

Above and Below: (Nut and Geb):

Kher Heb   My mother Nut: a double welcome to you, in this your living house.

Urt Hekau   *Mut-i Nut: en-ek iiui sep tu em per-ek pen en ankhiu.*

Kher Heb   My father Geb: a double welcome to you, in this your living house.

Urt Hekau   *Iti-i Geb: en-ek iiui sep tu em per-ek pen en ankhiu.*

East: Asar

Kher Heb   Hail Asar, Khenti Amentiu:

You rise up, you are not motionless.

You ascend into heaven, you are united to Ra.

To you belongs all that pertains to men and women.

To you belongs all that pertains to life and death.

You awaken in this sanctuary, it is filled with your light.

Urt Hekau   *Asar un nefer, Khenti peru, Ptah neb ankh, Asar her Akhut.*

South: Nebt-Het

Kher Heb   Hail Nebt-Het, Lady of the House of Ptah,

Dweller within Senu:

Eye of Ra whose brother is the Sacred One.

Within your house you protect the hearts of the living.

Divine sister, who is blue as Nut:

You accompany those who enter the barque of Ra.

You awaken in this sanctuary, it is filled with your light.

Urt Hekau   *Het Sekhem, Het Khasit, Ta Kehset per Mert, Ra Nefert, Hebet.*

West: Auset

Kher Heb   Hail Auset, who comes forth from the birth chamber:

Whose mouth is wise, the all-powerful one of the Hekau.

Lady and light giver of heaven, be mighty to protect this temple.

Mother of Heru Kha Kekhet, green goddess who brings forth life,

You awaken in this sanctuary, it is filled with your light.

Urt Hekau   *Sati Sopdet, Thenenet Anqet, Sekhet Renutet, Djet Ament Sah.*

North: Set

Kher Heb   Hail Suti, red god who dwells in the northern sky:

Your mouth is closed,

The red sky is opened with the Seb Ur in your hand

In your name of Great Divider.

You awaken in this sanctuary, it is filled with your light.

Urt Hekau   *Akhemu Seku, Set Nubti, Meskheti Khepesh.*

North: Anpu

Kher Heb	Hail Anpu, he who is on his mountain:
	Opener of the ways, presider over the chamber of embalmment.
	You art summoned to this place of purification,
	To make firm the altar of offerings.
	You awaken in this sanctuary, it is filled with your light.
Urt Hekau	*Apuat, Tep tu-ef, Khent Sehet am Ut, Sekhem em Pet, Sekhem Taui.*

III. Greetings

East:

Kher Heb	Hail splendor, dweller in the temple of the Ashemu gods:
	Beautiful rudder in the eastern heaven.
Urt Hekau	*A hemi aakhu heri ab het ashemu nefer en pet abtet.*

South:

Kher Heb	Hail, dweller in the temple of the Djesheru gods:
	Beautiful rudder in the southern heaven.
Urt Hekau	*A hemi khenti heri ab het djesheru nefer en pet resi.*

West:

Kher Heb	Hail, you who circles, guide of the Two Lands:
	Beautiful rudder in the western heaven.
Urt Hekau	*A hemi nekhen seshemu taui nefer en pet amentet.*

North: (Set)

Kher Heb	Hail darkest power, you who conceals the disc:
	Powerful rudder in the northern heaven.
Urt Hekau	*A hemi sekhem nefer en pet mehtet.*

North: (Anpu)

Kher Heb	Hail watcher, you who divides day and night:
	Powerful rudder in the northern heaven.
Urt Hekau	*A hemu sekhem nefer en pet mehtet.*

The Elemental Forces

Ceremonialists are familiar with the invocation of the elemental forces, another preliminary rite that invites the creative energies of nature into a ceremony—a necessary component in theurgy. When a divine presence is invoked, the physical elements that will constitute its appearance should ideally come from natural sources, rather than the vital force of the ritual participants.

In this practice, the invocation of the elemental forces may follow the consecration of the temple's four quarters as it did in ancient times, or it may be reserved for another appropriate time, such as the summer or winter solstice. These periods represent the exaltation and the concentration of the Earth's vital force, respectively.

The elemental forces are most often personified as five spirits, angels, or nature gods. And no matter which cosmogony is employed, they almost universally represent the five cosmic elements of Fire, Earth, Air, Water, and the Quintessence. In the Egyptian tradition, these are named *Am, Ta, As, Nu,* and *Sa.*

In this practice, "the four sons" of Heru—Imset, Daumutef, Qebsenuf, and Haapi—are the spirits that embody the elements constituting physical life. The fifth, Khepri (the deity of unceasing renewal), brings the Quintessence, or fifth element, into the ritual sphere. This element conveys the boundless emanation of Sa in the universe that is symbolized by the unique humming of the scarab's wings.

The four spirits who are known as "the four sons" are, in metaphysical terms, the issue of Heru's energetic constitution. In *The Book of Going Forth*, two important chapters disclose the nature and origin of these genii. In Chapter 112, they first appear following the loss of Heru's eye in his epic struggle with Set. Here, the young god calls upon his ancestor Ra for its restoration:

Endow me with two kinsmen in Pe and two in Nekhen,
Allow them to be my perpetual helpers,
So that the Earth may become green and turmoil may cease.

In response, Imset and Haapi come into being as the Souls of Pe, the primeval gods of Lower Egypt. Following that (Chapter 113), Daumutef and Qebsenuf come into being as the Souls of Nekhen, the ancestral spirits of Upper Egypt.

Qebsenuf
Fire • East • Hawk Head
Liver and Gall Bladder

Daumutef
Earth • North • Jackal Head
Lungs

Imset
Air • West • Human Head
Stomach and Large Intestines

Haapi
Water • South • Baboon Head
Small Intestines

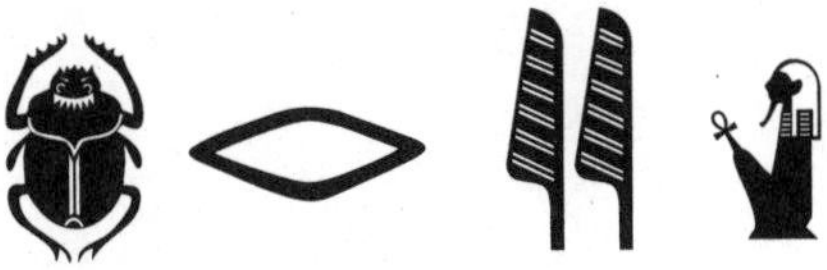

Khepri
Quintessence • Above • Scarabaeus Sacer
Heart

Figure 27—The Names of the Elemental Spirits

These four beings are given to Heru as his assistants in all future acts of magic, to restore the lost functions in both nature and human beings, an affirmation of the vitalizing powers of the elemental spirits. In cosmology, the four genii embody the four states of matter in the universe: solid (Earth), liquid (Water), gaseous (Air), and plasma (Fire).[4]

In the rite of invoking the elemental spirits, a substance that will contain the elemental force, regarded as a *receptor,* is brought forth during the invocation. Tradition usually dictates which substances are appropriate, and the Correspondences of the Five Elements (table 8) denotes the Egyptian forms. However, the water should be taken from a living (flowing) source if possible, and a portable brazier of metal or clay is preferable to a candle or oil lamp. Soil from a sacred precinct is the ideal substance for the Earth element, rather than salt or natron.

The elemental spirits are invoked in two stages: they are initially called, and they are then directed to the place of manifestation by intoning the hekau for empowering the four genii and Khepri. When they are called, the elemental receptors should be brought forth and placed on the altar: the lamp is lit, the water is poured, the incense ignited, and the salt/Earth is uncovered. For the fifth element, the temple oil is poured on the altar or anointed on an image of the Neter of the season. If the temple is fortunate enough to have its own land, foundation deposits may be implanted at this stage (see table 8 for the choice of materials).

---

4. In addition, astronomers at the University of Pennsylvania have recently proposed that more than half of the universe is comprised of a puzzling type of matter known as "dark energy," and is responsible for accelerating growth in the universe. This matter corresponds to the fifth element of the ancients, the Quintessence—the *Sa* of Egyptian cosmology.

Element	Fire	Earth	Air	Water	Quintessence
	Am	Ta	As	Nu	Sa
Direction	East	North	West	South	Above/Below
Stellar Asterism	Alifa	Yildun	Kochab	Phaecda	Thuban
Elemental Neter	Qebsenuf	Daumutef	Imset	Haapi	Khepri
Canopic Image	Falcon	Jackal	Human	Baboon	Scarabaeus
Receptor	Candle	Salt-Soil	Incense	Water	Oil
Offering	Fruit, Meat	Bread	Floral	Beer	Wine
Color	Red	Yellow	Blue	Green	Violet
Gem	Carnelian	Obsidian	Lapis	Malachite	Alexandrite
Stone	Granite-Basalt	Sandstone	Alabaster	Unbaked Brick	Schist
Figure	Pyramid	Cube	Sphere	Crescent	Egg
Organ	Intestines	Stomach	Liver	Lungs	Heart
Funerary Goddess	Selqit	Neit	Auset	Nebt-Het	Nut
Sacred City	Sais	Heliopolis	Mendes	Buto	Abydos
Wind	Henkhisesui	Qebui	Hutchaiui	Shehbui	Taurt
Sacred Bird	Bennu	Vulture	Sparrow	Owl	Ibis
Perception	Maa	Sedjem	Sia	Hu	Heka
Sense	Sight	Hearing	Speech	Taste	Theurgy
Instrument	Gong	Drum	Harp	Bell	Sistrum

Table 8—Correspondences of the Five Elements

Element	Fire *Am*	Earth *Ta*	Air *As*	Water *Nu*	Quintessence *Sa*
Vowel	A	E	I	O	U
Ceremonial Tool	Sword	Stone	Wand	Cup	Mirror
Metal	Gold	Lead	Quicksilver	Silver	Electrum

Table 8—Correspondences of the Five Elements

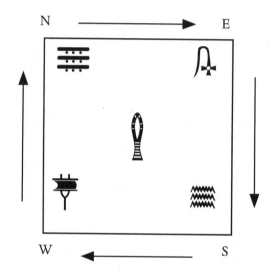

Figure 28—Elemental Invocation: The Diurnal Cycle: Fire-Water-Air-Earth-Quintessence, Am-Nu-As-Ta-Sa, East-South-West-North-Center.

In conclusion, a "pure offering" is made, which may consist of fresh fruit and floral trays that may be distributed to the participants afterward. And finally, if so elected, the erection of the temple pillars may now be performed since the elemental forces have descended to etherically constitute the Divine House. In lieu of pillars, the altar may be placed on the axis of the temple, and upon it the sacred stone of the temple may be brought forth—a representation of the sacred mound upon which the Neter has come to rest.

It does not appear that a strict order of calling on the elemental spirits was followed in ancient times. Some traditions follow the cycle of creation—Quintessence, Water, Fire, Earth, and Air. Others, probably in noting the passage of heavenly bodies over the horizons, follow the diurnal cycle—Fire/east, Water/south, Air/west, Earth/north, and Quintessence/center. The latter protocol is used in the following rite.

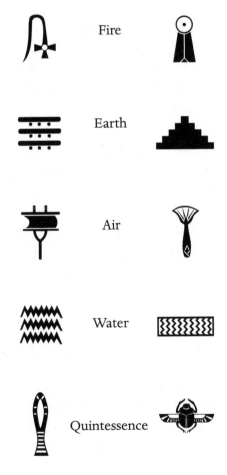

Fire

Earth

Air

Water

Quintessence

Figure 29—Element Sigils

Invocation of the Five Elements

I. Invocations

Fire—*Am*

> Awaken Qebsenuf: Lord of Fire and Flaming things,
> Brilliant one who illumines the Duat,
> Welcome in peace at this shrine.

Water—*Nu*

> Awaken Haapi: Lord of the Hidden Cavern,
> Whose body flows through the Two Lands on Earth and in the sky,
> Welcome in peace at this shrine.

Air—*As*

> Awaken Imset: Lord of wind who comes forth from Shu,
> Divine scent that emanates from Rostau,
> Welcome in peace at this shrine.

Earth—*Ta*

> Awaken Daumutef: Lord of Aker and the fields of Hotep,
> Whose body establishes the sacred mound,
> Welcome in peace at this shrine.

Quintessence—*Sa*

> Awaken Khepri: Lord of revolutions and all that becomes,
> Whose manifestations are continuous,
> Welcome in peace at this shrine.

II. Manifestations

Fire   *Met an Qebsenuf: Nuk se-ek Asar t-na un-a em sau-ek temt-a kesu-ek saq-a at-ek an na nek ab-ek, ta-a nek su her Auset-ef em khat-ek serut na pa-ek.*

Water   *Met an Haapi: Nuk Haapi se-ek Asar i-na un-a em sau-ek thes-ek tep at-ek, hui nek khe eta-ek kher-ek. Erta na nek tep t-etta.*

Air   *Met an Imset: Nuk Imset se-ek Asar, i-a un-a em sau-ek serut na pa-ek men sep sen utu en Ptah, ma utu en Ra t-esef.*

Earth   *Met an Daumutef: Nuk se-ek Heru Meriu-ek i-na net tef Asar em ta ari*
             nek-ef ta-a su kher ret-ek t-etta sep sen.

Quintessence
             Met an Khepera: Nuk pa Kheper em Khepera. Khepera Kheper Kheperu,
             Kheper Kheperu neb em Khet Khepera ashet Kheperu em per em re-a.

III. Offering and Placement of the Pillars or Mound

Homage to you, lords of Maat,

Anedj hra ten, nebu Maat,

Ancestral spirits who eliminate all defects,

Djatdjat tataiu sat em asfat,

Divine ones who are in the following of Hotepsekus:

Amiu khet Hotepsekhus

You eliminate all the defects of this place,

Ter ten tut neb en arutef,

You give birth to the Divine House.

Mesu-ef Per Neter.

IV. Opening the Mouth of the Temple

The temple is now established on the inner planes. It comes into the world of life
and becomes functional when its senses are awakened by the Opening of the
Mouth ceremony. This empowerment is outlined in chapter 7.

Chapter Three

COSMIC RESONANCE

Thus they say that Osiris was a general, that Canopus, from whom the star took its name, was a pilot, and that the ship which the Greeks call Argo, being made in imitation of the ship of Osiris, was, in honor of him, turned into a constellation and placed near Orion and the Dog-star, the former being sacred to Horus and the latter to Isis.
—Plutarch: *De Iside et Osiride*

In modern life, we no longer use our ancient sense of cosmic orientation, the means by which we once ordinarily related to the natural world around us. The daily passage of the Sun over the sky and the nightly procession of stars is no longer vital to our knowing the time or place where we are. Consequently, our sense of wholeness within a great system and our visual relationship with the outside world has receded. We do acknowledge that climatic and seasonal conditions affect our conscious existence in many respects—such as the rhythm of our work and play, our choice of clothing, diet, and travel. But we often overlook that our unconscious sense of timing and communication with the natural world is deeply affected by these factors.

All life in ancient Egypt was placed within the context of this cosmic orientation. We often marvel at the apparent serenity and spiritual confidence that the ancients possessed, forgetting that the tools they used—astronomy, geography, geometry, and architecture—were taught and used in an environment that encouraged a recognition of and a partnership with natural and divine forces. With these tools, a profound sense of cosmic orientation was maintained, and one's role in maintaining it was viewed as true spiritual work.

Although the Nile has long since ceased to produce an annual inundation due to the construction of dams in our era, understanding the profound rhythm of this natural event and others associated with it is essential to realizing the character of Egyptian ritual and ceremony. To restore our cosmic orientation, we must leave our temporal field of time and enter the visible universe of ancient Egypt, where the rhythms of cosmic powers governed the life of human beings, nature, and even the gods.

The concept of time was a powerful consideration in both secular and spiritual matters for the Egyptians. Though the realm of the gods was regarded as "timeless" time *(Neheh)*, it was also continuous, manifesting in cycles. The ebb and flow of cosmic life determined the appearances of the gods, but it was resolute and eternal. In the visible world, events took place in linear time *(Djet)* and were likewise determined by the ebb and flow of cosmic life through the mediums of heavenly bodies. Three rhythms—Lunar, Solar, and Stellar—were regarded as the principal forces affecting linear time, and they are embodied in the three dimensions of cosmic activity.

Lunar Deities

Asar • Djehuti • Het-Her • Khons

Solar Deities

Heru • Maat • Heru Ur • Ra

Stellar Deities

Sopdet • Nefertum • Seshat • Heru em Aakhuti

Figure 30—Cosmic Deities—Lunar, Solar, and Stellar: The Neteru associated with the Moon include Het-Her, representing the function of conception brought by the merging of Solar and Lunar powers in her fertile womb (First Quarter); Khons of the Theban Triad, who embodies the function of periodicity or change in the sky (Second Quarter); and Djehuti of the Hermopolitan Ogdoad, lord of measures and originator of cycles (Third Quarter). Asar is particularly associated with the Fourth and last Quarter of the Lunar cycle, the period of impending darkness.

I. The Lunar Rhythm

One of the spiritual realities transmitted in the esoteric traditions is that all life is dependent upon nature's rhythms, seasons, and cycles. Of these, the two luminaries—the Moon and the Sun—represent rhythms that are particularly relevant to human life.

Scholars believe that a Lunar calendar was the first invention for tracking time in ancient Egypt. Commencing with the first visible sliver of light from the crescent New Moon, a cycle of 29½ days was observed, the synodic period measured from New Moon to New Moon. This period is comprised of two hemicycles: 14½ waxing days and 14½ waning days of Lunar light. This monthly cycle is further divided into quarters of 7¼ days each. These measures are the basis for the Lunar week and month, used from ancient to modern times.

The flux of waxing and waning light in the sky is deeply embedded in the symbolism of Lunar phenomena. At the commencement of the Lunar cycle (the New Moon), the Sun and Moon are conjoined, at the same location in the sky. The ancients viewed this as the union of masculine (Solar) and feminine (Lunar) principles in the numerous legends of the mating of gods. One such theme in Egyptian ceremony is the union of Heru and Het-Her (deities of the Dendera Triad), memorialized in the great festival celebrated at their temples of Edfu and Dendera held on the New Moon of the eleventh month of the Solar year. This event is symbolized in the crown of the goddess, the Solar disc contained in the two horns (waxing and waning crescents) of the Lunar orb.

At the New Moon there is no visible light, but by day 3 following the Solunar conjunction the first crescent of light appears. By day 7 the first quarter is apparent with light illuminating half the disc of the Moon, and between days 14 and 15 the face of the Moon is fully illuminated by the reflected light of the Sun, which lies opposite in the sky. After this event, the Full Moon begins to diminish in the ensuing days, until it loses light altogether following the waning crescent in the sky.

The full cycle of Lunar days is visually depicted in one of the astronomical friezes in Het-Her's temple at Dendera. Here, the days of the Lunar month are noted along with Lunar festivals, though in unique terms. Recalling that the New Moon was determined from the first visible sliver of the crescent, this would occur after day 2 of the new synodic cycle. This explains why the Quarter Moon celebration was named the "Six Day Feast" (six days following the first visible crescent) and the Full Moon was named the "Fourteen Day Feast" (fourteen days following the first visible crescent).

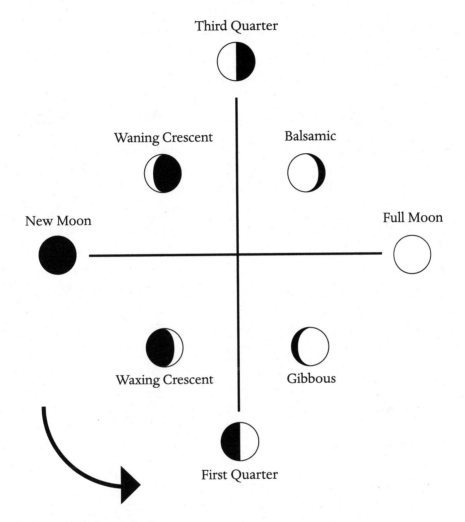

Figure 31—The Lunar Cycle

The Crown of Het-Her

Ra
The Sun

Khons
The Moon

Iah
The body of the Moon,
a name of Djehuti

Wehem Qet-et
Spirit of the Moon,
"renewer of form"

Figure 32—The Luminaries

Degree notations represent the ecliptical distance between the Sun and Moon.

●	Day 1 • 12° New Moon	Day 11 • 132°	Day 21 • 252°
●	Day 2 • 24° Waxing Hemicycle	Day 12 • 144°	Day 22 • 264° Fourth Quarter
●	Day 3 • 36° Visible Crescent	Day 13 • 156°	Day 23 • 276°
●	Day 4 • 48°	Day 14 • 168°	Day 24 • 288°
●	Day 5 • 60°	Day 15 • 180° Full Moon	Day 25 • 300°
●	Day 6 • 72°	Day 16 • 192° Fourteen Day Feast	Day 26 • 312°
●	Day 7 • 84° Second Quarter	Day 17 • 204°	Day 27 • 324°
●	Day 8 • 96° Six Day Feast	Day 18 • 216° Waning Hemicycle	Day 28 • 336°
●	Day 9 • 108°	Day 19 • 228°	Day 29 • 248°
●	Day 10 • 120°	Day 20 • 240°	Day 30 • 360°

Table 9—The Lunar Days at Dendera

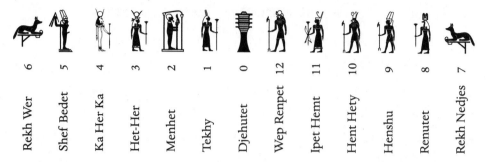

6	5	4	3	2	1	0	12	11	10	9	8	7
Rekh Wer	Shef Bedet	Ka Her Ka	Het-Her	Menhet	Tekhy	Djehutet	Wep Renpet	Ipet Hemt	Hent Hety	Henshu	Renutet	Rekh Nedjes

Figure 33—The Lunar Calendar: The Egyptian Lunar calendar as inscribed on the ceiling of the Ramesseum (Dynasty 19). The Lunar months are determined by the synodic period of 29½ days, the period from New Moon to New Moon. This scheme differs from the Solar (Civil) calendar of 12 months with 30 days each, though in some epochs the Solar and Lunar months shared some of the same names. The Lunar calendar commenced with the first New Moon following the heliacal rising of Sopdet (the star Sirius). The zero month, Djehutet, is the intercalary month of variable length, inserted between the last month, Wep Renpet, and the first month, Tekhy, for the interval between the end of last month and the rising of Sopdet.

Twelve Lunar months comprise a Lunar year of 354 days. This span of time is naturally shorter than the length of the Solar year that most are familiar with, and attempts throughout time by many cultures to reconcile the two calendar types of Lunar and Solar years have been attempted. The Egyptians were no different, and included a thirteenth Lunar month of variable length, as figure 32 demonstrates. The Lunar calendar was never abandoned, and in fact was the most consistently followed calendar throughout dynastic times. It determined most regional festivals for the temples, and marked the periods for making offerings at the tomb—at the Six Day Feast and at the end of the Lunar Year in a great ceremony of offering to all ancestral souls.

    The Lunar calendar followed by the ancient Egyptians is still in use today, though pertinent only to religious observances. In the Jewish tradition, Passover is calculated as the first Full Moon following the spring equinox; for Muslims, *Eid al Adhah* (the *hajji*, or journey to Mecca) is also determined by the first Full Moon following the spring equinox; for Christians, Easter is celebrated on the first Sunday after the Full Moon following the spring equinox. And in the oriental calendar, the New Year is determined by the first New Moon following the Sun's entry into Aquarius.

Though most cultures, including the Egyptian, viewed the Lunar rhythm as feminine in nature, the Lunar cycle of growth and diminishment is uniquely embodied in the saga of the Heliopolitan god Asar, a deity closely associated with the variable faces of the Moon. Egyptian legend tells that as first regent of Egypt in the mists of antiquity, Asar—along with his faithful sister-consort Auset—brought order and civilization to Egypt. However, the universal affection of Asar by all brought deep jealousy from his brother, Set. As a result, he became the victim of a number of nefarious acts, which ended in his murder and dismemberment into fourteen pieces by Set and his confederates. However, Asar was magically restored through the intervention of the gods and the magic of Auset. With his life renewed, he became governor of the shadow worlds—the vast, invisible regions beyond the material world where all ancestral souls reside. Consequently, it was believed that all return to the realm of this deity when physical life comes to an end.

The astronomical rhythm of the Moon is woven into this myth, from the reassembly of Asar's fourteen members—by Auset and their sister, Nebt-Het—to the Lunar eclipse following his demise that signaled the ascendancy of Set. Most importantly, Asar assumes the pulse of the Lunar principle in nature, as the function of reoccurrence in the life cycle and the power of transcendence. For even though the Moon is subject to waning and waxing light by virtue of its variable course, its repetitious return defeats the forces of dissolution by promising continued renewal. Thus Asar defeated Set by becoming whole and entering a realm beyond the temporal powers in nature.

In Egyptian ceremony, the diminishment of Asar's power and its return is observed throughout the Lunar cycle. At the New Moon his reappearance is celebrated, and at the Full Moon his restoration is commemorated. Following this, his dismemberment is solemnized, concluding with a rite of mourning and non-activity in the dark period before the next New Moon when his life returns. Throughout this cycle, Lunar ceremonies usually take the form of material offerings, acts of "feeding" that magically restore the Neter's waning powers until they return.

In the field of time represented by the lunar orb, the New Moon evokes the inauguration of enterprises and enhances the growth of new endeavors, such as the founding of the temple and the commencement of journeys. As the symbiosis of Sun and Moon, this period represents the planting of the physical seed in the womb of time, which will come to fruition at the Full Moon, when the body is inhabited by the spirit and dark matter is illumined by the powers of light.

Eclipses in ancient Egypt were regarded as periods of Set's ascendancy; temple ritual was suspended and ancient chroniclers report that the priesthood stayed within the confines of the Divine House. The Solar eclipse (occurring at the New Moon) was an event that recalled a legend involving Ra, the Sun god, and Auset. The diminishment of the Sun's face by the Lunar orb represents Ra's advancement in age and his enfeeblement. This allowed the goddess to administer a poison so that she could extort his secret name in exchange for neutralizing the affliction. By obtaining the name, she was able to pass it on to her son Heru, thereby ensuring the transmission of royal power to the pharaoh incarnate ever after. The Solar eclipse symbolizes the loss of the Sun god's powers and their restoration by Auset's magic. Hence, at the onset of this cosmic event the recitation of the seventy-five divine names of Ra was performed in the temple.

The Lunar eclipse (occurring at the Full Moon) is an event that recalls the murder of Asar by Set, symbolized by the face of the Moon that is diminished by the Earth's shadow. These were regarded as particularly nefarious and called for the highest magic to avert the reign of Set's powers of chaos. Rituals took the form of long vigils that emulated the mourning of Auset and Nebt-Het for their brother, and the restoration of his breath and revival of his form through the conception of his son Heru, fourteen days later at the following New Moon.

Every temple tradition followed a cycle of ceremonies that included daily observances, monthly rites, and annual festivals that were specific to the cosmogony of the temple and the particular events in the lives of the Neteru it served. The Lunar principle is honored through observance of *Khesu* ("rites" or "prescriptions"). These most often take the form of offering living goods throughout the Lunar cycle, nourishment derived from animal and plant sources. The Khesu also include daily purifications, which represent the renewal of the material form in cyclic periods. In all, the Khesu form the basic components of temple practice.

Heb Enti Pesedj
New Moon observance

Tepy Renpet
Beginning of the Lunar year

Dena Tep
First Quarter observance

Wag
Festival celebrated on the first day
of the Lunar New Year

Iah Meh Uadjat
"Filling of the Eye,"
Full Moon observance

Anep
Third Quarter or 20-Day observance

Figure 34—Lunar Phenomena

II. The Solar Rhythm

The principle of the Solar circuit through the sky had great significance to the Egyptians. The daily rhythm of sunrise, the Sun's culmination overhead, and sunset presented another reality to the ancient Egyptians that spoke of the ascent and descent of divine light that was in a continual flux with the *Duat* ("invisible sky" or "shadow world"). The Solar passage through the sky was especially important in the funerary literature, namely *The Book of Gates, The Spell of the Twelve Caves,* and *The Books of the Sky* (also known as *The Book of Day* and *The Book of Night*). In these works, the Solar journey through each of the hours of night and day is depicted as critical to the continuous renewal of life for the sojourning soul.

With the Lunar cycle that varied through the seasons, the Egyptians also instituted a civil calendar of 360 days based on the three seasons brought by the Nile. This calendar was closely associated with the Solar cycle of equinoxes ("equal night and day"), when the Earth's equator and the Sun's path coincide, and with the solstices ("Sun standing still"), when the Sun is farthest north or south on the horizon. Like the Lunar calendar, the Egyptian Solar calendar was comprised of twelve months, but each consisted of thirty days, with three weeks of ten days' duration in each month. To this was added the *epagomenae* (Greek: "added"), five days dedicated to the birth of the five Solar deities of Asar, Set, Heru Ur, Auset, and Nebt-Het. This calendar resulted in a total of 365 days, approximating the length of the tropical year (365.25 days exactly), the time between two successive spring equinoxes.

The Civil calendar was used to record events pertaining to the Royal House and acts of government, an appropriate protocol as kingship is governed by the Sun. It had some religious significance in the observation of the quarterly periods that called for the great festivals celebrated throughout the Two Lands, such as the Feast of Sokar, the Neter of latent vitality, held at the winter solstice (our December 22). The summer solstice (our June 21) was most important, as it coincided with the inundation of the Nile in ancient times.

The Tetramenes

The Egyptian Solar Calendar of Three Seasons

I. Akhet, "Inundation"—Nile Floods

1	Thoth	
2	Phaophi	
3	Athys	
4	Choiach	

II. Pert, "Going Forth"—Sowing

5	Tybi	
6	Menchir	
7	Phamenoth	
8	Pharmuthi	

III. Shemut, "Deficiency"—Harvest

9	Pachons	
10	Paoni	
11	Epipi	
12	Mesore	

IV. Hru Renpet, "Epagomenae"—Creation

1	Asar	*Am*—Fire
2	Set	*Ta*—Earth
3	Heru-Ur	*Sa*—Quintessence
4	Auset	*As*—Air
5	Nebt-Het	*Nu*—Water

Table 10—The Solar Calendar

Sep Tepi
The first occasion, primeval time

Hru
Day

Gereh
Night

Seshem Shu
Sun at dawn, one
of the deities of
the Duat

Ihy
Sun as a child on
New Year's Day.
Also, the name of
Horus at Edfu

Nek Hekh
Winter solstice Sun,
Ra as an old man

Hrui Renpet
Festivals of the epagomenae

Figure 35—Solar Phenomena

The Solar principle is embodied in the legendary exploits of Heru, son of Asar. Heru is essentially the incarnate Sun, descendant of the powers of light brought by the cosmic gods, hence his fourfold exalted name *Ra Atum Harakhte Khepri,* representing the four divisions of day in ancient times (dawn, noon, dusk, and midnight). As mender of discord, he subjugates the powers of Set in a series of battles and makes conscious the dark, unconscious side of human experience with his victory over "the adversary" (the shadow).

Heru assumes the pulse of the Solar principle in nature as restorer of order in the temporal world and the power of fusion in spiritual realms. As principle of ascension, he makes possible the constitution of a body of light through his function of mastery. This is the vehicle that is entered by the initiate in order to migrate to the realm of the gods on the stellar journey that begins when the exigencies of Earthly life are fulfilled.

The Horian principle of order is also regulated by the goddess Maat, who is depicted in a seat at the prow of the Sun barque. It is she who ensures that the course of the Sun follows the celestial path of vitality and truth, bringing illumination to all below. Other Solar deities include Heru Ur "the elder" of the Heliopolitan Ennead, who represents the latent powers of human experience that are awakened by the initiatory journey through the constellational year; and Ra, the source of light from the beginning of time.

In the temple, the Solar principle is honored through the observance of *Iru* ("festivals of the sky" or cosmic events, also called *Hebu nu pet).* These are celebrated as the Sun passes into new sectors of the celestial vault through the year, evoking the powers of cosmic beings whose "seasons" become active while the Sun is stationed in their constellational signs. The Iru also include the *Mesen* (foundation) ceremonies of establishing the four quarters and five elemental powers of the temple.

The Solar Seasons

Though the Egyptian Solar calendar reflected the three agricultural seasons of the Nile Valley, the cycle of the four celestial periods was recognized and viewed as the ascent and descent of Solar powers in the visible world. This is the Solar passage through the constellations along the ecliptical belt of the sky throughout the tropical year, beginning at the spring equinox, when night and day are equal in length, and symbolically, when body and soul are in balance between the visible and invisible worlds. In ancient times this period coincided with the return of the constellation Orion in the night sky, a harbinger of the powers of Asar becoming renewed.

The Egyptians were particularly watchful of the solstices, the summer solstice coinciding with the Nile's initial inundation and the winter solstice marking the time of planting after the waters had receded. Each was observed with elaborate temple festivities that honored the Neteru whose powers had become renewed and visible in the sky and on Earth. The autumnal equinox marked the lengthening of night and the gradual diminishment of Orion in the sky; hence, it was associated with the waning powers of the Solar gods and the incipient rule of dark forces.

The ingress (entry) of the Sun into the constellations is a metaphor of the soul's entry into the dimension of conscious creation. Ra, the divine creator, is the Neter who brings forth the five senses (Heka, Sia, Hu, Maa, Sedjem) and in the process endows all in the visible realms with the creative powers he embodies. The annual rhythm of the twelve Solar ingresses through the Zodiacal mansions represents the construction of the body of light, which is assumed by the temple initiate prior to meeting the gods in cosmic realms. The theme of the body correspondence with cosmic principles is still inherent in the astrological "rulerships" of the signs—their governing of regions of the body, physical functions, and metaphysical faculties.

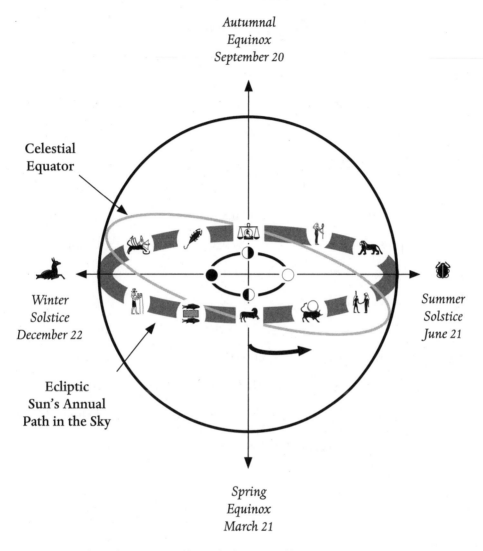

Autumnal
Equinox
September 20

Celestial
Equator

Winter
Solstice
December 22

Summer
Solstice
June 21

Ecliptic
Sun's Annual
Path in the Sky

Spring
Equinox
March 21

Figure 36—The Solar Seasons Through the Constellations

Astrological Rulerships

Fabrication of the Body of Light

Sign	Physical	Functional	Metaphysical Faculty
♈	Head, Brain	Autonomic	Regeneration
♉	Throat	Metabolic	Fusion
♊	Arms, Lungs	Respiratory	Transformation
♋	Stomach	Lymphatic	Conversion
♌	Heart	Circulatory	Individuation
♍	Colon	Digestive	Distillation
♎	Reins, Kidneys	Excretory	Transmutation
♏	Testes, Ovaries	Reproductive	Generation
♐	Thighs	Muscular	Purgation
♑	Knees	Osteopathic	Division
♒	Ankles	Neurologic	Elevation
♓	Feet, Skin	Somatic	Dissolution

Table 11—Astrological Rulerships of the Body

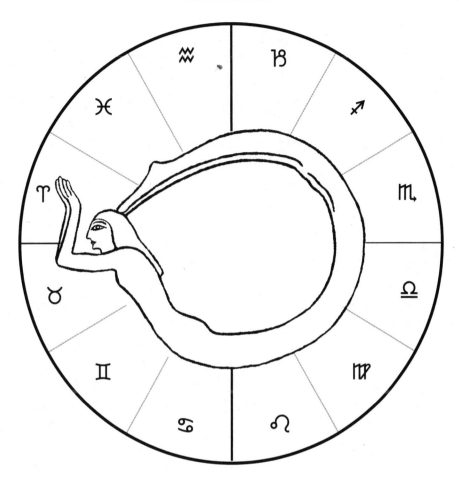

Figure 37—Zodiacal Rulerships of the Body

III. The Stellar Rhythm

Another spiritual reality the Egyptians recognized was the eternal, unchanging nature of divine life, independent of the cycles imposed on Earth by the two luminaries. The Sidereal (Stellar) year was known to them, the period of time between two successive appearances of a star at the same place in the sky, as seen on Earth (365.25636 days). The twenty-minute discrepancy between the Solar and Sidereal years is caused by the precession of the equinoxes, a phenomenon brought by the wobble of the Earth's poles and the very gradual backward movement of the spring equinox through the constellations along the ecliptic.

Four thousand years ago, the summer solstice in Egypt coincided with the heliacal rising[1] of the sacred star Sopdet—the cosmic form of Auset—and this event also heralded the beginning of the Nile's inundation. It was a time known as "the night of the teardrop," commemorating the legendary event of Auset discovering the death of her husband, and the tears shed by the goddess, which hastened the rise of the river. It is still celebrated in modern Egypt as *Lailat al Nuktah*.

Sopdet became the primary marker of the celestial sphere as a result of her synchronous appearance with the solstice and the inundation in ancient times. As a result, this star became the fiducial (starting point) for a Stellar calendar that calculated both time and the seasons with great accuracy. The Sothic calendar (from *Sothis,* the Greek name for this star) was used to record sacred time, events in temple ritual, and the movement of celestial bodies through the sky.

The mythological landscape of Sopdet is reflected in the transformative powers of Auset, mistress of magic, wife of the hibernating god, and mother of the victorious son of light. She represents the culmination of cyclic experience, from the periodic waxing and waning of physical power embodied by Asar, to the balance of dark and light moral forces personified by Heru. In her sphere, Stellar light is infused into the soul through the mystic processes of initiation, just as the goddess infused breath into the lifeless body of her husband. Through her the creative principle is aroused as the conception of Heru was effected by her powers of rejuvenation, enabling one to enter the region of cosmic life and become a member of the divine retinue.

In the temple, the Stellar principle is honored through observance of *Hebu Tep Teru* ("festivals" or "feasts" of the calendar). These most often take the form of special rites that endow the powers of the Neteru at peak periods. The Hebu also form the celebratory components of temple practice.

Sacred Time

Ancient timekeeping may have initially arose out of the necessity for ensuring that a predictable order exists and a method for understanding that order could be employed on a regular basis. In the temple, the ending of the dark hours and the appearance of light was one such requisite, as the deity was believed to awaken to the world of life and descend into the Divine House in periodic episodes dictated by the cosmogony of the temple tradition. This could be hourly,

---

1. Heliacal rising: a star or planet that rises before the Sun, allowing it to appear pre-dawn in the eastern sky for a brief period before it becomes obscured by the Solar light.

Usekh-t Shu
The Hall of Shu, sky, space

Usekh-t Geb
The Hall of Geb, Earth

Ikhem Sek
"Not knowing destruction,"
a name of the polestar

Wep et Renpet
Observance of the "Opening of the
Year," marked by the heliacal rising
of Sirius

Shet Shet
Vulva of the sky, Nut's body,
the place where the Sun is born

Meshtiu
Great Bear constellation; abode of
the soul of Set. Also represented by
(and referred to as) "the Bull's Thigh"

Gerh en Hatuiy
Night of the Teardrop (near the
Summer Solstice), bringing the
rain that causes inundation

Pert Sopdet
"Going forth of Sothis," the New Year
marked by the heliacal rising of Sirius

Sah
The constellation Orion

Shedju
The eight morning stars, constellation of the Tortoise

Figure 38—Stellar Phenomena

daily, monthly, or annually—but the return of the Neter from its celestial abode at an appointed time ensured the embodiment of divine life, and this was the essential function of the temple in ancient times.

As a result, the observation of the passage of the Sun took place during daylight, and the monitoring of stars moving across the vault of the sky throughout the night established the protocol of astronomer-priests who practiced their art in observatories on temple roofs. These specialists brought into being a system of timekeeping that we have inherited, along with the renowned sacred astronomy of Egypt. It is the latter system we have overlooked in modern times, resulting in our loss of knowing the periods and cycles of celestial powers that await our understanding and use.

As the Earth rotates daily on its axis, the full circle of stars passes overhead, though for approximately only half that time are the stars visible to the naked eye. The Egyptians recognized that certain groupings of stars appeared at different times on the horizon at dawn or dusk, depending on the time of the year. They were then followed by other stars, which shifted across the sky in a predictable manner. Careful observation revealed that the appearances of these stars were consistent with the passage of time, and so they became chronocrators—markers for a system of timekeeping that was associated with the appearances of divine forces. In this system every star is regarded as a *Ba,* or "divine appearance" of one of the gods, and this appearance has an influence on the world below. As such, the stars are indicators of beneficial or detrimental conditions for certain actions or enterprises, in both the sacred and secular realms.

Thirty-six star groups which lie in a belt at the southern expanse of the ecliptic (the Sun's path) became incorporated into this system. Each group acquired a name and associated spirit guardian, although the order and names vary somewhat according to the historical period when they were inscribed in tombs or on papyri in the temple archives. Nevertheless, a number of thirty-six remains invariable, and since these figures divide the 360° circle of the ecliptic into ten-degree segments, they are collectively referred to as *dekanoi,* the Greek term for "groups of ten." The time between the appearance of one dekan and the next on the horizon—at the equinoxes, when day and night are equal—would translate into forty minutes; this changes with the season and latitude of the observer. In this manner, the dekans served as markers for nocturnal hours as they transited the horizons.

Obviously, not all thirty-six dekans would appear visibly on the horizon because daylight obscures the stars for half the day. But they would have their turn on the night horizon at some point in the year, which to the careful observer will signal the beginning or ending of a season. Thus, the dekans also served as markers for the weeks (decades) and months of the year. The appearance of each dekan successively at dusk in the eastern sky at ten-day intervals signaled the beginning of a new week.

These two observational systems ("transit dekans" and "decades") were in use during pharaonic times, the former used at night (achronychal risings) to mark the hours, and the latter used at dawn (heliacal risings) to determine the beginning of the year and hence, the seasons and weeks. Each used a different star or asterism to mark its beginning.

The Hermetic writings of the Graeco-Roman period emphasize the influence of the dekanoi:

> *The force which works in all events that befall men collectively comes from the Dekans; for instance, overthrows of kingdoms, revolts of cities, famines, pestilences, overflowings of the sea, earthquakes—none of these things, my son, take place without the working of the Dekans.*
> —*Hermes to Tat*, Excerpt VI: 8

Such conditions are denoted by some of the dekan descriptions, others by the deities with which they were associated. Each dekan possesses a spirit guardian who characterizes its action, a Neter who governs it, and certain minerals or plants that embody its powers. For the most part, the Neter is often one of the deities of the Heliopolitan (Solar) rhythm, or one of the four genii of the Funerary Quaternary. Associations with the genii convey the elemental character of each asterism, in the realms of Fire (Qebsenuf), Earth (Daumutef), Air (Imset), and Water (Haapi). These attributes exemplify the essence of Egypt's sacred astronomy, which later disseminated to Greece and Rome as astrological magic.

Unlike the Zodiac (the twelve constellations that lie along the ecliptic, or Sun's path), the Egyptian dekanal belt was measured along the celestial equator, which is south of the ecliptic and parallel to it. Thus, only portions of the western Zodiacal constellations fall in the Egyptian system. We are not certain which stars comprised each dekan, as the lists vary in the description of the sky where they are located. However, the fiducial (starting point) is always indicated, and it usually falls in the region of the constellations Orion and Canis Major, parallel the constellations of Gemini and Cancer.

The marking and enumerating of the dekans was an important activity in the temples, as temple records show. These confirm that the observation of stars was integral to the timing of certain rites throughout the day and night, but the dekans had another magical purpose. Some tombs and funerary papyri include lists or representations of the dekanal hours as "guides" to mark the passage of the soul through the *Duat,* or night sky. The dekan spirits inscribed in the tombs symbolically assisted the deceased through the darkness so that the soul could make its way to be reborn with the Sun barque at dawn. It was believed that even in the heavenly regions nefarious forces could block the journey of the Sun, but the dekan spirits possessed the powers to dispel such obstacles. Given the proper timing, the soul could likewise proceed through the regions of the sky and become a celestial being.

The dekans, each representing $\frac{1}{36}$th of the celestial sphere (36 x 10 = 360°), marked time at night as they appeared in the east, culminated overhead, and set in the west. Approximately half (18) of the transit dekans would pass overhead on a given night (18 dekans x 40 minutes = 720 minutes). And since the Egyptians used a sexagesimal system of mathematics ($\frac{720}{60}$ = 12 hours), it became obvious that the Solar phases of night and day fell into 24 periods (12 hours x 2), the origin of our own system of timekeeping.

The calendar weeks commenced with the appearance of a new dekan rising in the night sky every ten days. The last day of each week was generally regarded as a "day of the dead," and funerary offerings could be presented on those days without deviating from the Lunar calendar of offerings. At Philae, the mourning of Auset for her dead husband was reenacted on these days, with a journey by a priestess of the temple to the adjacent island of Biga (the *Abaton,* Greek for "reserved place"), where the god was believed to have been secreted prior to his reconstitution at Abydos. Offerings of milk were made, and ancient inscriptions disclose that 365 offering bowls were filled in the sanctuary at each ceremony.

Dekans on two astronomical ceilings—that of the unoccupied tomb of Senmut at Deir el Bahri (1473 B.C.E.) and the Osireion temple of Seti I at Abydos (1303 B.C.E.)—represent the system used to mark the beginning of the ten-day weeks (the "decades"). Alternately, dekans inscribed in some of the later Rames-side tombs represent the system used to mark the hours ("transits"). The latter are also called "star clocks" because they visually depict the marking of time by the passage of stars from east to west in reference to an observer and a seated human figure—a valuable representation of the manner in which ancient astronomical observation was conducted.

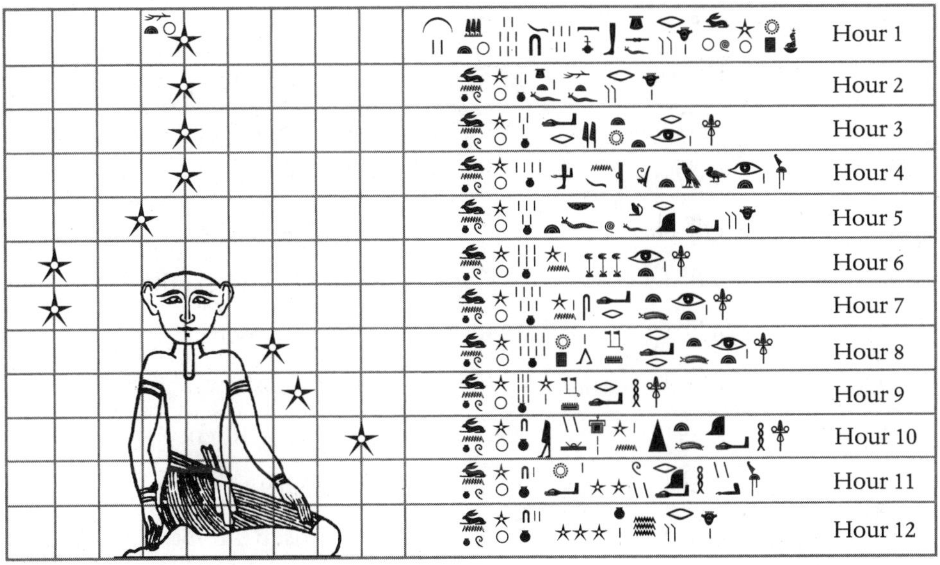

Figure 39—A Star Clock from the Tomb of Rameses IV

The transit dekans begin with Sopdet, the star whose heliacal rising marked not only the beginning of the Sidereal year, but the legendary beginning of the hours in timeless time. For this reason it stood apart from the rest of the dekanal stars as "leader" or harbinger of cycles. The foregoing list of transit dekans begins with the position of Sirius in 2780 B.C.E. along with the current era. It is divided into ten-degree increments from that reference point. It is important to note that the Egyptians recorded their stars as they gradually shifted from the vernal equinox over the ages, and did not use a stationary (tropical) system as most modern astrologers do. The position of Sirius for epoch 2000 is 19°15' of Gemini in the Sidereal (moving) Zodiac or 13°30' of Cancer in the Tropical (stationary) Zodiac.

Dekan	Sidereal Position B.C.E. 2780	Sidereal Position C.E. 2000	Dekan Spirit
1	24 ♊ 08	19 ♊ 15	Tepy a Sopdet
2	4 ♋ 08	29 ♊ 15	Sopdet
3	14 ♋ 08	9 ♋ 15	Anher Maat Tchai
4	24 ♋ 08	19 ♋ 15	Shetu
5	4 ♌ 08	29 ♋ 15	Djeriu Khepti
6	14 ♌ 08	9 ♌ 15	Ha Djat
7	24 ♌ 08	19 ♌ 15	Pehui Djat
8	4 ♍ 08	29 ♌ 15	Themat Khert
9	14 ♍ 08	9 ♍ 15	Uashati Bekati
10	24 ♍ 08	19 ♍ 15	Ipset
11	4 ♎ 08	29 ♍ 15	Sebshesen
12	14 ♎ 08	9 ♎ 15	Tepy Khent
13	24 ♎ 08	19 ♎ 15	Khent Hert
14	4 ♏ 08	29 ♎ 15	Imseti em Ibu
15	14 ♏ 08	9 ♏ 15	Temes en Khent
16	24 ♏ 08	19 ♏ 15	Sapeti Khenui
17	4 ♐ 08	29 ♏ 15	Hery Ib Wia
18	14 ♐ 08	9 ♐ 15	Shesmu
19	24 ♐ 08	19 ♐ 15	Kenmut
20	4 ♑ 08	29 ♐ 15	Tepy Asmad
21	14 ♑ 08	9 ♑ 15	Smad
22	24 ♑ 08	19 ♑ 15	Sert
23	4 ♒ 08	29 ♑ 15	Sa Sert
24	14 ♒ 08	9 ♒ 15	Khery Kheped Sert

Dekan	Sidereal Position B.C.E. 2780	Sidereal Position C.E. 2000	Dekan Spirit
25	24 ♒ 08	19 ♒ 15	Tepy Aakhui
26	4 ♓ 08	29 ♒ 15	Aakhui
27	14 ♓ 08	9 ♓ 15	Tepy Abaui
28	24 ♓ 08	19 ♓ 15	Baui
29	4 ♈ 08	29 ♓ 15	Khentu Heru
30	14 ♈ 08	9 ♈ 15	Khentu Djeru
31	24 ♈ 08	19 ♈ 15	Saui
32	4 ♉ 08	29 ♈ 15	Khau
33	14 ♉ 08	9 ♉ 15	Ayret
34	24 ♉ 08	19 ♉ 15	Remen Hery
35	4 ♊ 08	29 ♉ 15	Djes Uayrek
36	14 ♊ 08	9 ♊ 15	Uayret

Table 12—The Transit Dekans: The transit dekans were used to mark sacred time in temple and tomb. This list is among many, but is distinguished by the fiducial, Tepy a Sopdet, "the beginning of Sirius." Considered one of the oldest dekan groups, it is known as the Seti I-B list, and is found at the Dendera temple of Het-Her in two places: (1) in the main temple, inscribed on the ceiling of the outer hypostyle hall, and (2) on the walls of the ceremonial "Silver Room," located on the west side of the Hall of Appearings. These dekans are also inscribed in the Birth House adjacent to the temple.

The dekans in this set were observed to rise in the east as the Sun was setting (known as achronychal rising). In a linear frieze at the Dendera temple, they are depicted as deities on barques, sailing through the sky. Their successive appearance on the night horizon indicated the passage of time in sacred hours (chronocrators) and the flow of divine forces through the heavens.

This table may be used to gauge sacred time in the temple, though astronomical skill in locating the fiducial star is required. However, planetarium-type computer programs can easily provide the time for the appearance of Sirius on the local horizon, which commences the thirty-six dekanal hours.

We can see how, in the Egyptian timekeeping system, the dekans observed each night would, by their appearance in the eastern sky, mark the passage of hours. At the same time, the appearance of a dekan in the eastern pre-dawn sky (heliacal rising) throughout the year signaled another event, the beginning of a ten-day period when it would be seen in that location until replaced by a predictable successor. The dekan stars that appeared in this manner, properly called decades, designated the beginnings of the Egyptian weeks. This was the system used to observe the annual rising of Sopdet, which heralded the beginning of the sacred (Sidereal) year.

This secondary application of the dekans commences with the week of the summer solstice, which in ancient times coincided with the beginning of the Nile floods, and thus falls near the region of Sirius. It is this dekan set that merged with Hellenistic astrology and came to represent the variable powers working through the Zodiac.

The great temple of Het-Her at Dendera and the Temple of Khnum at Esna, last inscribed during the Ptolemaic period and considerably influenced by Greek astronomy, detail both dekanal belts in a number of Zodiacal schemes, both linear and circular. The well-known circular Zodiac at Dendera, the only one of its kind in Egypt, positions the dekans in their direction north and south of the ecliptic, while a linear Zodiac in another part of the temple positions them as they overlay the signs of the Zodiac.

It is the circular Zodiac that offers the most intriguing information about Egyptian sacred astronomy. The foregoing list describes the dekanal belt in this Zodiac, which represents a fusion of the transit dekans and the decades for the period in which it was inscribed (30 B.C.E.). For their positions in the sky, refer to the numbered circle of figures. The first dekan spirit, *Kenmut,* lies to the left of the temple axis, and the rest follow clockwise. The assignments of the dekans in this list to the Zodiac refer to the constellational signs, or the Sidereal Zodiac.

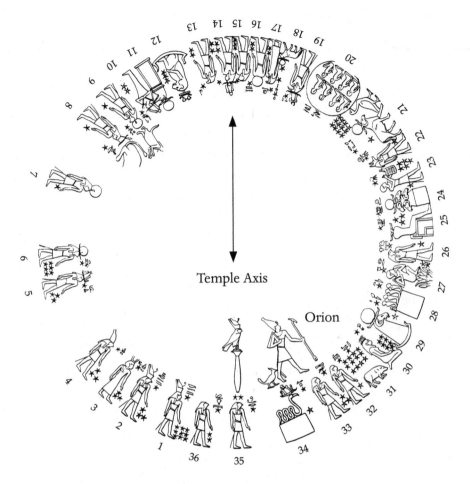

Temple Axis

Orion

Figure 40—The Dekan Spirits of the Dendera Zodiac: The dekan group of the Dendera Zodiac is distinctive of either the *transits* (achronychal rising dekans observed at night for timekeeping) or *decades* (heliacal rising dekans observed at dawn for determining the seasons). It may actually be a fusion of both systems in use during the Graeco-Roman period when the ceiling was inscribed.

The Dekan Spirits in the Dendera Zodiac

1. **Kenmut:** "the sacred baboon," is a spirit with a human head, wearing the double crown; this dekan is marked by nine stars. The last third of Cancer, its deity is Ba, the visible appearance of the Sun god, Ra. Above, a recumbent celestial cow reposes with Canopus, the navigator star, placed between her horns.

2. **Djeriu Khepti Kenmut:** "beneath the rump of Kenmut," referring to its position west of the celestial cow. A falcon-headed spirit wearing the double crown, it governs the first third of Leo and is marked by three stars. Its deity is Heru, son of Auset. This region contains the star Regulus, associated with Heru and the pharaonic tradition.

3. **Ha Djat:** "bow of the ferryboat," a human-headed spirit wearing a four-feathered crown, it is marked by three stars. Governing the second third of Leo, its deity is Shu, Neter of cosmic wind.

4. **Djat:** "the ferryboat," a falcon-headed spirit wearing a white crown, it is marked by three stars. Ruling the last third of Leo, its deity is Geb.

5. **Pehui Djat:** the "reed swamp of the ferryboat," a human-headed spirit wearing the Atef crown, marked by three stars. Ruling the first third of Virgo, its deity is Asar.

6. **Themat:** "the throne," a falcon-headed spirit wearing a Sun disc resting on horns, with a uraeus outside the disc. Governs the second third of Virgo and is marked by six stars. Its deity is Nefertum.

7. **Uashati:** the "place of darkness," a human-headed spirit wearing a Sun disc with uraeus in the disc, marked by one star. Ruling the last third of Virgo, its deity is Ra. This region contains the star Spica, depicted by the ancients as an ear of corn.

8. **Bekati:** "the pregnant," a human-headed spirit wearing the red crown with horns, marked by one star. Governing the first third of Libra, its deity is Asar. This region contains the star Arcturus, which formed the asterism *Menat,* the ritual collar of Het-Her that ensured breath for a soul in the Duat.

9. **Ipset:** "the assessor," a falcon-headed spirit wearing Sun disc with uraeus inside the disc, marked by one star. Ruling the second third of Libra, its deity is Ra.

10. **Sebshesen:** "guide or peacemaker," a mummiform spirit, carrying the pharaonic crook and flail, and wearing the crown of Asar. It is marked by two stars and the deity is Heru. Ruling the last third of Libra, at Philae the appellation "lover of sunlight" is given to this asterism, an allusion to the star Alpha Centauri, one of the brightest stars in the sky, which lies near this region.

11. **Tepy Shentet:** "before the spheres," a crocodile-headed spirit on a support with horns and Sun disc. Governing the first third of Scorpio, its deity is Asar. This region contains the star Antares, associated with Selqit, the scorpion goddess.

12. **Hery Ib Wia:** "middle of the boat," a baboon in a barque, marked by three stars. Ruling the second third of Scorpio, its deity is Iah, a mystic form of the Full Moon.

13. **Sapeti Khenui:** "the prophets," a serpent-headed spirit, marked by two stars. Ruling the last third of Scorpio, its deity is Heru, son of Auset. This region contains the stars of Ophiuchus (the serpent holder) and Serpens (the serpent).

14. **Shesmu:** "the winepress," a human-headed spirit wearing a crown of Asar with horns and uraei. Governing the first third of Sagittarius, it is marked by four stars, and the deity is Ra. This dekan spirit had a cult following from the Old Kingdom to the Roman period. At once a fearsome butcher in the Pyramid Texts to "master of perfumery" in temple inscriptions, Shesmu was foremost regarded as a distiller of essences, from plant to human. The galactic center is located in this region.

15. **Sa Shesmu:** "the offspring of Shesmu," a falcon-headed spirit. Ruling the second third of Sagittarius, it is marked by three stars.

16. **Kheri Kenem:** regarded as "one of the sacred baboons" that foretell the appearance of dawn. This dekan spirit takes human form with a Sun disc as its head. It is marked by two stars and governs the last third of Sagittarius. This region contains the star Facies, the "eye of the archer." It is traditionally associated with war, soldiers, and violence—the domain of Sekhmet-Bast in her protective aspect as patroness of the royal armies and as the "flaming eye of Ra."

17. **Tepy Asmad:** "beginning of the joiner," a serpent-headed spirit marked by two stars. Rules the first third of Capricorn; its deity is "Heru Who Loves."

18. **Pa Sba Uati:** "flaming star," a ram with a Sun-disc crown on horns. Governs the second third of Capricorn.

19. **Smad:** "what joins or unites," an ibis-headed spirit wearing the *Atef* (plumed) crown with horns, marked by two stars. Rules the last third of Capricorn.

20. **Sert:** "the goose," marked by twelve stars, governs the first third of Aquarius. At Dendera, this spirit is followed by a ram with a Solar disc between his horns, and is marked by one star. This region contains the stars of Aquila.

21. **Sa Sert:** "watcher of the goose." In this dekan, eight bound captives are contained in a disc. Rules the second third of Aquarius, though it is depicted before Sert because its stars lie below it.

22. **Tepy Aakhui:** "before the shining ones," this dekan is represented by a jackal-headed spirit, and marked by one star. Rules the last third of Aquarius.

23. **Aakhui:** "the shining ones," depicted as a human-headed spirit carrying a pectoral, marked by five stars. Rules the first third of Pisces, where the current Vernal point (the equinox of March 20) is located at 5°15' of Pisces in the Sidereal Zodiac.

24. **Tepy Abaui:** "before the souls." Four ram heads are placed on a support, with Sun disc on horns, marked by one star. Ruling the second third of Pisces, its deity is Herishef.

25. **Baui:** "the souls." A mummified, seated spirit, headless, with horns, marked by three stars. Governs the last third of Pisces.

26. **Khentu Heru:** "ship of Heru," a falcon-headed spirit marked by one star. Rules the first third of Aries. This region contains the stars of Cetus, the whale.

27. **Khentu Djeru:** "ship of sunrise," a naked youth on a lotus throne, with hand to mouth, marked by two stars. Governs the second third of Aries.

28. **Ked:** "the oarsman." Four uraei on a support designate this asterism, which includes the ideogram for "mooring post." Ruling the last third of Aries, its deity is Nefertum, Neter of divine scent.

29. **Saui Ked:** "watchers or guardians of Ked," a ram's head with multiple horns and a Sun disc, placed in a barque and marked by one star. Governing the first third of Taurus, its deity is Nefertum.

30. **Khau:** "the thousands," a kneeling, human-headed spirit with uraei on his head, marked by seven stars representing the Pleiades. Ruling the second third of Taurus, its deity is Asar.

31. **Ayret:** "the jawbone," a swine marked by twelve stars. Governs the last third of Taurus. Ayret was one of the serpent gods in the Duat who could be appeased with spells from *The Book of Going Forth*. This region of the sky contains the Hyades, associated with Set and chaotic powers.

32. **Remen Hery:** "lower shoulder of Orion." A human-headed spirit, marked by one star that represents Rigel. Ruling the first third of Gemini, its deity is Bastet, the benevolent cat goddess who brings domestic tranquility. This region was governed by the *Sahu,* the "ascended spirits" of the past who reside in the Orion constellation.

33. **Djes Ayreq:** "the girdle," a reference to the stars in Orion's belt. The spirit here is human-headed, marked by three stars. Governing the second third of Gemini, its deity is Sopdet. Royal predictions were often based on cosmic conditions occurring when Sopdet arose at the beginning of the year—events concerning the coming harvest, the peace of Egypt, and the deaths of royal persons are recorded.

34. **Remen Khery:** the "upper arm of Orion," an ibis-headed serpent marked by one star. Rules the last third of Gemini and is associated with the Neter of bandages, Taiyet. At Edfu she governs the royal linen and is called "Mistress of the Robes"; at Dendera she oversees the mummy swathings. In both spheres she represents the magical power woven into the linen garment of the king. In her serpent image she protects grain from vermin.

35. **Uayret:** "leg of Orion," a falcon-headed deity. Governing the first third of Cancer, its deity is Shepset, a goddess of the Memphite theology who is associated with birth and is one of the seven spirits *(Sahu)* of Orion. It is here in the Dendera Zodiac that the axis of the temple is marked by a falcon on a pillar, referring to the ancient Heru Shemsu ("followers of Heru"), who founded both the temple and the tradition to which it belongs. This place

in the sky also represents the abode of Sirius. The heliacal rising of this star was the major event in the temple's sacred calendar, and the culmination of Sirius in the sky established the direction of the temple's axis, according to tradition.

36. **Pehui Heri:** "the reed swamp of Orion." Here, a falcon-headed deity presides over the expanse of space governed by Orion. The asterism is marked by two stars. Rules the second third of Cancer.

Seasons of the Neteru

The sacred astronomy of ancient Egypt was visual and cognitive, and understanding its spiritual dimension requires that we place ourselves in that ambient field of experience. The Egyptians did this by combining the Lunar, Solar, and Stellar rhythms via ritual. In this system, the gods were endowed with their own seasons—periods of time that allowed their powers to be expressed and their influences to manifest in the phenomenal world to bring change, variation, and stability.

The Egyptian Civil (Solar) calendar, which does not allow for equinoctial precession, no longer coincides with the Sothic calendar as it last did in 139 c.e. For the year 2000, the heliacal rising of Sirius occurred on August 3 (Gregorian) in Egypt, the equivalent of the fourth month of Akhet (Choiach), day 14, in the Egyptian Civil (Solar) calendar. Thus, use of the Egyptian Solar calendar is not practical for following an appropriate protocol of spiritual practice in the Egyptian canon. Similarly, use of the Lunar calendar requires observation of the annual rising of Sopdet, upon which it depends for accuracy, and this event occurs on different days depending on the location of the temple north or south of the equator.

The foregoing table of cosmic events lists the months of the Solar calendar in line with their "ideal" times, synchronous with the Sothic calendar, which occurred in the years of the Sothic cycle (−4242, −2782, −1322, and +139 of the current era).[2] However, it becomes apparent that all three Egyptian calendars (Solar, Lunar, and Stellar) are reconciled by the Zodiacal "seasons," which overlap the Solar and Sothic events of the calendars, and from which the Lunar observances that fall between the months may be determined.

---

2. The Roman historian Censorinus reported that the heliacal rising of Sirius occurred simultaneously with the beginning of the Solar (Civil) calendar of Egypt (the first of Djehut) in 139 c.e. After four years, the event would transpire a day earlier in the Solar calendar, and after 1,460 years it would regress by one day through the entire 365-day Solar calendar. This gives rise to the astronomical period of the Sothic cycle.

Cosmic Events

Aries ♈
  Ceremonial Neter: Asar
  Tropical Ingress / Sidereal Ingress: March 21, spring equinox / April 14
  Egyptian Season: Pert
  Solar / Civil Month: (8) Pa en Renutet
  Greek / Coptic Month: Pharmuthi / Baramuda
  Observed Dates: 4 / 10–5 / 09
  Sothic Dates: 3 / 01–3 / 30

Taurus ♉
  Ceremonial Neter: Het-Her
  Tropical Ingress / Sidereal Ingress: April 20 / May 16
  Egyptian Season: Shemut
  Solar / Civil Month: (9) Pa en Khonshu
  Greek / Coptic Month: Pachons / Bashanz
  Observed Dates: 5 / 10–6 / 08
  Sothic Dates: 3 / 31–4 / 29

Gemini ♊
  Ceremonial Neter: Djehuti
  Tropical Ingress / Sidereal Ingress: May 21 / June 16
  Egyptian Season: Shemut
  Solar / Civil Month: (10) Pa en Inet
  Greek / Coptic Month: Paoni / Ba'una
  Observed Dates: 6 / 09–7 / 08
  Sothic Dates: 4 / 30–5 / 29

Cancer ♋
  Ceremonial Neter: Nebt-Het
  Tropical Ingress / Sidereal Ingress: June 22, summer solstice / July 17
  Egyptian Season: Shemut
  Solar / Civil Month: (11) Ipip
  Greek / Coptic Month: Epiphi / Abib

Observed Dates: 7/09–8/07

Sothic Dates: 5/30–6/28

Leo ♌
Ceremonial Neter: Heru

Tropical Ingress/Sidereal Ingress: July 23/August 17

Egyptian Season: Shemut

Solar/Civil Month: (12) Mesut Ra Harakhte

Greek/Coptic Month: Mesore/Misra

Observed Dates: 8/08–9/05

Sothic Dates: 6/29–7/28

Births of (1) Asar, (2) Set, (3) Heru Ur, (4) Auset, (5) Nebt-Het
Epagomenae/Nisi 9/06–9/10
Heriu Renpet 7/29–8/02

☆
Ceremonial Neter: Sopdet

Tropical Ingress/Sidereal Ingress: August 3, Heliacal rising/August 3

Egyptian Season: Wep Renpet

Solar/Civil Month: (0) Heriu Renpet

Greek/Coptic Month: Epagomenae/Nisi

Observed Dates: 9/06–9/10

Sothic Dates: 7/29–8/02

Virgo ♍
Ceremonial Neter: Geb

Tropical Ingress/Sidereal Ingress: August 23/September 18

Egyptian Season: Akhet

Solar/Civil Month: (1) Djehut

Greek/Coptic Month: Thoth/Thut

Observed Dates: 9/11–10/10

Sothic Dates: 8/03–9/01

Libra ♎︎
  Ceremonial Neter: Auset
  Tropical Ingress/Sidereal Ingress: September 23, autumnal equinox/October 18
  Egyptian Season: Akhet
  Solar/Civil Month: (2) Pa en Ipet
  Greek/Coptic Month: Phaophi/Beba
  Observed Dates: 10/11–11/09
  Sothic Dates: 9/02–10/01

Scorpio ♏︎
  Ceremonial Neter: Anpu
  Tropical Ingress/Sidereal Ingress: October 24/November 17
  Egyptian Season: Akhet
  Solar/Civil Month: (3) Het-Her
  Greek/Coptic Month: Athys/Hatur
  Observed Dates: 11/09–12/10
  Sothic Dates: 10/02–10/31

Sagittarius ♐︎
  Ceremonial Neter: Sekhmet-Bast
  Tropical Ingress/Sidereal Ingress: November 23/December 17
  Egyptian Season: Akhet
  Solar/Civil Month: (4) Ka Her Ka
  Greek/Coptic Month: Choiach/Keiach
  Observed Dates: 12/11–1/09
  Sothic Dates: 11/01–11/30

Capricorn ♑︎
  Ceremonial Neter: Set
  Tropical Ingress/Sidereal Ingress: December 22, winter solstice/January 15
  Egyptian Season: Pert
  Solar/Civil Month: (5) Ta Iabet
  Greek/Coptic Month: Tybi/Tuba
  Observed Dates: 1/10–2/08
  Sothic Dates: 12/01–12/30

Aquarius ♒

  Ceremonial Neter: Maat

  Tropical Ingress/Sidereal Ingress: January 20/February 14

  Egyptian Season: Pert

  Solar/Civil Month: (6) Pa en Mekhir

  Greek/Coptic Month: Menchir/Amshir

  Observed Dates: 2/09–3/09

  Sothic Dates: 12/31–1/29

Pisces ♓

  Ceremonial Neter: Nut

  Tropical Ingress/Sidereal Ingress: February 19/March 15

  Egyptian Season: Pert

  Solar/Civil Month: (7) Pa en Amumhotep

  Greek/Coptic Month: Phamenoth/Baramhat

  Observed Dates: 3/10–4/09

  Sothic Dates: 1/30–2/28

Table 13—Cosmic Events

The Zodiacal seasons are determined by the Sun's passage through the twelve constellations, visible at dawn throughout the year; i.e., the constellation of Leo appears on the eastern horizon at sunrise between August 17 and September 18. The Zodiacal season begins with the ingress of the Sun into the constellation, and the observation of a New Moon and Full Moon in that constellation. For example, in the month of January 2002, the Sun will ingress into the constellation of Capricorn on the 15th, followed by the Full Moon of Capricorn that will take place on the 28th (Lunar phenomena is available from most modern calendars). The New Moon of Capricorn follows on February 12, and the Sun will then ingress into the next constellation of Aquarius on February 14, concluding the season of Capricorn. It should be pointed out here that the natural sequence of the New Moon followed by the Full Moon in the same constellation does not always occur due to the fluke of the Moon sometimes trailing rather than leading the Sun in the sky. However, each season will have a New and Full Moon in the same constellation, though the latter may occasionally precede the former as in our example.

We know that the ancients used the Sidereal (moving) Zodiac as opposed to our predominantly Tropical (fixed) system, but it is not requisite to follow a rigid scheme of the Sun's precise entry into the visible constellations—a plan that is not even possible since the constellations have no agreed beginnings or endings. Indeed, the Egyptians allowed overlapping of celestial space when observing sacred places in the sky, and their philosophical approach was always one of inclusion rather than arbitrary demarcation or exclusion. From the realms of their deities to the meshing of their calendars, the ancients invited both fluidity and synthesis in their religious practice. It is also important to remember that it in Egyptian esotericism, it is the cosmic resonance that provides the energy dynamic for the ceremonial plan to work and not its visible mechanics, a view that most ritualists can support.

Thus, ceremonies in the Egyptian canon may be performed at the inception of any cosmic event: diurnally (at each of the twelve hours of day or night, calculated in the method of planetary hours), monthly (at the New Moon and/or Full Moon), or throughout the year (at the Solar ingress into each sign or constellation). For purists, the ingress dates for the Sun in the constellations compare to the manner in which the ancient Egyptians used the sacred astronomy (refer to the "Sidereal" dates in table 13), though astrologers who adhere to the Zodiac may observe the alternative (refer to the "Tropical" dates in table 13). The equinox and solstice dates are not calendar dependent.

Metaphorically, the twelve constellational seasons represent the twelve stages of constituting the divine body—of both the gods and the spiritual aspect of the initiate. A liturgical calendar that marks these seasons and evokes the particular powers of their associated Neteru will be presented, using the ancient canon of ritual and temple tradition.

The ceremony of each Neter in this scheme is the articulation of a cosmic principle that has both come into being in timeless time and taken form in the moment of the here and now. This reality, though ever present in the cosmic environment, manifests in our dimension with the Sun's passage through the Zodiacal realms. In each season, the particular force of each Neter rises like the sap in plant life to become manifest in the mundane world and to assist in the construction of the spiritual body in the celestial world.

The Solar cosmology of Heliopolis constitutes the theme of this liturgy, with twelve ceremonies that have been adapted from ancient observances for these Neteru. Each of the twelve ceremonies represents a station in the cosmic calendar that emanates a unique power on Earth, and each infuses its participants with the vital components for entry into divine life. The Egyptians believed that this was the fundamental inheritance of human beings and the ultimate goal of a fulfilled existence.

Of the forty-two Neteru, those who illustrate the twelve principal functions of the Zodiacal cycle are incorporated into the liturgy. Their assignments to the twelve signatures of the Zodiac are based on the imagery of the Sun (Ra), who travels through the circuit of the sky through the heavenly vault (Nut's body) daily. Her children (Asar, Auset, Set, and Nebt-Het) and their progeny (Heru, son of Asar and Auset, and Anpu, son of Set and Nebt-Het) would necessarily have a close relationship with this phenomenon as well as Nut's consort, Geb. The remaining four signs of the Zodiac are assigned to Het-Her, because she is associated closely with Heru as his counterpart/wife; Djehuti and Maat, because they are the only two celestial Neteru who communicate through all worlds and are concerned with circuits and cycles; and Sekhmet-Bast, because of her close association with the Sun as daughter, wife, and protector. Nut is the last sign of the Zodiac because she is the beginning and the end of the Sun's circuitous path, just as Pisces is depicted as the two fish (or the two sycamore trees of Nut) that face both directions in the sky.

While these twelve ceremonies have been designed for performance at the ingress of the Sun into the Zodiacal signs, it is entirely appropriate that they may also be performed at the New Moon within each Solar season, with one caveat: the rite of Communion should be reserved for the Full Moon in the season, which is truly the time in the Lunar month when the spiritual forces initially invoked at the New Moon become manifest. Lunar theurgy is truly more successful when the groundwork is laid at the beginning of the cycle (New Moon) and the fruit of the work is harvested at its culmination (Full Moon).

Figure 41—The Domains of the Neteru

In the season of Aries, the winter's hibernation has passed and the carnal body becomes the seed for the body of light. In ancient Egypt, this coincided with the return of the constellation Orion in the east at dawn, signaling the return of Asar, bringer of renewal and the vital power for a season of rejuvenation. The body of light is born in the celestial realm.

As the Sun moves into Taurus, the fertile soil is filled with the vitality of the rising life force in the Earth while the rhythms of nature are ascending in newly sprung life. The goddess Het-Her presides over the event of nature's initial proliferation at the return of the growing season, and she brings together the elemental forces that conceive life and augment its form.

With the passage into Gemini, the networks of physical and psychic life are joined together through the natural magic of sound alchemy. Djehuti transmits the pattern of growth through symbol and language, which allow innate intelligence to come forth and the spiritual senses to awaken.

The realm of Cancer brings fruition to the natural form and feeling to the body of light as it is nurtured by the goddess Nebt-Het. As patron of initiates in new realms, she welcomes the soul into the world of cosmic activity by stimulating new perceptions—second sight, precognitive dreams, and communion with natural forces.

In Leo, authority in the phenomenal world is symbolized by the powers of kingship that are bestowed upon Pharaoh. In the cosmic realm, such powers confer mastery over the limitations of matter and the ability to subjugate the lower forces, so that they may become incorporated into spiritual life. Heru, the victorious son of light, must resolve the balance of matter and spirit, but he elevates the former and gives substance to the latter, making possible divine appearances on Earth.

In the season of Virgo, Geb personifies the natural powers that have made the mature harvest of spiritual life possible. As ancestral father and creator of organic life, this Neter provides all the physical and spiritual nourishment that allows the pattern of nature to continue proliferation and the body of light to take physical form. He also implants the ancestral memory of divine descent into the initiate, so that it may grow into a reservoir of wisdom that is transmitted in noble acts.

In the season of Libra, the consecration of spirit and matter is personified by Auset, whose wanderings to discover the lost body of her partner represent the search for the divine unity brought forth in primeval creation, though lost with the sundering of spirit and matter in Earthly life. In the legend, Auset's devotion to her husband brought magic, renewal, and the time-honored tradition of pharaonic succession to Egyptian civilization. But this is a metaphor of the divine succession that follows the restoration of spirit and matter in the *mysterium coniunctionis* ("divine union") of Asar's renewal through Auset's magic.

When the Sun enters Scorpio, the vital force created by the union of spirit and matter in Libra is transmuted into a form that becomes psychic nourishment for a journey into cosmic life. New powers arise in the initiate from this, which are brought by Anpu to the soul so that it may consume divine forces in a mystic communion of fusing with the powers of creation.

In the season of Sagittarius, the body of light is purified of its Earthly needs so that experience in divine realms may proceed without the hindrances of the carnal body—hunger, thirst, and desire. The sacred fire of Sekhmet-Bast purges the soul of its subtle connections to the physical world so that it may exercise its powers in unison with the natural rhythms of the universe. This act actually refines the physical body and bestows the ultimate restoration from the supreme goddess of healing.

In Capricorn, the soul departs from physical life and joins with the ancestral soul in a period of hibernation that allows resolution of past, present, and future. Here, Set separates the initiate from the realm of time so that the landscape of creation may be entered.

In Aquarius, the worlds of creation are ascended in a series of purifications symbolized by the declarations of truth required by Maat, Neter of divine order. She brings the laws of harmonious existence with natural life to the initiate, who becomes integrated into the cosmic order and a power acting within it.

In the season of Pisces, there is both conclusion to the cosmic journey and preparation for a new rhythm of experience, simultaneous endings and beginnings. Nut was regarded as the prototypal mother, and her image was painted on the ceilings of tombs and coffins to represent the body through which life both enters and departs. She is both the beginning and ending of existence, who gives birth to the soul on Earth and welcomes the soul to the sky when it returns. The water jar on her crown symbolizes the incubating womb that continually brings incarnations to the initiate, and allows the soul transition to new realms.

Realms of the Neteru

The sublime images and powers of the Egyptian gods often appear remote and far removed from our obscure, individual lives. But this was far from the attitude of the ancients, and thousands of relics have been found in modern times that prove this. Amulets, shards of pottery, and scraps of papyrus inscribed with personal prayers, and simple votive statues for the home and tomb were produced in great quantity over the millennia in Egypt. In all, they reflect the close bond that the Egyptians felt with their gods. No petition was too petty or insignificant for divine beings to consider in those times, and simple, subjective thinking was not the basis for this. Rather, the Neteru were understood to interact in the human sphere as a necessity, to enhance their divine functions through their appearance in the physical world.

Understandably, certain of the Neteru honored in this scheme of twelve ceremonies may not resonate with some individuals, due to personal or cultural idiosyncrasies. To remedy this, those deities that are cosmically or terrestrially associated with the twelve Heliopolitan divinities have been included, and their images may be honored during the relevant cosmic season. Those images are augmented by the use of the Neter's corresponding stones, colors, metals, incenses, perfume scents, and wood. Special note should be made of the animals associated with the Neteru, as they often appear through ritual in their forms from nature, an indication of their presence.

Understanding the cosmic principle of each Neter also gives us direction in the use of its energy dynamic. For example, Asar represents the principle of renewal, and any situation or condition that requires renewal will find a source in Asar. The function of the Neter is another important consideration; it provides information about the influence and results that can be expected when invoking the Neter. Here, we know that Asar's presence will cause some aspect of the situation or condition to germinate and "spring forth" as one of his names, *Un Nefer,* implies.

Correspondences of the Neteru

Aries ♈

  Neter: Asar

  Stone: Malachite, *Wadju*

  Color: Green, *Wadj*

  Metal: Iron, *Baa*

  Incense: Cypress, *Kebes*

  Scent: Cinnamon, *Ti-shepses*

  Tree: Acacia, *Shenedj*

Taurus ♉

  Neter: Het-Her

  Stone: Turquoise, *Mafkat*

  Color: Blue-Green, *Khedeb*

  Metal: Copper, *Hemet*

  Incense: Myrrh, *Antiu*

  Scent: Mimosa, *Shendet*

  Tree: Tamarisk, *Iser*

Gemini ♊

  Neter: Djehuti

  Stone: Agate, *Meh*

  Color: Gray-White, *Hedj*

  Metal: Lodestone

  Incense: Eucalyptus, *Nehaut Sentra*

  Scent: Neroli, *Khesa*

  Tree: Pomegranate, *Inhemen*

Cancer ♋

  Neter: Nebt-Het

  Stone: Alabaster, *Shes*

  Color: Blue, *Irtiu*

  Metal: Silver, *Het*

  Incense: Lily of the Valley, *Nehem*

  Scent: Lotus, *Sesheshen*

  Tree: Willow, *Tcherat*

Leo ♌

  Neter: Heru

  Stone: Obsidian, *Tehnu*

  Color: Yellow, *Khenet*

  Metal: Gold, *Nub*

  Incense: Temple Incense, *Kyphi*

  Scent: Sandalwood, *Djeba*

  Tree: Olive, *Djedet*

Virgo ♍

  Neter: Geb

  Stone: Amber, *Manu*

  Color: Brown, *Djeriu*

  Metal: Bronze, *Ut*

  Incense: Patchouli, *Hebut*

Scent: Olive, *Baq*

Tree: Persea, *Ished*

Libra ♎

Neter: Auset

Stone: Carnelian, *Seher*

Color: Maroon, *Marsh*

Metal: Electrum, *Djam*

Incense: Jasmine, *Ankham*

Scent: Rose, *Uarta*

Tree: Cedar, *Ash*

Scorpio ♏

Neter: Anpu

Stone: Serpentine, *Themes*

Color: Black, *Kem*

Metal: Brass, *Tehast*

Incense: Cassia, *Khasit*

Scent: Camphor, —

Tree: Date Palm, *Bener*

Sagittarius ♐

Neter: Sekhmet-Bast

Stone: Flint, *Djes*

Color: Orange, *Menshet*

Metal: Tin, *Tran*

Incense: Balsam, *Khet Aadjer*

Scent: Civet, *Basa*

Tree: Juniper, *Wan*

Capricorn ♑

Neter: Set

Stone: Haematite, *Dedi*

Color: Red, *Desher*

Metal: Lead, *Djhet*

Incense: Natron, *Hesmen*

Scent: Musk, *Seshsau*

Tree: Ebony, *Hebeny*

Aquarius ♒

Neter: Maat

Stone: Amethyst, *Hemagat*

Color: Violet, *Tekhit*

Metal: Platinum, *Katam*

Incense: Orris, —

Scent: Frankincense, *Nenib*

Tree: Papyrus, *Mehyt*

Pisces ♓

Neter: Nut

Stone: Lapis Lazuli, *Khesbet*

Color: Indigo, *Khesbedjti*

Metal: Aluminum, *Ibnu*

Incense: Storax, *An*

Scent: Ambergris, *San en Wadj Wer*

Tree: Sycamore, *Nehet*

Table 14—Correspondences of the Neteru

♈ Asar

In reading through many of the prayers and hymns of Egypt's sacred literature, it becomes apparent that the hope for life's continuance is addressed to Asar, god of both afterlife and renewal of the living. Yet this is not an indication that Asar possessed more of a following than the other Neteru. Rather, he was recognized as the exemplar of all mortals—even all sentient beings—who must eventually relinquish physical life and pass into the shadow worlds. As such, Asar's commemoration, experiences, and words are metaphors for our existence and should be viewed as such. What the god of renewal presents to us is both the inevitability of our mortal existence, along with the promise of survival in a sublime realm, one peopled by other spirits, gods, and natural forces that belong to us and to which we belong.

Principle: Renewal. Asar reconstitutes that which has been broken, disassembled, or diminished. He is the Neter of new life, beginnings, and second chances.

Function: Germination. This Neter brings forth the creative forces that are innate to living beings. He allows this force, which may have been hindered or blocked, to return and infuse vitality, appreciation for life, and recovery.

Associated deities: Hapi, the recurring Nile god; Sokar, the hibernating life force; Andjety, the nome spirit who endows the crook and flail of sovereignty; Anher, "the striding one" who is an image of Orion in the sky; Khentiamenti, "foremost of the Westerners" who leads souls into the afterlife from the holy land of Abydos.

Animals: Ram, hare.

♉ Het-Her

As goddess of fecundity and nourishment, Het-Her embodies the incubating womb for the life that has become renewed in Asar's realm. Within her sphere, all things flourish and progress through their natural cycle of embodiment. This Neter represents the rhythmic pulse of creation, and in her temples the sound of sistra and drum emanated through halls and chambers that celebrated her powers as consort of the Sun, the younger Heru. She is patroness of the artistic realm and especially favors the activities of music, dance, art, and performance. Her radiant physical beauty is always recounted in ancient hymns and poetry, one of her names being *Nubet,* "the golden one." She was often called upon in these love poems to draw the beloved, as she embodies the ideal of feminine magnetism and evokes intense states of erotic desire and passion.

One of the functions of Het-Her's temple in ancient times was healing, as she also brings great peace to the troubled mind. Her Lunar powers allow dreams to present remedies and solutions to conflicts in the emotions and thoughts.

Principle: Fertilization. The energy dynamic of Het-Her brings separate forces together and houses (her name means "House of Heru") divergent powers in an atmosphere of harmony and growth.

Function: Conception. This Neter has influence over lovers and young families. She assists in bringing mating rituals to successful conclusion and heals sexual dysfunctions. Her presence brings celebration, though it can also encourage inebriation and overindulgence. She is patroness of weddings and reunions.

Associated deities: Wadjet, the cobra goddess who protects the Royal House; Bat, the regional Neter at Dendera who embodies her fruitful aspect; Renutet, who is royal nurse and a protective cobra in the afterlife; Hesat, the divine cow of heaven whose milk nourishes the royal person; Bes, the Nubian spirit of fertility and joy who protects the integrity of the home; Meretseger, patroness of offerings at the Theban necropolis in Upper Egypt.

Animals: Bull, cow, hooded cobra.

♊ Djehuti

As recorder of the Akashic record, Djehuti is the source of all knowledge pertaining to the past and present. He brings dignity to learning and assists in tests of skill. This Neter is also prosecuting attorney in the law court of the gods, the counselor and judge on behalf of Heru's petition when Set made false claims on the throne of Egypt. As such he allows just claims to be made and false accusations to become null.

Principle: Resonance. The energy dynamic of Djehuti breaks through mental barriers; it allows facts to become known and secrets to be revealed. His powers are concerned with cosmic memory and access to ancient wisdom.

Function: Communication. Djehuti assists in the delivery of messages and information, and the discovery of lost knowledge. He is one of the patrons of divinatory activities, but he communicates more directly with the mind rather than through oracular tools such as magic mirrors and geomantic figures. He may be called upon when learning new skills and languages (especially symbol systems), as he is patron of scholars and scribes. He eases mental confusion and will come to the aid of the person who diagnoses or repairs equipment, tools, and machinery.

Associated deities: Khons, the Lunar deity of transitory phenomena; Shu, the Neter of cosmic space and wind; Seshat, the measurer and architect; Tekhi, regulator of times and seasons.

Animals: Ibis, baboon, giraffe.

♋ Nebt-Het

Nebt-Het is always depicted as the faithful companion and loyal guardian—to her sister Auset, her brother Asar, and the young Heru, to whom she was nurse. One of her important roles is watcher and custodian. When the body is inert or suspended—while under surgical treatment, hypnosis, or accident—her powers protect the vital functions and ensure that life will return.

Principle: Secretion. The energy dynamic of Nebt-Het brings nourishing benefits to conditions that are newly inaugurated. Her influence will feed, comfort, supply, and aid where there is want or danger. As nurse, she protects and nurtures the young so that they may awaken to their divine mission with courage and commitment.

Function: Sustenance. Nebt-Het provides both material and spiritual food. As patroness of offerings, she ensures that the domestic table is always provided for and that food which enters the body will benefit its growth and maintenance. Hence, she restores health and is helpful in diet and nutrition.

Associated deities: Taiyet, the goddess of swathings and divine coverings; Nebet Hetepet, the Heliopolitan consort of Atum and mistress of *djefau* (sacred offerings); Renutet, the nursing deity who attends the births of royal children; Nekhebet, the archaic vulture goddess who protects the Royal House; Hatmehyt, the dolphin goddess of Mendes and consort of Ba Neb Djedu.

Animals: Vulture, tortoise, dolphin.

♌ Heru

Two distinct images of Heru appear in the ancient legends—Heru Ur "the elder" and Heru Behutet, the avenging son of the Heliopolitan family. He also assumes other aspects as divine child *(Heru pa Khart),* lover *(Ihy),* king and uniter of the Two Lands *(Sma Taui),* and chronocrator of the Sun's daily passage over the two horizons *(Heru em Aakhuti).* All of these images are metaphors of the Solar principle on Earth, the divine light that enters the mundane sphere and brings its particular illumination to every dimension of human experience and nature.

Heru Ur (the "Elder"), the fully matured heir to the divine birthright, shares the Kom Ombo Temple in Upper Egypt with Sobekh as healer, and is here regarded as patron of medical procedures and healing, similar to the tradition of Apollo's healing temples in ancient Greece. Heru Behutet (the "Younger") is the triumphant contender to the throne of Egypt, continually threatened by the nefarious acts of Set and his confederates. In becoming the victor, he personifies the ideal of kingship, the model for valiant behavior, responsible government, and dedication to honorable tradition. The king was also viewed in ancient times as a primary source of virile power, fertilizing the land with his vitality, the ideal of masculine strength.

Principle: Ascension (Younger Heru) and Exaltation (Elder Heru). Heru's energy dynamic brings courage and confidence to one's convictions, allowing progress to take place despite obstacles, jealousies, or interference from meddling family members.

Function: Mastery (Younger Heru), Initiation (Elder Heru). As patron of high office, Heru brings rewards to great effort and dedicated work. His influence brings sound decisions when managing the affairs of others in business or family. Advancement and acknowledgment come through the intercession of Heru.

Associated deities: Ra, the Solar ancestor; Min, the god of potency and sexual prowess; Herishef, a nome spirit who represents the ideal of manliness; Mont, Neter of successful battles; Heru's four "sons" or energetic helping spirits: Imset (conscious thought), Daumutef (instinct), Qebsenuf (inspiration), and Haapi (sensation); Dunawy, a protective initiatory figure known as "the one with the outstretched talons."

Animals: Hawk, falcon, phoenix, bee.

ﾜ Geb

Geb is the ancestral father of Egyptian civilization, the fountainhead of its culture, and custodian of the land. As consort of Nut the sky, he represents the stability of the Earth that balances the continually changing forces in the heavens. He bestows the birthright of his children—the guardianship and maintenance of the Royal House—and when it comes under threat, he intervenes and resolves conflict. He is also a virile figure, though his vitality is directed more to nature rather than human beings.

The powers of Geb, which manifest divine ideas into material reality, bring about successful conclusions and amicable agreements, and allow conditions to reach resolution.

Principle: Creation. As one of the fabricators of human form, he may be called upon to heal physical infirmities and correct defects, especially for the young. And if there are divisions in the family, his intercession can bring agreement to all sides. Being the wise arbitrator in the family dispute between Heru and Set, he is patron of judges and mediators. Building projects and business plans may go forward under his influence, with all sides being fairly compensated.

Function: Vegetation. Geb is primarily a Neter of the harvest, and ensures a continual supply for the home and business. His influence also allows the artisan to become prolific and successful.

Associated deities: The androgynous figures of Neit, the healing goddess of the Lower Kingdom who constitutes the body; and Ptah, the divine artificer who inspires the builder and fabricator. Other Neteru include Khnum, creator of the

Ka, who fashions the ideal form for the body and corrects defects; and Hotep, lord of the offering table, who brings abundance and freedom from want.

Animals: Goose, duck, mongoose, lizard.

♎ Auset

The greatest of the Neteru, leader of the powers that govern terrestrial life and come to its aid, Auset has been regarded for millennia as the source of divine intervention and magical processes. The season of Libra highlights those powers and her companion divinities who bring forth new life, restore lost vitality, and ensure divine protection. She is the source of hope when all appears to be lost, and her intercession can reverse the most dire circumstances. Auset always answers an appeal, and invoking her attention should be done with certainty and sincerity. She is patroness of the priesthood, as her fidelity and service to the slain god is the model of attentiveness and spiritual devotion.

Principle: Fruition. The energy dynamic of Auset brings conditions to their utmost realization or completion, allowing all that is potentially life-producing to come into being. Her powers can circumvent great obstacles, and will banish harmful influences and feelings.

Function: Birth. This goddess is the archetype of maternal life. She gives birth and nurses the child, protects it from danger, and in her greatest act, guides the youth Heru to consummate his ultimate destiny—resolve the death of his father and assume the powers of life in the mundane world. She does this by teaching the proper use of personal power and the careful practice of high magic in a respectful environment. She brings dignity and closure to tragic circumstances.

From her legendary power to elicit the secret name of her father Ra, and dispel the poison from her son Heru and help restore his lost eye in a series of battles with Set, Auset is also an effective healer and restorer of vital functions, especially the breath. She is patroness of midwives, emergency medical practitioners, and hospice workers.

Associated deities: Sopdet, the star goddess of initiation; Meskhenet, Neter of the birth house; Selqit, vanquisher of poisons and "she who relieves the windpipe" in the Pyramid Texts.

Animals: Swallow, dove, female falcon.

♏ Anpu

As son of Set and Nebt-Het, the loyal attendant Anpu embodies the protective nature in psychic life. His genealogy implies very powerful, destructive potential, as he is the doorman to the shadow worlds and mediator to the denizens who reside within. However, his prudent devotion to the Solar gods prevail in his legendary exploits, and Anpu personifies the good that arises from the proper use of theurgy. These qualities are imbued in his images of the faithful domestic hound and the watchful wolf of the necropolis; his warning sound is echoed in the night cry of the desert jackal.

Principle: Transmutation. The energy dynamic of Anpu transforms conditions, especially those that appear in a state of confusion, dissolution, or decay. He brings the powers of conversion into the environment, allowing the positive to arise from negative influences. As one of the lords of divination, he assists in discerning secrets and hidden agendas, communicating with ancestral souls, and diagnosing difficult cases. He also guides those who are lost or missing back home.

Function: Digestion. The healing powers of Anpu can accelerate a return to health and restoration of clear mind and optimistic feeling. He is called upon to bring the appropriate remedies to psychic afflictions (especially fear) and expert assistance in situations that do not respond to ordinary courses of action.

Associated deities: Apuat, the "opener of the ways," sentry of the shadow worlds and wolf of Lycopolis who guides the soul through darkness; Heka, Neter of theurgy and lord of magic; Khepri, bringer of renewed life and transformation.

Animals: Hound, jackal, wolf, scarabaeus.

♐ Sekhmet-Bast

According to the ancient Egyptian legend *The Deliverance of Mankind,* it was the goddess Het-Her, summoned by the Sun god Ra, who destroyed the desert people after they offended their maker with hostile behavior. In this deed, the goddess assumed her form as Sekhmet-Bast, the "sound eye" of her father, fiery and burning, the avenging power of all that brought disorder to the land of Egypt.

"I have prevailed over men and my heart is satisfied," she reported to Ra when the slaughter was completed. Thus bathed in the blood of mortals, she became known to the gods as the dreaded vindicator of wrongdoing, the fierce protectoress of sacred territory.

But this goddess also holds the keys to healing the wounds that she is capable of inflicting, especially those brought by her powers to dispel unwanted influences. Thus, she governs processes that eliminate, for once and for all, the poisons that come from unwise living, thinking, and feeling. In ancient times, her priests were trained to the highest skills in medical treatment, surgery, and exorcism.

Principle: Purification. Sekhmet-Bast's energy dynamic is directed toward removing invasion, intrusion, and disorder. Her influence is formidable and should never be called upon for frivolous purposes. Rituals of her temple were known to utterly destroy those they were directed toward, and may have been the only ones that employed blood sacrifice, though none have survived the ages. She is protector of soldiers, law enforcement, and psychic healers.

Function: Purgation. As healer, Sekhmet-Bast removes impurities from the body, though her presence may bring fever and eruptions of the skin. However, she brings the appropriate medical assistance when invoked, and she is patroness of all healers, therapists, and physicians.

Associated deities: Bastet, the Neter of domestic felicity; Paket, "she who claws," the avenging aspect of the goddess; Imhotep, the renowned Old Kingdom healer and source of medical wisdom; Amunhotep, son of Hapu, the Middle Kingdom deified healer and priest of Sekhmet-Bast.

Animals: Large cats, domestic cat, hedgehog.

♅ Set

The visage of Set may evoke fear in the ritual landscape, but his function was always regarded as a vital component in the cosmic scheme. Set's raw physical powers gave rise to his name *Seb Ur* ("greatest strength"), the title of his cosmic sceptre that stands at the pole of the Earth in the form of the Big Dipper. He is also lord of Earthly forces, embodied in the metals of iron and lead that fashioned his awesome tools—the adze and ceremonial blades used in the transformative Opening of the Mouth ceremonies. All must be reconciled to the powers of Set, and though they are formidable, they are the forces that govern the essential laws on Earth and within the mortal form itself. Thus, he oversees the realm of corruption and decay, an important phase in the life cycle of the phenomenal world.

Principle: Fixation. The energy dynamic of Set imposes physical restraints that may inhibit free movement and thought. His influence brings conditions to a standstill that may require extended periods of remedial action, such as repeating efforts, experiencing bureaucratic delays, and facing opposition. However, his own powers have limitation, and will subside when natural laws are obeyed. Set may assist in health matters that have been misdiagnosed or disguised by symptoms; he allows conditions to present themselves openly.

Function: Corruption. Set brings adversaries to one's attention without compromise and he assists in facing irresolvable situations that may appear formidable and overpowering. He provides mental endurance and physical stamina, allowing the weak to come back with renewed vigor.

Associated deities: Apep, "the devourer," who governs cyclic phenomena on the organic plane; Sobekh, the crocodile god whose powers heal the deformed; Taurt, goddess of proliferation; Sokar, deity of hibernation and the winter solstice.

Animals: Goat, crocodile, hippopotamus, antelope, gazelle, oryx (all desert animals).

⌇⌇ Maat

As goddess of justice and order, Maat organizes the chaos brought by Set and ensures its timely return whenever disruptions have altered the natural order. Ironically, the structure that Maat embodies is the adaptable, free-flowing matrix of nature. This is her most important role, and universal justice is dispensed by her when mortal laws have been circumvented.

This Neter is also associated with astrology and the divinatory arts. In the sky, she sits at the prow of the Sun barque to ensure that it will stay on course of the *Meten* (ecliptical path of the Sun). As the material aspect of Djehuti, she translates divine ideas, and is therefore consulted as intermediary to the gods when the answer to a question is sought or advice is required.

Principle: Order. Maat's energy dynamic quickly reorganizes conditions that have become seriously disrupted or out of objective control. She also ensures the orderly progress of long-range plans, including building, commerce, and education.

Function: Structure. This Neter brings fair judgment in legal cases, and new rules and approaches to seemingly unsolvable situations. However, one must be willing to work with the structure that arises from her response; it may not be the conventional solution, but it will normalize the situation expediently. She is also the celestial tutor, and assists in understanding complex issues and ideas.

Associated deities: Seshat, the divine architect and dispensator of measures; the forty-two Maati, each of whom represents the balance of law in the natural order of life, as articulated in the renowned Declaration of Innocence recited by priests on entering the temple and the deceased on entering the afterlife.

Animals: Heron, ostrich, owl.

♓ Nut

The mother of the sky is both the beginning and ending of human experience, but her great power allows life to continue, in cycles, through endless periods of realization and reflection. Nut is the source of new ideas, the endless reservoir of possibilities. She is also associated with astronomy, as the ancient temple priests viewed the sky as her material body, accurately calculating time and the cyclic periods of celestial phenomena from a sophisticated system of observation and notation. She associates with the deities of divination, as all past and future events take shape from the firmament in her visible form.

Principle: Augmentation. The powers of Nut provide increase, allowing the seed of thought and the fruit of labor to reach its utmost limit. She is the incubator *par excellence,* and assists in the successful completion of any endeavor.

Function: Gestation. Nut's watery realm is also the source of peace and recuperation. She brings healing dreams and insights, and allows intuition to come forth when required. This Neter also possesses a fertile nature, which may be called upon to alleviate difficulties in conception, pregnancy, and childbirth.

Associated deities: Atum, "the all," the primeval creator and ancestor of Nut; Tefnut, Neter of cosmic moisture and guardian of the horizons; Nun, the primordial water that rejuvenates the spirit and restores the body; Nefertum, the divine youth whose scent inspires spiritual visions; Mut, incubating mother who protects the royal child; Heqet, an attendant birth goddess in the form of a frog.

Animals: Serpent, frog, eel.

The Egyptians regarded the passage of the Sun over the sky as a divine journey that ensures Maat (order) and continuity. As the Sun god Ra makes his daily passage through the heavens, divine vitality is distributed through the visible worlds, and as he performs his annual circuit through the constellations, "seasons" of that vitality becomes accessible to the temple.

Recognizing that the twelve-signed band of constellations was not incorporated into temple iconography until the Graeco-Roman period, an understanding of the parallels between celestial rhythms and acts of theurgy was nevertheless the fundamental premise of temple work in ancient times and should be our guide in the present. Following the astrological scheme fulfills that aim and allows the initiate to experience the powers of the celestial seasons and the Neteru who bring them to conscious life.

Chapter Four

THEURGY

To know how to make the proper gesture in the correct milieu at the right cosmic moment: this is sacred magic . . . In this way, often unconsciously, we are magicians. Wisdom consists in knowing how to be consciously so.

—R. A. Schwaller de Lubicz, *The Egyptian Miracle*

The Neoplatonists, a philosophic body that developed over several centuries at the end of the ancient era in the Graeco-Roman period, promoted a combination of Egyptian spirituality with the schools of Plato, Pythagoras, Aristotle, and the Stoics. The fusion of religious and metaphysical concepts that arose from this endeavor preserves some of Egypt's esoteric tradition, but favors the Greek approach to spiritual practice—a cognitive dialogue between the conscious mind and immanent soul, an approach that delegates feeling and sensation to the realm of irrational experience.

In spite of its withdrawal from the sensate and intuitive aspect of spirituality, Neoplatonic philosophy acknowledged the importance of divine experience, and expressed it in terms of *theurgy* ("divine work"). Though the term is generally applied to divine or supernatural intervention in human affairs and is often used to allude to the magic and sorcery practiced in the Graeco-Roman age, it imparts the spirit and intent of ancient Egyptian spiritual practice.

Theurgy can fulfill the natural inclination in a spiritual practice to employ the senses, along with the conscious mind, to experience the sacred. More importantly, it is an approach to spiritual practice that conveys benefits to the practitioner, a "grace" that is exchanged between the god and the theurgist—sacrament.

The fundamental premise of theurgy is that nature and natural forces are intelligent, and communication with them is not only possible, but desirable—approaches forwarded by both the priestly tradition of pharaonic Egypt and the later Hermetic philosophy of the Alexandrian sages. Acts of communicating with these forces—the gods—fulfill many of the needs that human beings possess, which the Neoplatonic philosopher Iamblichus (fourth century C.E.) described in several ways:

> . . . *the presence of the Gods, indeed, imparts to us health of body, virtue of soul, purity of intellect and in one word elevates every thing in us to its proper principle.*
> . . . *the dispositions of the soul of those that invoke the Gods to appear receive, when they become visible, a liberation from the passions, a transcendent perfection, and an energy entirely more excellent, and participate of divine love and an immense joy.*[1]

But the pursuit of this interaction is not one-sided. The ancients believed that the Neteru are as attracted to the mundane sphere as much as human beings seek knowledge of divine life. This is because the gods embody nature and convey the natural forces that are interdependent with human existence. In this, the gods have a threefold need to interact with us—the first being the *theurgic necessity.* Here, the Neteru seek to reveal—through vision or appearance—their existence, thereby increasing their power and extending their realm of visible manifestation. Consequently, the second purpose arises as the *magical necessity.* The Neteru must manifest through material mediums, so that their natural powers increasingly associate with, rather than separate from, the physical world. Here, their existence is continuously integrated with natural life and is thus bound to it.

The third purpose for the Neter's interaction with Earthly life is the *goetic necessity.* The power of the Neter that has animated the material form imprints and modifies it—and thus elevates it. A consequence of this phenomenon is that the

---

1. *De Mysteriis,* translated by Thomas Taylor (San Diego, Calif.: Wizards Bookshelf, 1977) 95, 101.

modified material form serves as a medium; it may be "read" or "interpreted" by human participants for divination, prophecy, and healing. Here, the Neter's imprint continues to refine the matter that it embodies.

What then were the Egyptian sacraments? And which of the necessities—theurgic, magical, and goetic—were served when they were performed and received?

These are questions often posed when we examine the temple tradition, and even for scholars they are the most elusive to answer. However, from the ritual texts that comprise the known liturgies, several acts that evoke the powers of the gods that are passed on to recipients appear on the landscape of religious ceremony throughout all periods in Egyptian history.

Ritual establishes a relationship, and in the Egyptian context it renews the human connection to natural life through the Neteru, the divine intermediaries. Hence, the landscape of the natural environment is an essential component of the temple—the phenomena of the sky and Earth are an integral part of its spiritual work.

For the sake of clarity, this work will refer to *rite* and *ritual* as purposeful words and actions performed in the sacred environment that have been prescribed by tradition, such as the Rite of Offering. In turn, a series of rituals dedicated to a specific goal or deity is here regarded as *ceremony* or *observance,* such as the Ceremony of Opening the Mouth, which involves offering as well as other rites. The Egyptians also celebrated festivals, and in the context of their tradition, such events commemorated the appearance or acts of the Neteru. Festivals involved many rituals, ceremonies, and other incidents, such as journeys (the Ipet Festival of Amun's barque traveling from the Karnak temple to the Luxor sanctuary), processions (the annual entombment of Osirian effigies at Abydos), and communal celebrations (the Festival of Intoxication at Dendera).

Khesu—Rites

Prescribed rites, for daily observances as well as for ceremonies called by other occasions, rarely deviated from tradition, and this encompasses a span of thousands of years. The cultures surrounding Egypt in ancient times recognized this, and attributed the great power of Egyptian religion to its antiquity and fidelity to past tradition. These basic acts, the *Khesu* ("prescriptions" or "rites"), were performed in the home, temple, tomb, and public festival. All ceremonies, great and small, featured variations on these time-honored rites. The Khesu, loosely described, fall into two categories: *Hotepu* and *Wabu*.

Hotepu—Offering Rites

In the Egyptian tradition, acts of offering are basic and fundamental to every rite. Daily in the temple, periodically in the tomb, calendrically in the sacred astronomy that determines Solar, Lunar, and Stellar events, offerings are made on behalf of the living, the dead, and especially to the gods. This sharing of goods is a vital component of social and religious observance in every agricultural society, but it is especially particular to Egyptian ceremony. The interdependence of life is acknowledged through this act, as well as the metaphysical transference of power from material to spiritual form and its reversion to the mundane world once more. Formal offerings nurture the bonds between the visible and invisible worlds by acknowledging power and sharing the fruits of labor.

Offerings took a number of forms, and each had its ceremonial value. The offering of consumable goods is most often described in temple and tomb, with a regular and consistent program of such offerings being established for the god or the deceased—as a cult. Votive offerings were also made at temple and tomb, being finely made or sentimental objects that honor the gods or the deceased. They could also commemorate sacred days or events, and represent important tools that the gods may empower for the owner—physicians instruments, jewelry, architect's tools, scribal supplies, etc. Such offerings are occasional and not subject to the cult rules of other offerings, where, for instance, fish was never offered in the ceremonial environment.

The most important aspect of the offering gesture is the expectation that it will be returned in another form. Here, the goetic necessity is operative—the material that is offered becomes transformed by its contact with the divinity. The Egyptians believed that making use of this converted substance completes the circle of offering and perpetrates the divinization of matter. Hence, the communal feasts following funerary ceremonies and the reversion of offerings after temple ritual.

Khesu
Common Rites (Day)

Iru
Ceremonies (Month)

Hotepu
Offerings

Kheperu
Transformations

Wabu
Purifications

Mesen
Founding

Hebu
Festivals (Year)

Sa Akhu
Initiations

Figure 42—Temple Observances

Wabu—Purification Rites

Egyptian ritual is replete with rites of purification that precede every ceremony or festival. The concept of purity is not, however, arising from a belief that the participants are impure or unworthy in any manner; rather, these acts are an acknowledgment that a new world has been entered and an exalted state is recognized. As a form of rebirth, these observances emulate the renewal of the land by the river's inundation, or the entry of the child into the world with its initial bathing and donning of new apparel.

In the daily ritual of the temple, those who entered the Divine House were required to be physically and ritually clean. This encompassed individual bathing, anointing in the Divine House, and the recitation of texts that declared moral purity. Even the deity shared in these acts—a ritual cleansing, clothing, and feeding of the Neter's image took place in the daily ritual, a need that arose out of its descent from celestial realms in the night and reentry into the mundane world in the day.

Gestures of purity are a restatement of dedication to divine work on a number of levels, but they also convey the transcendent purpose of theurgy. These acts provide the opportunity for renewal and revision of behavior or attitude that becomes aligned to divine purposes. Purification is also a reminder of the innate perfection of creation that is being realized through all ritual.

The Khesu may be designed for practice according to the convenience and preference of the practitioner. Such rites, being very basic to temple ritual, are best performed in the morning on arising as they were in ancient times, but this is not requisite.

Iru—Ceremonies of the Sky

The creative worlds become accessible through the rhythms of cosmic life—the Solar, Lunar, and Stellar resonances of the sacred astronomy. These rhythms provide the powers of the temple and renew them cyclically.

The *Iru* ("fabrications") are temple observances that take place during these times—at the New Moon and Full Moon (Lunar), Solar ingresses, solstices, and equinoxes (Solar), and Stellar events such as the heliacal rising of Sirius or the return of the temple's particular star to the pre-dawn sky. Also included in these ceremonies are any events that denote the inception of new cycles, such as the *Wag* festival for the beginning of the Lunar New Year. The times for observing these ceremonies may vary each year and must be calculated using the temple's system of sacred astronomy.

The function of the Iru is to capture the outpouring of the Neter as it is released cosmically, and direct it to enhance human and natural life. In the Egyptian world view, divine life is believed to be resident in all phenomena, and exists in its most powerful form in celestial bodies, where even the souls of exalted human beings could journey.

Hebu—Festivals

Festivals of the "times" (calendar) were often called *feasts* and were numerous in ancient Egypt. These included the days that commemorated the divine births of the five children of Nut and Geb, and heroic acts such as the defeat of Set by Heru. They were usually held on fixed dates, and included traditional events like pharaonic crownings, celebrated on the first day in the month of Tybi.

Calendric ceremonies (*Hebu,* plural for *Heb,* "festival") provide openings between the visible and invisible worlds where the exchange of energy and information may take place. This fulfills the magical necessity that integrates the natural realm with the realm of the Neter.

Hebu are also observed when required by the temple or its members, such as a funeral or marriage. These events fulfill the theurgic necessity that extends the realm of the Neter, from the celestial to the mundane sphere. This is because the acts of the gods, when emulated, allow their powers to become integrated into the daily life of participants and elevate the environment.

Kheperu—Transformations

There are other significant human events that fall within the realm of the Hebu, though they represent the ultimate aim of theurgy—the transition from mundane to divine experience. In ancient Egypt, these high rituals were reserved for members of the Royal House and the priesthood, though at times other members of society had access to them through extensive temple training and accomplishment in certain disciplines, such as medicine, theology, and astronomy. Spells and sorcery also fall under the realm of Kheperu.

Mesen ("Founding") Ceremonies

These are specific rituals intended to prepare and welcome the recipient into a new life, whether it be for a specified period or for eternity. These include the inauguration of the Divine House, namegivings, and the enigmatic Sed festival, a thirty-year pharaonic celebration that commemorates the original crowning into the monarchy. These events impart a new identity and arrival into a new realm of existence.

Sa Akhu ("Initiation") Ceremonies

These rituals intend to empower the initiate with new faculties, powers, and responsibilities. They are known from records of pharaonic and priestly investiture, and ceremonies that represent the processes described in Hermetic literature as "making gods." This genre of Egyptian spiritual work includes the transformative forces conveyed in the Opening of the Mouth and Book of Breathings. They are pivotal ceremonies that represent the endowment of creative power from the gods to human beings. Recipients for these events include the living, the suffering, the dead, divine forces, and the temples themselves. *Sa Akhu* means "to make glorious" and "to perform sublime rites."

The Daily Ritual

One of the most cited of the Egyptian temple observances is the daily ritual of the temple, delineated in modern times as *The Ritual of the Divine Cult*. It is recorded at the temples of Karnak and Abydos, and many of its components are included in funerary and the dedicatory ceremonies of Egyptian monuments. However, it was consistently performed at dawn in the temple and employed a great number of personnel, most of whom were resident in the Divine House for at least a season of the year. A generous array of offerings were presented in this daily event, along with individual rites—from awakening the deity and presenting its Earthly nourishment to transferring its power via the officiants to divine images or human recipients. Fifty-three individual rites are described, and each was followed every day in the temple, never deviating from tradition. However, in the great temples, rites were elaborated with additional hymns and offerings particular to the deity of that locale. For instance, when the statue of the deity in the shrine wore a uraeus crown, a separate censing and libation were made to the serpent goddesses—Wadjet, Meretseger, and Renutet.

The day began with the awakening of the deity and welcoming it into the mundane world. The event was observed in every temple, from the humblest local shrine to the great city-temples along the Nile. The primary officiant of this rite was the *Kher Heb* ("lector priest"), who represented Pharaoh as son of the gods, welcoming the Neter into the sanctuary. The royal person was the living descendant of the gods, and as such was spiritually qualified to perform divine labors. Among these, the duties of feeding and clothing divine beings were essential. But the royal person's duties could be performed, if necessary, by spiritually appointed surrogates, and in most cases they were. Certain clergy of the temple were dedicated to this task, and enacted those labors according to the traditions exclusive to the god of the temple.

The ritual followed in this time-honored order:

1. *Striking a Fire:* The brazier of the sanctuary is lit. A pair of deep stone cauldrons, filled with embers, usually flanked the sanctuary entrance of the temple to provide a continuous supply of incense coals.

2. *Presenting the Censer:* The censer in which the incense is burned is first presented to the Neter. The *An Heru* ("hand of Heru") is fashioned in the form of a long rod ending in a hand or falcon's claw that grasps the incense bowl.

3. *Dedication of the Incense:* The temple incense, which is composed of small, rolled spheres of precious materials (storax, benzoin, frankincense, myrrh) is presented to the Neter.

4. *Placing the Incense on the Fire:* This is a solemn act, one that initiates the sanctification of the naos.

5. *Advancing to the Holy Place:* This act is performed with the "call to awaken the deity" in the form of chant and litany.

6. *Breaking the Cord of the Seal:* The naos had been sealed with a tied papyrus cord and stamped clay seal on the previous night, in the belief that the Neter would repose in its celestial realm until dawn, when it would descend into the temple.

7. *Breaking the Clay Seal:* Spells were recited to protect the officiant from any harm that results from breaching the temple seal.

8. *Removing the Seal:* Brushes and ceremonial brooms carried by attendants were part of the seal-breaking rite, to ensure absolute cleanliness and order in the sanctuary.

9. *Opening the Face of the Deity:* The door of the naos is opened, and litanies of the divine names are recited. The head of the officiant is bowed in respect.

10. *Looking on the Face of the Deity:* The highlight of this ritual comes when the face of the Neter is exposed to its servant. Recitations of prayer and acknowledgment of the god's powers are spoken.

11. *Smelling the Earth:* The officiant and attendants prostrate themselves before the Neter.

12. *Embracing the Earth:* The sanctuary ground is kissed in respect for the appearance of the Neter.

13. *Rising Up:* The temple musicians proceed to pay homage to the Neter.

14. *Bowing Down:* A recitation of praises and hymns are sung to the Neter.

15. *Presentation of Honey:* The Neter's meal begins.

16. *Presentation of Incense:* A censing of the Neter's image proceeds.

17. *Entering into the Sanctuary:* The Neter's image leaves the secluded naos.

18. *Entering into the Shrine:* The Neter's image appears within the sanctuary to all attendants.

19. *Withdrawing from the Shrine:* The Neter leaves the sanctuary room.

20. *At the Steps of the Sanctuary:* The Neter enters the Hall of Appearings, immediately outside the sanctuary.

21. *Uncovering the Deity in Festival:* The clothing of the previous day is removed from the image of the Neter.

22–29. *Opening the Mouth:* In this "rite within the rite," the image of the Neter is reanimated with the tools of the *Un Ra,* the ceremonialist whose specialty is confined to performing this ritual.

22. *Smiting the Face:* A ritual gesture that concludes the Opening of the Mouth.

23. *Presentation of Water on the Table of Offerings:* Nile water is sprinkled upon the offering table.

24. *Pouring the Libation:* Precious oils are poured into offering bowls at the table.

25. *Censing the Table of Offerings:* The offerings and oils are censed in a final sanctification of the god's morning meal.

26. *Presentation of the Table of Offerings:* For each Neter, the morning meal was prescribed according to the temple tradition, and this differed by region and the function of the Neter's house. Each component of the offering was articulated in a presentation litany.

27. *Incense Offering to All the Deities:* The images of the subsidiary gods of the temple are now censed.

28. *Food Offering to All the Deities:* The offering table is taken around the temple to the shrines of the subsidiary gods.

29. *Image of the Deity Withdrawn:* Hymns are sung as the image returns to the sanctuary room.

30. *Censing, Hymns, the Presentation of Maat:* In the name of Pharaoh, the officiant censes the Neter's images while hymns are sung by the temple chanters; the image of Maat (truth and order) is shown as proof that ancient protocol is followed and the primeval pattern continues.

31. *Censing of the Deities in the Sanctuary:* A final censing of all the images is performed.

32. *Laying of Hands on the Deity:* In this mystic act, the officiant receives the power of the god through a transference. This power (Sa) may in turn be transmitted to other images, persons, or objects at the conclusion of the ritual.

33. *Opening the Box of Purification:* The casket containing ritual vases and substances is opened so that the divine toilet may begin.

34. *Purification by Four Nemes Vases of Water:* A bath of water poured from green vases brings the powers of proliferation into the ritual.

35. *Purifications by Four Deshret Vases of Water:* A bath of water poured from red vases brings the life force into the ritual.

36. *Purification by Natron:* A cleansing by natron proceeds, by sprinkling the powder on a cloth and rubbing the divine image.

37. *Presentation of Apparel:* The new clothing for the Neter's image is initially presented.

38. *Donning of White Apparel:* The image receives its first piece of clothing, and a strict order of presenting the materials by color is employed.

39. *Donning of Green Apparel:* This color represents the proliferation of life and ensures the prosperity of the Neter while in its sanctuary.

40. *Donning of Red Apparel:* This color brings the powers of animation to the Neter.

41. *Donning of Headdress:* Regalia in the form of crowns are placed upon the Neter's image.

42. *Presentation of Oils:* Ten flasks of precious oils are presented to the Neter, each anointed on the brow. The ten oils are the same used in the purification rite of the temple priest.

43. *Presentation of Copper Cosmetic:* The Neter's eyes are painted with this substance, which possesses both medicinal and magical powers for sight.

44. *Presentation of Lead Cosmetic:* The eyes are outlined with galena, to acquire the power to see through the halls and chambers of the Divine House.

45. *Scattering the Sand:* The sanctuary floor receives a light scattering of sand followed by a thorough sweeping.

46. *Circumnavigation of the Sanctuary:* This is performed clockwise, four times.

47. *Presentation of Bet Incense:* The sanctuary is censed while circumnavigated.

48. *Presentation of Natron Vase:* The sanctuary is symbolically purified while circumnavigated.

49. *Purifications:* Recitations to eliminate hostile forces purify the atmosphere of the sanctuary.

50. *Presentation of Divine Food:* A small offering of the Neter's in the symbolic form of statuary or carved representations is placed in front of the naos.

51. *Presentation of Water Vessel:* A small offering bowl of water is placed in front of the naos.

52. *Presentation of Natron:* A small offering bowl of natron is placed in front of the naos.

53. *Burning of Myrrh:* A final censing takes place as myrrh is placed in the temple braziers and the door of the naos is closed. It will be sealed following the evening service.

Similarly, the individual's awakening, conscious participation with the present, and active spiritual functions should be engaged in an event that is observed each day. Several daily rites (Khesu) comprise this—Purification, Offering, and Reversion of Offering (Communion).

The temple is a living entity, and its powers—for rejuvenation, harmony, and wholeness—wax and wane over time. The benefit that emanates from these powers is accessible, and it comes from consistent observance. It is the Khesu that fulfill this, beginning with personal purification that awakens the divine nature, and proceeds with an offering ceremony that restates the unity of the Neteru with nature and human life. The reading or recitation of the temple cosmogony and its perpetual renewal may also be included in an individual's Khesu at the end of the day, and this is presented in chapter 7.

It is ultimately the officiant who benefits most from these acts, and who in effect plays the central role in the daily transformations that arise from the Khesu. In this manner, temple ritual is an emulation of the timeless, creative order that brought forth life and enables it to continue. In this process, one becomes a participant in the dynamic flux of nature, a co-creator. As it is often said in the sacred literature, ". . . it benefits the one who knows it, it excellently equips the soul."

Daily Practice

Wabu—Purifications

The ancients believed that the human body is a microcosm of cosmic life. The spinal cord, regarded by the Egyptians as the vehicle for Earthly stability, was even possessed by the gods. The mystic dismemberment of Asar is an allegory of these ideas, and his spine, the *Djed,* was an important fetish in the form of a pillar, in ceremonies honoring the god's reconstitution and renewal.

The neck, which contains seven cervical vertebrae, corresponds to the seven visible planets in the sky; the twelve thoracic vertebrae embody the twelve constellations illumined by the Sun's path in the sky; and the five lumbar vertebrae represent the five elemental powers. The sacrum, located below the lumbar vertebrae and joined to the pelvis, consists of five fused vertebrae—the five directions or cardinal points of the mundane sphere. And the coccyx, or tailbone, is located below the sacrum and consists of three to five fused, rudimentary vertebrae in humans, symbolizing the kingdoms of nature to which we belong: animal, vegetable, mineral, elemental, and angelic.

Preparation for every ceremony begins with a basic purification for participants that not only cleanses the body, but symbolically removes all the mundane influences from the soul so that the divine presence may be approached. In ancient times, priests began the day in the great temples by bathing in the sacred pool, followed by the donning of new clothing and sandals. Particular attention was given to cleanliness of the hands and fingernails.

But cleanliness was not the sole motivation for these elaborate rites. The rite of purification is a reenactment of the primeval genesis, where the theurgist symbolically comes forth in purity from the primeval territory to approach the Neter. Purification is a restatement of the creation and the expectation of rebirth through divine agencies.

Scent is a vital component in the sacramental repertoire of the temple. Incense, *sti neter,* is the "scent of the gods," and one of the benefits of ceremony is *seneteri,* "to make things divine." The latter is usually accomplished through elaborate body censings, where the censer is placed around the recipient so that the perfumed air may waft into the clothing, hair, and pores of the body.

Shesmu, associated with the Neter Sokar in the Memphite tradition and the spirit of the eighteenth dekan, is the deity regarded as the "master of perfumery." He represents the mystic process of extracting the essences from plants to make wine, perfume, and medicines. Similarly, Nefertum, son of Ptah and Sekhmet-Bast, is regarded as the patron of scent itself. He also signifies the process of divine inspiration and elevation received from sacred plants, especially the lotus, which he personifies. And closely related to these deities is Sokar himself, who according to legend, mixed aromatic substances for the gods. He represents the process of infusion and the transformation of botanicals into sacred elixirs. He was also a fashioner of silver bowls, used in the temples for sacred offerings. Thus, he represents the process of fermentation, and the alteration of base materials into elevated substance—ideas that embody both the purification and offering rites of the temple.

Anointing rites serve an important role in theurgy. Besides purification, these acts empower certain forces to enter the center where invocations are focused. Archeologists who enter Egypt's tombs discover that wall paintings and inscriptions have been anointed during the installment ceremonies performed thousands of years ago, in order to "bring to life" the images, along with the statuary and sceptres used in the mystic rites of the funeral. In the enigmatic Pyramid Texts, utterances #72–81 elucidate the anointing of the initiate's brow with seven holy oils, followed by a presentation of kohl prior to ascension into the realm of the sky gods. We are unable to identify these oils, save their names: Sti-Heb, Hekenu, Sefetch, Nehemen, Tuwawet, Ha-Ash, and Tet en Tehenu. During the performance of the Opening of the Mouth ceremony, the oils were either anointed, presented in alabaster flasks, or poured/sprinkled in the hollows of an anointing tablet. Reference to the "eye of Heru" alludes to the legendary account of the restoration of Heru's eye, which every sacramental offering emulates. Each utterance was recited four times:

72: *I fill your eye for you with Sti Heb* (festival perfume).

73: *Assume this eye of Heru, which arises from his image* (Hekenu oil).

74: *Assume this Eye of Heru, which alleviates the god's suffering* (Sefetch oil).

75: *Assume this Eye of Heru, which grants protection* (Nehemen oil).

76: *Assume this Eye of Heru, which supports the gods* (Tuauwet oil).

77: *Divine essence, arise and open the Eye of Heru, that you may make him a spirit, that you may cause power to rise in his body. That you may evoke awe in the eyes of the spirits who see him* (Ha Ash, pine oil).

78: *Assume the eye of Heru, which you take upon your brow* (Tet en Tehenu, Libyan oil).

79: *I restore the eye of Heru upon your face* (green kohl).

80: *I restore the eye of Heru upon your face* (black kohl).

81: *Your eyes are intact, you see with them. Eye of Heru: awaken in peace!*

(A communion follows.)

Purification is a basic component of daily practice and temple ritual. The following rites are intended for personal purification in private or for inclusion in the monthly ceremonies (Iru). The correspondences of the Neteru (table 14) may be consulted for selecting the appropriate oils, but application of all oils on the corresponding body center may not be possible for the participant, in which case the recitation may be made and a slight touch of the oil placed under the nostril. The "small anointing" employs the seven substances of funerary tradition, and the "great anointing" uses the ten oils of temple purification. There is no strict association of scents in this rite, as the Egyptians made use of materials that were pertinent to the locality, time, and tradition of the temple as much as the association of plants with the Neteru. Plain olive oil may be substituted for all floral and plant extracts, a substance highly prized in ancient times for its purity.

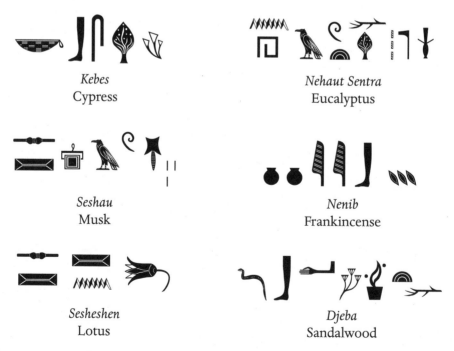

Kebes
Cypress

Nehaut Sentra
Eucalyptus

Seshau
Musk

Nenib
Frankincense

Sesheshen
Lotus

Djeba
Sandalwood

Figure 43—Scent Alchemy

Center	Sign	Neter	Amulet	Spiritual Dimension
Hands	—	Atum	♎	Akh: the exalted, "divinized" body
Footsoles	♓	Nut	☥	Sa: universal life force
Ankles	♒	Seshat		Maat: order, harmony
Knees	♑	Set		Khat: physical form
Sacral Plexus	♐	Sekhmet-Bast		Sekhem: personal power
Pubis, Prostatic Plexus	♏	Anpu		Heka: the creative force
Epigastric (Solar) Plexus	♎	Auset		Ba: the soul, astral body
Stomach, Intestines	♍	Geb		Sahu: ancestral spirit, oversoul
Heart, Cardiac Plexus	♌	Heru		Ab: the "heart soul," seat of passions
Lungs, Pulmonary Plexus	♋	Nebt-Het		Ren: name, personality
Mouth, Pharyngeal Plexus	♊	Djehuti		Djed: power of speech
Nape of Neck	♐	Four Genii		Maa, Sia, Hu, Sedjem: the four senses
Throat, Cavernous Plexus	♉	Het-Her		Khaibit: elemental body, shadow
Crown	♈	Asar		Ka: vitality, etheric body

Table 15—Correspondences of the Spiritual Bodies

The "small" (Gasu Nedj) or "great" (Gasu Ur) version of the anointing rite is also elected at the preference of the individual, though constraints of time and materials should be taken into consideration. If performed in the temple, all of the anointings may be placed on the crown of the head during ceremonies. The oils may be combined together in one offering bowl, or a special temple oil may be created using the scents particular to the Neter of the season or the temple itself.

Gasu Nedj—"Small Anointing"

Each of the seven centers corresponds to one of the vital bodies in the metaphysical constitution of the initiate. In this rite, the anointing reconstitutes and fuses these bodies to create the *Akh*, the "body of light" that is the spiritual aim of all theurgy.

Center	Recitation	Hekau
Mouth	I become pure,	*Uab Kua,*
Hands	I become a soul,	*Ba Kua,*
Pubis	I become strong,	*User Kua,*
Heart	I become glorified,	*Khu Kua,*
Nape of Neck	I become divine,	*Djeser Kua,*
Brow	I become a god,	*Neter Kua,*
Crown	I am the soul of creation.	*Nuk Ba Khepera.*

Gasu Ur—"Great Anointing"

The body is washed, from head to feet in a circular motion, and dried. This anointing proceeds with the cleansing of the hands, and the body is purified from the feet upward. The scents associated with each center are laid out on an offering table similar to a scheme used on anointing tablets that have been uncovered at mortuary and temple centers. These tablets are permanently inscribed with the names of the sacred oils and feature carved wells into which those oils were poured for the anointing. For practicality, this method seems useful for the ceremonial environment, where the opening, pouring, and closing of flasks is clumsy and time-consuming.

The rite is performed facing east and in the outermost part of the temple.

I. Purification of Hands: Atum

O Atum who possesses my flesh and spirit,
Let me not decay nor know corruption, but live as Khepri each day.
I am the soul of Ra Atum, who comes forth from the two horizons,
Nuk ba Ra Atum, pert em aakhuti,
Sovereign of the gods, who gives birth to himself, lord of life.
Suten neteru, mesu djes-ef, neb ankh.
I am restored. *Suten ta hetepu.*

II. Purification of the Feet: Nut

Come, thou form, Stabilizer, who covers me in the house of gold:
Grant to me the power to endure forever.
I am the soul of Nut. *Nuk ba Nut.*
I am restored. *Suten ta hetepu.*

III. Purification of the Calves: Maat

Come, thou form, Stabilizer: who knows truth throughout:
Bring me to the chamber of fair judgment.
I am the soul of Maat. *Nuk ba Maat.*
I am restored. *Suten ta hetepu.*

IV. Purification of the Knees: Set

Come, thou form, Stabilizer, who fixes me firmly upon the Earth:
Establish me in the the sacred places.
I am the soul of Set. *Nuk ba Suti.*
I am restored. *Suten ta hetepu.*

V. Purification of the Thighs: Sekhmet-Bast

Come, thou form, Stabilizer, who purifies the offerings:
Enter the gate that guards the sacred fire.
I am the soul of Sekhmet-Bast. *Nuk ba Sekhmet.*
I am restored. *Suten ta hetepu.*

VI. Purification of the Pubis: Anpu

Come, thou form, Stabilizer, who is upon the secrets:
Guard the gate that establishes my form upon the Earth.
I am the soul of Anpu. *Nuk ba Anpu.*
I am restored. *Suten ta hetepu.*

VII. Purification of the Plexus: Auset

Come, thou form, Stabilizer, who creates the reviving wind,
Make ready the place where my Ba returns.
I am the soul of Auset. *Nuk ba Auset.*
I am restored. *Suten ta hetepu.*

VIII. Purification of the Stomach: Geb

Come, thou form, Stabilizer, who hastens the fields to come forth:
Let me go up from the Earth with the day behind me.
I am the soul of Geb. *Nuk ba Geb.*
I am restored. *Suten ta hetepu.*

IX. Purification of the Heart: Heru

Come, thou form, Stabilizer, who conquers the spirits in the night battle:
Come to the place where I rise from the deep.
I am the soul of Heru. *Nuk ba Heru.*
I am restored. *Suten ta hetepu.*

X. Purification of the Throat: Nebt-Het

Come, thou form, Stabilizer, who rests upon the mound of her brother:
Bring me to the place where my breath is restored.
I am the soul of Nebt-Het. *Nuk ba Nebt-Het.*
I am restored. *Suten ta hetepu.*

XI. Purification of the Mouth: Djehuti

Come, thou form, Stabilizer, who speaks truth throughout:
Guard the place where my name speaks for me.
I am the soul of Djehuti. *Nuk ba Djehuti.*
I am restored. *Suten ta hetepu.*

XII. Purification of the Brow: Het-Her

Come, thou form, Stabilizer, great of power in her father's barque:
Where your Heka restores the hidden eye.
I am the soul of Het-Her. *Nuk ba Het-Her.*
I am restored. *Suten ta hetepu.*

XIII. Purification of the Crown: Asar

Come, thou form, Stabilizer, lord of life who comes forth
Into the place where my Ka may exist without hindrance.
I am the soul of Asar. *Nuk ba Asar.*
I am restored. *Suten ta hetepu.*

XIV. Purification of the Nape of the Neck: Sons of Heru

My flesh came into being by the design of the Neteru,
I am made perfect before them, without defect.
I am purified, truth and order are in my body.
Wabu-a, au maat en khat-a.

Hotepu—Rites of Offering

The word for offering, *hotep,* has additional meanings, including "satisfaction," "wholeness," and "peace." The gods were believed to eat and drink, and to possess all other human functions in addition to their supernatural powers. In this view, they take great pleasure in the fruits of the Earth, but they will reject offerings from sources that are hostile to their domain.

Many view the ancient ritual of offering to have been sacrificial in nature, motivated by a desire to appease an injury or to reconcile for a past error. But in ancient Egypt, the offering rite in both temple and tomb had one essential intention: to reinforce the bonds that human beings and divine forces share (and in fact, this intention formed the foundation for all Egyptian ritual). As such, the only sacrificial attitude present should be the abandonment of the mundane ego, a relinquishment that allows one to enter into the original state of primeval unity with nature and the gods.

Both animals and natural forces are regarded as actual emanations of the Neteru in Egyptian thinking, but sacred images are included; they are seen as their static representations. The latter may become divine embodiments through a threefold theurgic process. Initially, the image is consecrated to the Neter for its exclusive use; it is then animated with the Neter's power through a ritual. Lastly, the image maintains its embodiment through the continuous infusion of nourishment provided by offering rites. These function to honor, support, and fortify the Neter while it exists in the physical world.

Three types of offerings are presented to the Neteru in the temple:

- Those presented in rites of theurgy, such as the Opening of the Mouth, to restore vital functions. These offerings contain specific vital forces that may be liturgically transferred to fuse the components of the light body (the Ba, the Ka, and the Khat) and thereby animate life in one of the realms of existence, Earthly or celestial. Such offerings heal, restore, and endow vitality.

- Those presented as Khesu (daily or standard rites), such as the morning ritual and offering rites in the necropolis. These are intended to maintain the spiritual bodies of the deity, person, or infused object while it is in the physical sphere.

- Those presented in dedication to the gods or ancestral spirits, intangible qualities that represent a form of commitment to the gods. Such offerings took the form of Maat (order and justice), Ankh (literally: one's life), Uas (influence), and Ren (one's name or identity).

These three types of offering—vitalizing, sustaining, and dedicatory—are performed to maintain the connection between the material and immaterial worlds. In this process, contact made between the Neter and this nourishment (whether physical or symbolic) transforms the offering into divine substance, *djefau*. Thus, while the Neter receives the spiritual aspect of the offering, its material aspect remains for the ceremonialist, and here the ritual association between offering and communion is made. In the Egyptian temple, the return of the offering by the Neter "after it is satisfied" becomes the reversion of offering, a rite that symbolically disperses the divine vitality that has entered the world through the ritual sphere. Here, the full circle of divine embodiment is made, and the forces between all the worlds are assimilated by all participants.

The Egyptians viewed the consumption of food as a metaphor for absorption of divine powers, a magical symbiosis. Offerings were ritually dictated by size, shape, and origin, being the elements of psychic reconstitution for both the gods and the dead. According to legend, the gods were associated with particular offerings, and festivals would often honor the offerings themselves as emanations of the divinity. For example, beer was sacred to Het-Her, arising from the drunken rampage she undertook to punish Ra's ungrateful children in *The Deliverance of Mankind*. However, her excess was considered justified, because Set's drinking solely for its own end gave rise to one of his derogatory names, "the inebriated one."

But the true mystic significance of the offering ceremony is embodied in the legendary loss of Heru's left eye (a Lunar symbol, alluding to his father's origins), resulting from one of his epic battles with Set. According to tradition, the eye was restored by Djehuti (another Lunar principle), but only after a series of reconstituting acts performed by Auset and the other gods. The restoration of this eye became the paradigm for all offerings made in ancient Egypt, and offering rites in temple and tomb will usually be preceded with the recitation "Receive this Eye of Heru . . ."

The symbolism of restoring Heru's eye has other profound implications. Bringing wholeness to the deity brings wholeness to the ceremonialist, who gathers together the diverse forces of nature with the offering to restore the broken unity of creation. Here, the duty of human life to divine life is fulfilled.

While offerings in the temple setting are presented to the Neter, each should conclude with mention of the ancestral body and specific individuals in one's family or social sphere who will also benefit from the ceremony.

Offering to the Neter

Observance

In high ritual (the Iru and Hebu), the Offering to the Neter is usually preceded by an elaborate censing that welcomes it into the temple and presents it initially with divine scent. This may be performed on a smaller scale for the daily offering, though it is optional.

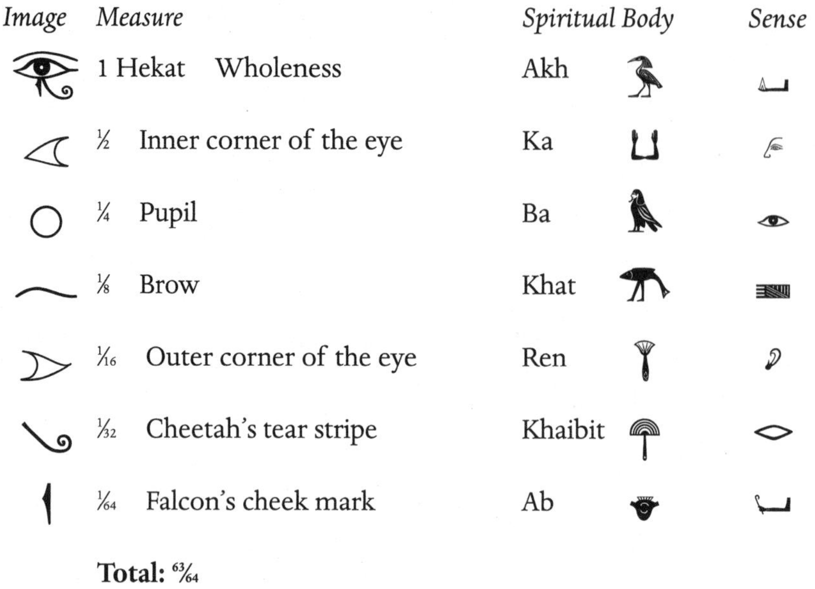

Image	Measure		Spiritual Body		Sense
👁	1 Hekat	Wholeness	Akh	𓅆	𓂋
◁	½	Inner corner of the eye	Ka	𓂓	𓂀
○	¼	Pupil	Ba	𓅃	👁
⌒	⅛	Brow	Khat	𓄘	𓏥
▷	1/16	Outer corner of the eye	Ren	𓏤	𓏙
〰	1/32	Cheetah's tear stripe	Khaibit	𓇳	◇
⎮	1/64	Falcon's cheek mark	Ab	𓄤	𓂋

Total: 63/64

Figure 44—The Eye of Heru: Each component of Heru's eye is associated with the sense functions of touch (Kha) 1/64; taste (Hu) 1/32; hearing (Sedjem) 1/16; thought (Sia) ⅛; sight (Maa) ¼; and smell (Sensen) ½. The remaining 1/64 is restored by the Heka evoked in the Offering ceremony. This "missing portion" is what constitutes the *Akh,* the body of light that is "restored" by the conscious joining of all the immaterial bodies through the spiritual alchemy of initiation.

Food offerings may be minimal (a piece of fruit or flower), or they may include the entire family meal, which is first presented to the Neter and returned to the normal place of consumption. They may be made at sunrise as was the custom in ancient Egypt, or they may be made at every occasion that meals are prepared in the home.

A tray reserved for offerings (the Hotep tray) should be consistently employed for the offering ceremony. It should be deep enough to prevent items from sliding off and water aspersions from dripping. Following the rite, the food that has been offered should be consumed, distributed to those it will nourish, or returned to nature as soon as possible. Floral offerings may remain throughout the day, but should be taken elsewhere at nightfall.

I. Introduction

Homage to you (Neter),

Whose crown is exalted this day,

Who is given sovereignty in this shrine.

May the divine company make way for you.

Receive on your table of offerings

What is given by one who honors you.

And may dominion be given to you,

That you may be mighty in your transformations in the holy places.

(The Hotep tray is presented at the altar and censed.)

II. Food Offering

I have brought forth that which opens the mouth of (Neter),

I offer pure things, giving:

An-na em tui un ra-ef em (Neter), Iu wabu, di:

Irep	wine	*Wadju*	herbs
Henket	beer	*Hotepi*	flowers
Seneter	incense	*Semu*	vegetables
Merhet	oil	*Neshem*	meat
Menket	linen	*Hesa*	milk
Hebsu	raiment/clothing	*Biuk*	grain
Hesmen	natron	*Aped*	fowl
Ta	bread	*Mu*	water

(The Hotep tray is sprinkled with water.)

Everything good and pure upon which a divinity lives.

Khet nebet neferet uabet ankhet neter em.

Receive at this hour of your appearing

These goods from the domain of Hotep.

And as you receive life, may you give life,

And as you make manifestations in your shrine,

May all men and women and beings of Earth

Give honor to your name (Neter).

III. Temple Offering

I bring forth the sacred stone,
As Atum brought forth the Ben Ben,
Which rests upon the great mound in Iunu.
(Neter) has come to rest upon it,
And lead the divine train on this day.
(The temple stone and other objects are anointed with oil.)

IV. Uadjeb Neter Hotep—Reversion of Offering

Want does not come for me,
I am satisfied by the bread of Heru which I have eaten.
I assume my strength.
I will not be thirsty because of Shu,
I will not be hungry because of Tefnut.
Imset, Daumutef, Qebsenuf, and Hapi expel my hunger and thirst.[2]
(The offering is distributed.)

V. Remembrance

To the memory of (name) . . .
En Ka eny (name) . . .

(The Hotep tray is removed from the altar.)

Many who view the art of Egypt in temple inscriptions or hieroglyphic texts are struck by the stiff, formal gestures that are often depicted. Much of this art gives the impression that Egyptian ritual was a somber affair and emotions were alien to the ceremonial setting. However, most of what is inscribed or painted in the temple and tomb reflects gestures that are "frozen" in the moment of greatest ritual intensity, and are far from the restrained images they appear to be. It is perhaps the liturgies that convey the truth about how the Egyptians felt about their gods and the divine work of the temple, and in this realm true passion is expressed. We hear supplications of rescue from all the mortal fears that beset ordinary human beings, as well as the desire for acceptance and belonging in the heavenly regions.

---

2. Adapted from the Pyramid Texts, Utterance #338.

Name	Gesture	Function
Dua		Adoration Reciting hymns or giving praise
Sen		Respect Honoring the Neter and royal persons
Hesy		Repose Arms clasped on chest denote cessation of thought, meditation
Dua		Devotion Paying homage
Hemsy		Supplication Requesting favor (prayer)
Henu		Triumph Commemorates the victory of Heru's forces over Set
Diuwi		Invocation Invoke, call, summon. The right hand is extended with the palm facing upward, the left hand is at the side
Hai		Rejoicing The expression of joy and celebration
Sa seseneb		Transference of Sa (vitality) to a recipient for healing; left hand on the nape of the neck, right hand on the sacrum
Sebehu		Mourning for funerary rites and observances such as the Lamentations

Table 16—Ceremonial Gestures

Much of this emotion is translated in ceremonial gestures, and many of the traditional hieroglyphic signs convey this. Related to these signs are the sacred gestures attributed to the animals that the Egyptians associated with divine beings. For instance, the baboon announces the dawn with loud shrieks and upraised arms, and this was viewed as the animal's expression of Djehuti, who is cognizant of all celestial phenomena. The hieroglyphic sign that conveys this depicts a man with upraised arms and is the determinative for "adoration," as the baboons appear to be acting at sunrise. In fact, most animals indigenous to the Nile Valley were seen as evocations of some specific divine power, incarnate only in those species.

The Inner Court

Egyptian society maintained no defined divisions between religion, government, commerce, or social interactions, because both its spiritual canons and mundane laws were believed to have been endowed by the gods.

Religious conduct in the form of ritual was the subject of early training in ancient Egypt. Didactic literature from many eras, such as the following New Kingdom instruction, describes the ideal attitude of the student for spiritual practice:

> *Do not raise your voice in the god's house, he abhors loud speech.*
> *Pray alone with a loving heart, safeguard your words.*
> *He will grant your needs, he will accept your offerings.*
> *Offer to your deity, do not offend his presence.*
> *Do not question his forms, do not make demands when he appears,*
> *Do not become disorderly in his procession or interrupt the oracles.*
> *He gives power in a million forms.*
> *The one who magnifies him is magnified.*
> *The god of this Earth is the Sun in the sky,*
> *While his images are on Earth.*
> *Offer them daily incense as food,*
> *And the lord of risings will be satisfied.*
>
> —Instruction of Ani, Dynasty 18

The Egyptian temple was manned by a diverse company of attendants, clergy, students, and laypersons who performed the daily task of maintaining the temple, and organizing and participating in the daily and periodic festivals of the Neter. The core personnel were dedicated to service for life, while members of the community served periodically in voluntary shifts which the Greeks called *phyloi*. These usually lasted for a season of three to four months out of the year, with a return to secular life afterward.

The modern temple may emulate this arrangement, though for obvious reasons the number of participants may be considerably less depending on the scope of the temple facilities and membership. Nevertheless, the traditional roles are valuable guides to re-creating the results of ancient ceremony, which were designed to reinforce the bonds between human and divine life and to spiritually refine the physical constitution of its participants—to become "godlike."

Obviously, the more participants involved in a rite, the greater the vital force and desired results. However, one person can read and meditate on the ritual scripts with an excellent outcome; in fact, spiritual contact is usually established expediently in this manner, as it eliminates the interference of the many unfocused thoughts that is often brought by a large number of persons in a group setting.

Despite the impression left by Victorian-era writers that only men served in high offices at the temples of ancient Egypt, there is ample evidence that both women and men equally shared dignified positions and responsibilities in the service of the Neteru. An Old Kingdom tomb at Giza records that the lady Peseshet was a physician and overseer of temple training in the healing arts, while Taimhotep, a priestess living in the time of Kleopatra VII, married the high priest of Ptah at Memphis and gave birth to a son after invoking the god for his favor. Priestess oracles were also in operation at the temples of Neit in the Delta and the house of Het-Her at Dendera in Upper Egypt throughout the millennia. And in the New Kingdom, a revival of the "ancestor priestess" in the Heliopolitan tradition resulted in the establishment of the office of Divine Adoratrix at the Theban temple of Amun. It appears that only women of royal blood assumed this office, and they or their representatives (nonroyal blood priestesses) may have replaced Pharaoh in the daily rites of the temple.

In addition to the records of women participating in divine service, Egypt is replete with records of a remarkable social equality for ancient times. Land and business ownership was the same for both sexes, and though both privilege and responsibility were equal, the differences between men and women were honored. In the modern temple, the same view should be cultivated, as both priest and priestess working together are essential to the successful practice of Sacred Science. The citation of inferiorities regarding gender were even more rare in ancient Egypt than they are today.

There are basically twelve priestly functions *(Hemu)* in the traditional temple, and these are outlined to provide a view of the responsibilities for members of a Divine House "in the making." These roles naturally affiliate with the Neteru by virtue of the skills and knowledge required to execute their assignments, who may be viewed as the "patrons" of each priestly office. The twelve are certainly, in turn, associated with the energetic qualities of the Zodiac. Other divinities are associated with the priestly offices, and some of them share dimensions of influence among the Zodiacal rhythms.

In the following descriptions, appending the *t* to the name represents the female form of the title, while appending the *u* denotes the plural form (ex.: *hem, hemt, hemu).*

♈ The Hem(t) Ka: Spiritual Servant —Patron: Asar

All individuals possess the *Ka* (the etheric form or vital nature), and this subtle body always finds its refreshment in the Divine House. The *Hem Ka* ("priest of the Ka") welcomes every participant into the temple and ensures that the guidelines, teachings, and announcements relevant to each ceremony are explained and understood. In this manner, spiritual refreshment is the first offering made to the temple seeker.

In ancient Egypt, the Hem Ka acted much in the same manner as the vicar or parish priest. Seeing to the needs of both the living and the dead, the Hem Ka advised, counseled, and performed rites for individuals and families. This priest was also mediator and consultant, referring petitioners to other "specialists" when the occasion required, such as healing and teaching.

Mer
Overseer of the temple

Kher Heb
Reciter, lector, keeper
of the sacred books

Uab
Pure one, asperger,
libationer

Hem Neter
Servant or incarnation of
the god, ceremonialist

Maa
The Seer

Hem Ka
Priest of the Ka, over-
seer of the tomb

Sentyt
Clairvoyant, oracle

Ur Hekau
Magician, master of
powerful words and
gestures

Senu
Physician-priest

Sau
Guardians, magical pro-
tectors, reciters of spells

Khener
Chanter, one who
proclaims

Setem, Sem
Keeper of offerings,
priest of the dead and
the necropolis

Figure 45—The Hemu

The Hem Ka is usually the first individual encountered in the temple setting; as such, the responsibility of cultivating the membership and providing the means of recruitment is assigned to her. This office is associated with Asar, the first of the terrestrial divinities in the ennead (company of nine) of Heliopolis. In ancient Egypt, all who entered the Western Land (physical passing) incorporated their Ka with that of Asar, as he is the repository of ancestral memory and organic energy. He is the divinity who possesses what is common to all, and at the same time distributes to all freely the divine vitality that allows everything to live.

In the liturgy, the Hem Ka performs the rite of Communion, fulfilling the responsibility of distributing spiritual benefit to the living. Patrons of this role include Hapi, Anher, and Sokar.

♉ The Khener(t): Hymnodes
—Patron: Het-Her

Of all the senses that are employed and focused in a ritual environment, sound and scent are equally powerful. Of the former, we know from temple records and the resumés inscribed in the tombs of notable persons that every major Egyptian temple was served by thousands of male and female singers, musicians, and chanters. Their service was performed for the morning and evening rituals and in the sanctuary throughout the day. Special events, from public processions to pharaonic investitures, employed the temple musicians.

In the performance of the liturgy, the chanter may not be disposed to actually singing or chanting, and may prefer to initially intone the words until familiarity with the material is established. But recitation of the opening hymn, which initiates each ceremony, is essential to conveying the spirit of the Neter being invoked and honored. Consequently, a careful study of the names, attributes, and associations of the deities is important.

Accompaniment by drum, sistrum (rattle), gong, or clapping is also appropriate. The Hymnodes is charged with the care and use of all temple instruments, and the knowledge of evoking divine states through sound. In the modern temple, the choice of background music and cueing it to synchronize with certain rites is under her charge.

The ceremonial function of the Hymnodes should never be underestimated; the evocation of divine images is dependent upon an ambient environment, and this role provides the pivot upon which successful rituals come into being.

The office of the Hymnodes is associated with Het-Her, who governs sacred rhythm in music and dance. She is the female branch of the Dendera Triad, which bonds spiritual and physical principles together through feeling. Patrons of this role include Bat, Wadjet, Bes, and Meretseger.

♊ The Kher Heb(t): Keeper of the Book —Patron: Djehuti

The skills of the scribe were regarded as the means *par excellence* of attaining status in ancient Egypt. Writing, transmitted to the human race by Djehuti, Neter of divine resonance and sacred script, was a proficiency that ensured entry into the temple, the government, and all of the elite professions. In the Divine House, record keeping, copying, and archiving all required scribal proficiency as well as the knowledge of which ritual formulas were used for temple ceremonies and how they were to be performed. Thus, the Kher Heb was a teacher as well as a ceremonialist.

The ritual book of the temple was regarded in ancient times as a sacred relic, and the lector priest was in possession of it both in procession and ceremony. In the latter, the lector provides the ritual script to participants and coaches the recitations. Knowledge of the sacred names, and their pronunciation and meaning, are important skills for this class of priest.

The Kher Heb is associated with Djehuti in his role as progenitor of the divine word. A deity of the upper worlds, he performs the first act of physical creation in the cosmogony of Hermopolis. Here, the sacred resonance is the initial impulse that gives life to all things, and the Kher Heb provides this function in the ceremony by reciting the divine Litany of the Neter. The development of a pleasing, rhythmical voice adds to the power of the Litany, and it should be practiced as much as possible to become like second nature.

If the participants prefer, the Kher Heb may be the sole person holding the rite book during the ceremony, which may be passed around in turn to those who require it for their recitations. This frees the attention of everyone to the metaphysical dimension of the work, while allowing the Kher Heb to focus on the protocol of the rites.

For public ceremonies, the Kher Heb may pause during the rite to explain the meaning of certain actions to the audience, or to prompt participants in the next course of ritual action.

Following all ceremonies, the Kher Heb is expected to maintain and keep the record book of the temple, which notes the relevant facts of each meeting, ceremonial or social. The importance of this record should not be underestimated; it serves as a reminder to all of the spiritual progress made throughout the temple's endeavors, and draws attention to unfinished business or unanswered questions that must be resolved. Patrons of this role include Shu and Khons.

♋ The Hem(t) Neter: Divine Incarnation —Patron: Nebt-Het

In ancient times, the *Hem Neter* was usually the senior of the temple, or a master of the temple's tradition. *Hem,* meaning "distinguished," was also a word indicating "incarnation" or "presence," alluding to the deity's nature that is spiritually assumed by the dedicated servant. This priest is the chief ceremonialist, and is expected to know the full order of ceremonies and the procedures for all the rites.

In particular, the Hem Neter is also charged with keeping the fire of the sanctuary and providing the incenses, herbs, and resins required to maintain the pleasing environment of the Divine House. The ancient Egyptians believed that scent drew divinity into the temple; its consistent provision is an essential component in fulfilling that aim. The maintenance of light is also the responsibility of the Hem Neter, along with the overall organization of the sanctuary prior to ceremony and its cleaning afterward.

Theurgy is the science of divine evocation. In temple ceremony, this work is performed by the Hem Neter in the rite of Invocation, where the ritualist as divine enunciator is co-creator of the Neter's manifestation. This is why rites of purification are so essential prior to all ceremonies. The ancient Egyptians had specific procedures for this, from cleansing the mouth to painting sacred images on the tongue. These actions stemmed from the belief that words of invocation must come out of a ritually pure mouth that is dedicated—at least for the length of the ceremony—to bringing forth divine life.

The Hem Neter literally performs the work of bringing forth the god, and may be called upon to teach and train in this aspect of ceremonial service. Nebt-Het, the deity who assisted Auset in the birth of Heru and ever afterward was regarded as the divine midwife and nurse, is associated with this priestly role. Other patrons include Taiyet, Renutet, and Nebet Hetepet of Heliopolis.

♌ The Maa: Seer —Patron: Heru

Supervising the spiritual protocol of temple ritual is the *Maa*, or "Seer." This word also refers to the sense of sight, and in the context of ceremonial magic, implies the special ability to view the ritual and its participants with spiritual insight. Clairvoyance has always been the end product of deep metaphysical training, and contact with spiritual forces is believed to enhance this gift. That is why the Maa's duties come into play after the god is invoked. In the Dedication of the Temple, she must direct the divine presence to maintain its existence in the sanctuary and to provide the benefits requested. Extended communication with the deity may also take place, and the Maa may intercede for inexperienced participants with the god. In essence, the Maa performs the two-way function of communicating with the deity once it has become manifest. She also represents the temple as a whole in the divine worlds during the ceremony.

The Maa's patron deity is Heru, in his form as sacred falcon. This bird is known particularly for its acute visual ability and swiftness. In the Osirian myth, Heru's eye was torn away by his adversary Set, but it was restored by Djehuti and in its renewed form provided great power to the god. Heru's images are found in the mythological tenets of Heliopolis, Memphis, and Dendera. Other patrons include Ra, Mont, Min, the initiatory deity Dunawy, and the four genii—Imset, Daumutef, Qebsenuf, and Haapi.

♍ The Setem(t): Steward
—Patron: Geb

Every temple in Egypt had a group of provisioners who performed the daily tasks of arranging sustenance for the god. After food and drink were offered in the sanctuary, the provisions were distributed to temple personnel, in a rite regarded as the "reversion of offerings."

The Setem, "keeper of offerings," prepared and presented the nourishment and gifts—clothing, jewelry, and cosmetics—for temple ceremonies. The god's entry into the mortal sphere was believed to necessitate all the equipment for daily existence, and every item that a revered guest might require was furnished to the Neter through a daily welcoming rite in the sanctuary.

Purity of offerings was a priority, and physical cleanliness was not the only criterion. Inferior goods were not deemed proper gifts in the Divine House, but if the intention by the presenter was honorable, then prudent redistribution was employed. Prior to the ceremony, the Setem collects all goods that will be presented to the Neter, including those that may be placed on the altar only for the duration of the rites to receive its blessing. The offerings should be inspected, cleaned, or ceremonially cleansed (the Uab may assist in this duty). They are then presented formally during the rite by the Setem and distributed to the congregation by this priest at the conclusion.

The Setem's patron is Geb, regarded by the ancients as *Urpa*, "great provisioner." As father of the terrestrial gods at Heliopolis, he was regarded as the ancestor of the living on Earth. Other patrons include Hotep, the creatrix Neit, and the divine artisan Ptah.

♎ The Ur(t) Hekau—Magician
—Patron: Auset

The sacred names of the Neteru and their words of power were viewed as privileged knowledge in the Divine House. As vocal resonance was believed to evoke life since the beginning of time, the use of this skill was reserved for the highly trained and dedicated in the temple.

The Ur Hekau ("great of magic") performs the rite of Meditation in temple ceremony, an act that employs both verbal and silent skills of communication, the power of *Djed* ("speech"). In the ritual setting, this is the art of verbal articulation, the power to transmit life through the manifestation of the divine word. For the Ur Hekau, the ability to subtly guide the attention of participants to the divine presence and engage in communication with the divinity is essential; it is truly theurgy in action.

Observation of the participants and the temple environment is also critical to this work. A successful invocation will produce results, and the meditation that follows will reveal those results. The temple magician must know how to interpret all sorts of phenomena that may take place, and be able to maintain calm despite any strange occurrences. Her function is, in essence, to lead the spiritual attention of the assembly.

The patron of the Ur Hekau is Auset, the sublime embodiment of magic in ancient Egypt, "the great enchantress" and "lady of powerful words." As the leading divinity in the ennead of Heliopolis, she has been regarded over the millennia as the most powerful goddess in the Egyptian pantheon, and not without reason. Auset hears all prayers and answers all inquiries, and so her priests must be mindful of all that takes place in the Divine House. Other patrons of this role include Selqit, Meskhenet, and Sopdet.

♏ The Sau(t): Watcher —Patron: Anpu

In ancient times, the temple possessed sentries who stood watch in the sacred precinct throughout the day and night. On occasion policing was necessary, but the spiritual role of the *Sau* ("watcher") was to act as doorkeeper of the sanctuary area, ensuring that only dedicated clergy entered the consecrated space. In temple work, this priest also observes the spiritual climate during ceremonies and may provide interpretations to participants afterward.

The engagement of a doorkeeper in the modern temple eliminates concerns about interruptions from the outside world, from telephone calls to noisy pets. On the inner planes, the Sau is expected to place herself before any disruptive force that may impose itself in a ceremony, and should be in possession of the invocations that banish such influences. In the ancient temple, the Sau were also known as "reciters," continuously chanting protective spells to maintain the peace of the sanctuary.

The Sau performs the Closing rite in the temple, so that the cosmic order evoked by the ceremony can be maintained and taken into the world of the living where it will vitalize the environment. Her patron deity is Anpu (the divine jackal), guardian of all sacred places and reserved knowledge. Other patrons include Apuat "opener of the ways," Heka, and Khepri.

♐ The Senu(t): Physician
—Patron: Sekhmet-Bast

In ancient Egypt, the Senu were physicians of both body and soul—priests who healed both physically and spiritually. Those consecrated to Sekhmet-Bast were surgeons, invested with the flint knife of the goddess. The Sekhmet-Bast priests were also exorcists, assigned to deal with the most malevolent forces that could adversely affected large groups of people, such as armies and expeditions.

In the modern temple, the Senu arranges the special rites that follow the standard liturgy. Most of these are concerned with healing and the extension of benefit to temple participants. A special study of occult healing is encouraged when serving this priestly function, because the constructive use of spiritual force that comes from the powerful results of ceremony is the ultimate aim of temple work. Such study may include alternative disciplines such as herbalism, magnetic manipulation, hypnosis, nutritional therapy, and homeopathy—all related to the healing tradition of ancient Egypt.

The Senu's patron is Sekhmet-Bast, goddess of medicine and surgery. Other patrons include Imhotep; Amunhotep, son of Hapu; Pakhet; and Bastet.

♑ The Mer(t): Overseer
—Patron: Set

Every Divine House requires a ways and means person, someone who will solve the basic problems of furnishing the sacred space, feeding participants and visitors, and raising funds for special needs. In ancient times the Mer served as overseer, negotiating the sale or barter of temple goods for supplies needed by temple personnel. In the modern temple this priest likewise administers to the physical planning and execution of the divine work.

The Mer is not expected to perform all the duties required to make ceremonial events run smoothly; rather, she should have the skill to select those who possess the talents to provide for certain requirements, and direct them to appropriately fulfill those needs. For instance, if floral offerings may be needed for certain ceremonies, the Mer would find the supplier, negotiate payments or barters, and arrange for their timely delivery. The records of temple goods and finances are also maintained by the Mer.

The Mer's functions are governed by Set, who is concerned with material life and its continuance. It should be remembered that though this deity was regarded as malevolent in the Osirian mythos, he was honored throughout Egyptian history and in some temple traditions was a principal divinity. Some of the most accomplished and respected royal persons were named in his honor, such as Seti I, father of Rameses II and refurbisher of the glorious Osireion temple at Abydos. Other patrons of this role include Taurt, Sobekh, and Apep.

ᗯ The Sentyt: Oracle —Patron: Maat

Knowledge of sacred periods was essential in most ancient cultures for determining the appearances of the gods, commemorating their festivals, and responding to both benefic and malefic forces that follow the rhythms of nature. The Sentyt is charged with this work, along with specializing in any or all of the divination sciences that allow foresight of and insight into sacred events. A timetable for upcoming events should be made available to the temple by the Sentyt, outlining the times of the Solar, Lunar, and Stellar cycles. She should also be versed in several forms of divination, such as scrying and reading sacred images like the Tarot. In ancient Egypt, the casting of lots was considered unseemly in the temple environment, so the use of dice and runes is not appropriate. However, a form of divination using the casting sticks of the sacred game Senet was used, and this tradition has been passed down through time in the practice of geomancy. The most respected form of divination used in Egypt was dream interpretation, which entails not only an understanding of symbolism and psychology, but a well-developed intuitive skill and empathy with the dreamer.

In temple ceremony, the Sentyt performs the rite of Pronouncement, giving the words of the invoked god to the congregation. The patron of this priest is Maat, who is consort of Djehuti in the cosmic world. He provides the sound or vibration for creation, while Maat provides the vessel or matrix its embodiment. Thus, she was regarded as "mistress of truth," knowing the perfect forms of all things. Seshat and the forty-two Maati (goddesses) are also patrons of this role.

♓ The Uab(t): Asperger —Patron: Nut

The name *Uab* means "pure one" and is the same word used to denote water. Hence, it is not surprising that the role of this priest encompassed the purifications and ceremonial cleansings that were traditionally performed before offerings were made in the temple and tomb. Water was the primary agent for these rites; all water was believed to have originated from Nun, the primeval abyss. As such, it carried the power to renew and rejuvenate, just as the gods could cyclically return to their watery origins and come into being once again. Equally important was the use of natron (a naturally occurring desert salt) and incense—substances that are natural disinfectants.

The Uab prepares consecrated water, and in the absence of a dedicated well it is usually taken from a natural source (river, lake), filtered, and stored in protective containers. She then performs aspersions, the sprinkling of consecrated water on offerings, amulets, and any space that will be used—permanently or temporarily—for ceremony. This ensures that the environment is sanctified, even though it may not have been ritually consecrated as a whole.

The Uab may also assist in ablutions that are performed prior to ceremony by other temple members or for guests. This includes providing the water, sacred oils, and any accessories required for anointing and purification. She must also be well versed in the rites of purification, including the body censings performed for initiations and healing.

The patron of the Uab is Nut, Neter of celestial existence. Others include Nun, Nefertum, Shesmu, and Tefnut.

Season	Patron Deity	Priest/ess	Meaning	Temple Function
♈	Asar	Hem Ka	Spiritual Servant	Counsellor
♉	Het-Her	Khener	Hymnodes	Chanter
♊	Djehuti	Kher Heb	Keeper of the Book	Lector
♋	Nebt-Het	Hem Neter	God's Incarnation	Censer
♌	Heru	Maa	Seer	Teaching
♍	Geb	Setem	Steward	Provisioner
♎	Auset	Ur Hekau	Great of Magic	Theurgist
♏	Anpu	Sau	Watcher	Doorkeeper
♐	Sekhmet-Bast	Senu	Physician	Healer
♑	Set	Mer	Overseer	Administrator
♒	Maat	Sentyt	Oracle	Divination
♓	Nut	Uab	Asperger	Purifications

Table 17—The Hemu of the Per Neter

The Temple Master

While we recognize that Egypt was governed by a monarchy, the royal person was also a metaphor of the consciously realized individual, because she was viewed as a direct descendant of the gods. The elevation of the royal person represented the cultural aspirations of society, the stability it sought for the present and future, and the continuity of the past. In ancient times, the system relied almost exclusively upon family lineages, as the Egyptians believed that divine blood flowed through the Royal House, from an archaic period when the gods lived on Earth and founded Egypt. And while certain individuals were recognized as descendants of divine beings, the system was not infallible, as history has shown. Numerous nonroyal individuals, male and female, arose at critical historical periods to introduce new cultural mandates and represent spiritual objectives that superseded ones of the past. They did so not only with the support of the temples that perpetuated this tradition, but also with the consent of the gods, if such records can be believed.

An example of this is the reign of Hatchepsut, the female pharaoh who has aroused such curiosity and speculation in modern times. A legitimate descendant of the Thutmosside royal house, she nevertheless broke with tradition and assumed not only the office of monarch, but the role of pharaoh and not queen. At her glorious mortuary temple of Dier el Bahri on the western bank of Thebes (*Djeser Djeseru,* the "most holy place"), inscriptions disclose that Amun himself came to her mother and she was conceived as the Neter's divine descendant, destined to rule Egypt. The same theme is repeated in the Luxor temple for the conception and birth of Amunhotep III, where in the birth chamber his conception is symbolized between the god Amun and his mother, Mutemwiya.

In modern times, the representation of one individual for the spiritual undertakings of the whole is not possible within the constructs our societies have created. At most, teachers and interpreters of spiritual traditions can exemplify such undertakings. But in the democratic spirit of our age, it is possible for the individual to step into divine territory and call upon the ancestral spirits of the past and claim their powers, when it was once only the privilege of divine descendants. For after all, are we not all enfolded in the miracle of divine creation, now melded into a family of gods in the making?

The role of spiritual kingship is not only achievable in the present, it is also a vital goal in spiritual practice. Modern individuals have earned this opportunity— and responsibility—through the development of conscience that the ages have provided, and the striving for the common good that is built into our everyday consciousness. Thus, practitioners should never be discouraged if they cannot work with a full cadre of temple personnel. Two or three persons may assume the duties and scripts of the traditional twelve ritualists, as long as everyone understands what each role is expected to do and in what sequence. For instance, the *Sau* ("watcher") is expected to be vigilant during rites for outside interference, while the *Ur Hekau* ("magician") ensures that spiritual focus is maintained by all present during the interval of meditation. The same person can perform the tasks of both Sau and Ur Hekau, since attention and close observation are required of both roles.

And it should be emphasized that, in keeping with ancient tradition, these roles should be rotated periodically for a number of reasons. Skill in the full repertoire of ceremonial service is a mark of true accomplishment for each member, and the arrangement of working in phyles discourages the concentration of authority in one or a few individuals—a situation that could be harmful to all. If one individual pursues the work of each priestly role for the phyle period of four months (an Egyptian season), a total of four years will have been spent in temple service, a period that closely matches ancient training in the Divine House—and also provided the model for modern undergraduate study.

There were other classes of priests. Some arose at certain historical periods out of the transient needs of the times, while others are distinguished by special talents or powers required by certain rites. For example, the *Iunmutef* ("pillar of his mother") is closely associated with the transforming ritual of the Opening of the Mouth both in temple and tomb, and appears only at this ceremony. The role is associated with Heru and was filled by a close relative in the funerary scenario, and in temple ritual by a senior member of the clergy. The *Sameref* is another ceremonial role associated with Djehuti and literally means "his beloved son," though it also refers to "kinsman" and "close friend." Djehuti's function is similar to that of sponsor in Masonic ceremonies, and he appears as patron of the temple initiate.

But the priest of ancient Egypt did not exercise any greater moral authority than others in the community. His or her vital role required only adherence to tradition dictated by the ancient record of the temple. Rules or decrees were set only by the royal person of the time, who was viewed as the only authority in religious matters while living. As such, the priestly roles outlined here should not be viewed as separate functions that segregate one class of priest from another. They encompass a set of responsibilities that must be fulfilled in unison with the rest of the temple body, along with a continual study and practice that aims for flawlessness in all roles. Each priestly title brings an integrity to the practitioner that cannot be compared to a job or duty in the secular world. The maintenance of the temple through the spiritual commitment of the priesthood enriches every dimension of one's life and the lives of all who enter the Divine House.

Temple Dress

The record on temple dress was very specific in ancient Egypt, and the costume never deviated from a design that was adopted in the Old Kingdom. Extremely fine linen (inscriptions show it to be gauzelike) was the fabric of choice, and cloth derived from animal sources was not used for temple dress, particularly wool. Though cotton and hemp were not yet introduced, they are an acceptable substitute for linen. In all cases the fabric was bleached white.

Footwear in ancient times consisted only of woven papyrus sandals, though white cloth sandals were also used in processions. Both types can frequently be found in modern import shops. In the sanctuary area, however, bare feet are portrayed in inscriptions.

The shaven head is a well-recognized feature of the Egyptian priesthood. Climatic conditions dictated this custom for the most part, though the dedication of a pure body to the Neter's house was the underlying theme of relinquishing all worldly adornment, of which the hair was most essential in ancient times. While this may not be practical today, the hair should be tied away from the face for safety, since the presence of fire and smoke is an important consideration. One style that was employed throughout all periods was the "sidelock of youth," emulating Heru as a royal child. The hair was elaborately plaited and gathered at the left side of the head. Women are often depicted in temple scenes wearing wigs, plaited hair, or hair held back from the face by plain headbands of cloth, tied at the back of the head.

There were few features that distinguished the types of priests other than shawls or sashes worn across the shoulders; a belt often attached the sash to the gown. In some inscriptions, the shawl was worn over the head when outdoors. Colors have particular meaning, and some choices for priestly functions are known.

Red, the color of vitality and generative power, was rarely used in the temple environment as it possesses a hostile character associated with the destructive side of Set and the material world. Alternately, it reflects the powerful return of vitality that Sekhmet-Bast brings when combined with yellow (her Solar function). These colors are appropriate for the Mer and the Senu, respectively.

Blue and its various hues (turquoise, indigo) reflect the powers of the heavenly sphere and the primeval flood. These colors may be used by the Hem Neter and the Uab, whose functions include censing and purifying in the Divine House. Violet combines the powers of the heavens (blue) with the vital life force (red), realms of the Sentyt.

Color	Name	Realm	Priest
Red	Desher	Physical world, material goods	Mer
Blue	Irtiu	Spiritual world, cosmic beings	Hem Neter
Yellow	Khenet	Cyclic phenomena, light	Khener
Green	Wadj	Nature's powers, propagation	Hem Ka
Orange	Menshet	Vital force, physical regeneration	Senu
Violet	Tekhit	Cosmic life, divination	Sentyt
Indigo	Kesbedj	Creative life, renewal	Uab
Brown	Djeriu	Earth's harvest, provision	Setem
White	Hedj	Dedicated life, purification	Kher Heb
Black	Kem	Unseen worlds, protection	Sau
Spotted	Abi	Celestial existence, prophecy	Maa
Gold	Nub	Reflective world of the Neteru	Ur Hekau

Table 18—Priestly Apparel

The colors of nature, green and brown, correspond to the functions of feeding and providing that the Hem Ka and the Setem provide. Yellow represents Solar forces and the dawn, which is evoked by the mystic chants of the Khener. White, also associated with divine beginnings and the sacred, represents the purity brought by duty to the gods overall, embodied by the ibis-god Djehuti and his priest, the Kher Heb.

Gold, the divine color, is appropriate for the Ur Hekau, who comes in direct contact with the gods. Kem, one of the names used to describe Egypt's fertile, black soil, is associated with night and the powers that dwell in dark regions, hence its attribution to Anpu and his priesthood, the Sau. And the black-on-gold spotted design is always associated with the Maa. Silver, because of its corrosive nature, is not used in the ritual environment.

For specialized priests, the Iunmutef is distinguished by the the leopard skin over the shoulders and the sidelock, representing Heru as officiant at his father's reconstitution. Since this type of apparel is obviously impractical in modern times, the use of humanmade materials is acceptable, especially since animal prints by some manufacturers appear almost identical to nature.

In temple inscriptions, the high priest of Memphis is shown with an elaborate collar and hair plait emulating the patron deity Ptah, and the high priest of Heliopolis wears the panther skin decorated with golden stars, an allusion to his role as *Ur Maa,* "greatest of seers," the astronomer-prophet.

Iunmutef
Conducts the Opening of the Mouth ceremony

Figure 46—Iunmutef

Chapter Five

LITURGY

And it is the lot of men to live their lives and pass away according to the
destiny determined by the gods who circle in the heavens, and to be re-
solved into the elements . . . And every birth of living flesh, even as
every growth of crop from seed, will be followed by destruction; but all
that decays will be renewed by the measured courses of the gods who
circle in the heavens.

—Hermetica: Libellus III, 4

The foundation of every spiritual practice is its liturgy, one that articulates the cosmology, philosophy, and metaphysical goals of the practitioners. Egypt's spiritual tradition provides us with hundreds of examples of prayers, invocations, and litanies that were carefully recorded for use in both temple and tomb. Along with these writings are included the rubrics (instructions or rules), which explain the context in which the liturgy is to be used.

Liturgical programmes rarely changed throughout the extended history of ancient Egypt. The ceremonial acts performed in temple and tomb were believed to be handed down from antiquity, and were so honored for their veracity, correctness, and power. Pursuant to this belief, the walls of the temples record the liturgies that were recited in each division of the Divine House, along with lists of the daily and seasonal festivals, and the historical antecedents or founding event of the particular Neter's sanctuary.

At Edfu, the walls in the inner hypostyle hall record the founding ceremony of the temple, at which the legendary Imhotep, the Dynasty 3 sage and healer, presided. Elsewhere in the hall of appearings the morning litany is inscribed, sung each day by the *kheneru* to open the temple. And for the observance of festivals, calendars record the sacred days at Karnak, Esna, and Abydos. In all, the protocol of timing, location, and the acts that spiritually sustained the temple determined its activity every moment, throughout the ages.

The following liturgy is an annual cycle of twelve ceremonies (Iru) that may be used in conjunction with the Solar calendar. They combine an orderly monthly plan of observances for each Neter in the Solar cosmogony of Heliopolis, each comprised of twelve separate rites (Khesu) that reflect the ceremonial protocol of the ancient temple. When performed, they provide the components for developing a conscious and vital interface among the living worlds—the human, divine, and nature. Note that the standard Khesu rites are indicated in each of the Iru ceremonies, but their performance outline can be found in chapter 4.

Each ceremony also includes an optional observance or festival (Hebu) that honors the specific powers of the Neter of the season. Depending on the amount of time and resources available to the modern temple, these observances may be tailored to fit the occasion.

Elaborations on the Iru ceremonies can certainly be introduced, especially if they coincide with several cosmic events, such as a New Moon that takes place on the day of the Sun's ingress into a new sign of the Zodiac. Additional observances may include special offerings or activities for the temple family, such as a communal meal in lieu of the reversion of offerings, or the production of temple oil and amulets.

Menu
Dedication

Temau
Closing

Mau
Meditation

Hesi
Hymn

Pert Kheru Neter
Pronouncement

Hotep
Offering

Hekaut
Invocation

Sekha
Contemplation

Wehem
Litany

Gasu
Anointings

Figure 47—The Khesu

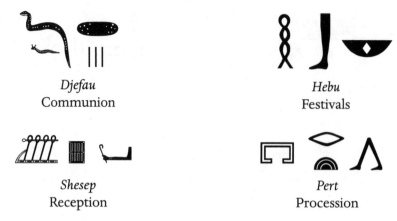

Djefau
Communion

Hebu
Festivals

Shesep
Reception

Pert
Procession

Figure 47—The Khesu

I. *Hesi*—The Hymn

Every ceremony opens with an initial greeting that evokes the divine feeling and image of the Neter. The *Hesi* ("hymn"), which may be accompanied by music or temple instruments such as drum and sistra, sets the ritual tone of the ceremony and calls attention to the participants of the sacred nature of the event.

Hymns are inscribed in every temple and tomb, and certain hymns to the Neteru were included in the papyrus rolls that were placed near mummies so that the deceased could continue to recite the divine attributes and acquire them in the afterlife. In the Divine House, the *Khener* (hymnodes or chanter) intoned the hymns, which were often sung in a procession approaching the sanctuary prior to the commencement of ceremonies. Likewise, the modern temple should feature at least one chanter to perform or lead the all-important opening of the ceremony.

II. *Wehem*—The Litany

The science of sound alchemy in ancient Egypt arose from knowledge of the occult law that sacred names incorporate the essence of a being, and possession of such names provides both knowledge of and access to divine forces.

Litanies to the Neteru are found in both temple and tomb. They are comprised of sacred names, images, and sayings associated with the god or goddess, and spoken together they form a powerful invocation. Many are of great length, enumerating the sacred forms by which the Neteru are known, while some are short but powerfully effective. The Litany (*Wehem*, "repeating") may include some of the magical names of the divinity, which should be spoken with the knowledge that possession of the name transmits the powers of the named.

Recitation of the Litany actually marks the beginning of a temple ceremony and calls the Neter's attention to the action. And though it is traditionally performed by the *Kher Heb* ("keeper of the book"), participants may also recite the Litany, especially if their priestly offices are governed by the Neter being called. In other instances, such as in the ceremonies of Heru and Anpu, the Litany consists of recitations by the Kher Heb with responses from the participants.

Ancient liturgies specified that a ball of incense was dropped into the temple brazier each time the deity's name was called. If the invocation is long, this procedure may not be suitable for a confined or unventilated space, but the Litany is an appropriate time for the Hem Neter to begin censing the temple.

III. *Gasu*—The Anointings

For high ceremony, individual purifications are performed before the event, usually in the form of *Gasu Ur* (the extended anointing). In the ceremony itself, the *Gasu Nedj* (brief anointing) is performed, usually employing only the temple oil.

Anointing joins all participants together in an act that has always been regarded as sacred. When taking office, both royal persons and the clergy are anointed; in the transitional stages of life—childbirth, baptism, and passing—anointing rites *(Gasu)* are traditionally performed. The symbolism of anointing is also obvious: the opening of psychic centers or senses is implied as the sacred substance is applied to a specific area of the body. In addition, protection is extended to the anointed by virtue of the powers inherent in the oil itself.

The *Uab* ("asperger"), whose duty encompasses the purification of all objects that are brought into the ceremonial environment, performs the Anointings. In ancient Egypt, cones of waxed perfume were customarily placed on the head to produce a pleasing scent as they gradually warmed and melted. In a similar fashion, the forehead or crown of the head is anointed in this rite with temple oil. Temple inscriptions show the Uab holding the oil flask with the right hand while anointing images of the deity with the left hand. The ancient prescription calls for application "with the smallest finger" in a circular motion. Care should be taken to use only a small amount for each participant, as oil expands with body heat and can drip into the eyes.

The anointing is performed for all ceremonial participants, but it should be decided before the event whether or not guests will receive the anointing.

IV. *Sekha*—The Contemplation

The participants are now ready to approach the god. Prior to taking this step, a preliminary form of meditation provides the opportunity to develop intention and resolution to go forward into the divine sphere and summon the divinity. The rite of Contemplation *(Sekha)* allows participants to reflect on the unique qualities of the Neter and develop a rapport with its visible aspect.

In virtually every ancient culture, the embodiment of the god's visible aspect was expressed in sacred dance, and depictions of these events are abundant in Egypt's monuments. Postures, gestures, and creative movement combined to transmit the qualities of the divine being to the audience. The power evoked by this art could transform both the performers and the spectators with the spirit of the deity, and this is still regarded as a spiritual practice today in Egypt. The Sufi tradition, along with the centuries-old art of evocative dance, preserves Egypt's unique approach to contemplation of divine principles. Thus, the inclusion of sacred dance in this portion of the ceremony re-creates the ancient custom.

During this rite, the *Mer* ("overseer"), who is charged with possession of the temple goods, may unveil an image of the Neter, show a drawing of the deity or photograph of its temple in Egypt, or present symbolic elements of the god on the altar, such as its plant, stone, or cloth in its sacred color (see table 14 in chapter 3). She then recites the *hekau*—often an ancient prayer to the Neter that elucidates its powers.

V. *Hekaut*—The Invocation

When invoking the divinity, it is commanded to come forth and re-create itself. The Invocation *(Hekaut)* re-creates the birth of the god by sending forth its divine names to prompt its entrance into the sacred precinct. The Invocation also assures the deity that the environment has been duly prepared and consecrated, and is, in essence, a receptive womb through which it will enter the world of life.

The ancient texts instruct the theurgist to "Send forth your voice . . ." Likewise, the rite of Invocation should be rendered with strength and assurance, because any hesitation will invite failure to bring the divinity into communion with the temple. Fear, suspicion, or a lack of reverence in the environment also deters the divine presence.

The *Hem Neter* ("god's incarnation") performs the Invocation, being the theurgist closest to the sanctuary, the place of divine manifestation. But the Invocation entails far more than calling forth the deity. Knowledge of the ritual postures to direct subtle energies into specific areas of the sanctuary, and the use of the appropriate wands and ritual staffs, was an ancient art of the Hem Neter, whose function is to focus the divine presence in the environment. In this manner, the Hem Neter serves both as a conduit and a source of energy for the manifestation. In the truest sense, the Hem Neter is a channel for divine forces, and must possess the detachment to serve as such.

VI. *Mau*—The Meditation

In Egyptian spiritual practice, ritual is the ultimate form of meditation. The focus of everyone's attention and feeling into the ceremonial environment provides a tremendous concentration of energy that peaks quickly and powerfully, and can transform participants in profound ways. This must be directed by a theurgist with excellent stamina to banish undesirable influences. These may range from the surprise that comes from those who are unprepared for the mental or emotional stimulation brought by the ceremony, to fear from the uninstructed, and mistrust from the inexperienced.

The *Ur Hekau* ("magician" or "theurgist") must take command of this portion of the ceremony thoughtfully and dynamically. Working with the Sau, participants should be observed, and any unusual manifestations, such as light and sound, should be noted carefully. Following the ceremony, the Ur Hekau may report such occurrences and translate their meaning to the recipients.

It is not unusual for certain phenomena to take place in a ritual environment. The combination of scent, sound, ceremonial recitations, and, above all, the cosmic timing of the event all combine to produce unique circumstances. After all, the purpose of the ceremony is to provide an opportunity for divine manifestation; it should not surprise participants when this actually takes place. The rite of Meditation actually represents the stage of divine reception, when the deity is manifest in the environment and begins to communicate its nature to those present.

The meditation *(Mau)* is guided and timed by the Ur Hekau. If the participants so elect, a guided meditation may include the reading of the meditation script or silence (the preferred method) that is concluded with the reading. The length of this rite is optional; conclusion of the meditation may be signaled by raising the lights, playing background music, or firing new incense in the temple brazier.

VII. *Hotep*—The Offering

The Neter is welcomed into the Divine House with sustenance and gifts. The offering is both an acknowledgment of the divine presence and an expression of gratitude for its arrival, but it is most importantly a gesture of sharing that most ancient societies possessed. A sense of the collective life and the need to maintain it permeated everyday existence in Egypt; interdependency among all the lifestreams was acknowledged. As a result, stunning labors were undertaken—such as the building of the pyramids—with great confidence and mutual support. Needless to say, such efforts were a great success in the face of tremendous obstacles.

Similarly, the rite of Offering *(Hotep)* is a gesture of presenting all that we value to the Neter, with the confidence that it will be replaced continuously by the powers of the god through nature. The rite of Offering is performed by the *Setem* ("steward"), who presents the sustenance, followed by gifts to the temple, and items for blessing that will be charged with the god's power through the ceremony.

VIII. *Djefau*—The Reversion of Offerings (Communion)

The distribution of divine benefit is the peak of ceremonial work for the participants. In ancient times, this was a temple rite known as *Uadjeb Hotep Neter*, the "reversion of offerings," when the deity returned the honors presented in a different form. After temple ceremonies, the offerings were redistributed to temple personnel and, in many instances, to those in the outer court—guests and visitors. In this rite a communion with the god is performed both literally and symbolically. The Egyptians believed that the *Ka*, or vital essence of the food, and other presented gifts were absorbed by the deity, and in the process, the very nature of the offerings was changed from being in contact with divinity. To partake of this transformed substance *(Djefau)* is a great privilege.

The consumption of food is not advised in the ceremonial environment for aesthetic reasons, but the reversion of offerings provides much needed "grounding" for the participants. The temple ceremony is at this point only half completed, and refreshment is a necessary reprieve from the emotional and intellectual demands of ritual.

The *Hem Ka* ("spiritual servant") distributes the offerings in the form of a communion rite. In ancient times, her function was to serve as an intermediary—between the temple and the outside community, and the living and the dead. She performed the periodic offering ceremonies in the name of the family at the tomb.

IX. *Menu*—The Dedication of the Temple

This portion of the ceremony restates the goal of the temple and its participants to serve as a vehicle for divine life. Here, the hekau reinforces the initial founding of the temple with the dedication of the cardinal quarters and elemental forces at the *Mesen Het Neter*. It is the Neter's powers that fill those stations and components once more through this rite, thereby reinforcing the temple's etheric structure. If there is a founding stone for the temple (a Ben Ben or symbolic mound), it is brought forth or uncovered at this time.

The Dedication *(Menu)* is performed by the *Maa*, "Seer," whose role requires the use of spiritual sight and an uncompromised willingness to communicate with the divine presence.

X. *Pert Kheru Neter*—The Pronouncement

Divination was always taught and provided by temple priests in ancient times as a benefit of the Divine House. A number of techniques were employed in Egypt to fulfill this—astrological portents, scrying by water in vessels and mirrors of silver and obsidian, dream interpretation, and the decoding of omens.

The Pronouncement, *Per Kheru Neter* ("voice offering of the god"), is a salutary form of divination, providing words and information from the Neter, as recorded in ancient times, to guide the participants afterward. It is performed by the *Sentyt* ("oracle"), who speaks in the voice of the god to pass on its message.

If there is an urgent need for spiritual guidance by one or more members of the temple, the Sentyt may perform a *Tep Ra* ("mouth of the god") at this time, a special divination that she is proficient in. However, the results and interpretation of this act should be disclosed after the ceremony's conclusion, so that attention remains on performing the rites with merit and precision.

XI. *Hebu*—Festivals

Every season brings a particular energy that is emanated by the Neter. Some of these forces are evoked by special observances, such as the divinatory powers brought by honoring Djehuti and the protective forces that come with invoking Anpu. A great advantage exists in making use of the energies as they are released cosmically.

Each ceremony in the liturgy features an additional, special observance or festival *(Heb)* that is often particular to the Neter of the season (these are delineated in chapter 6). The performance of these rites is optional and may take place within the ceremony or at another time in the season, such as at the Full Moon. An example of this would be the *sejeryt,* or vigil, with a recitation of the hekau from the Book of Hours at the Full Moon in the season of Nut. As this would take place in the time of Pisces (the last sign of the Zodiac) and at the start of the waning hemicycle of the Moon, the conclusion of the Solar year and the Lunar month would be simultaneously observed by this rite. In this instance, *The Book of Hours* reenacts the vigil the gods kept over the body of Asar, which will rise to renewal in the next season of Aries and the next Lunar cycle at the New Moon.

The *Senu* ("healer") may take charge of the performance of the Heb. Since it is mostly concerned with the distribution of the Neter's special benefits, the Senu is best able to plan and oversee the rite fairly and objectively. In lieu of the Heb, a *Sa Seseneb* ("transference of Sa") healing rite or commemorative gesture for one recently passed may be performed. The names of the recipients may be recited or inscribed on paper and placed on the altar or offering tray. In this manner, some of the energy evoked by the ceremony is distributed to those in need or to those who are remembered.

XII. *Temau*—Closing of the Ceremony

The closing rite *(Temau)* is merely a formality, a reminder to the participants that they must return to the mundane world, though the Neter goes forth with them. In the Western esoteric tradition, spiritual forces are usually dispersed or "returned" to their origin to close the ceremony. This is certainly not so in the Egyptian temple, where the consecrated space remains so until physically and ritually dismantled in a formal ceremony—a necessity only required by calamity.

It is appropriate that the *Sau* ("watcher") announces the end of the ceremony with the last praises to the Neter. The Sau also speaks the concluding portion of the liturgy for all who have participated, and reminds them of the spiritual benefit they have received.

Following the recitation, the Sau may indicate the appropriate exit for participants, or lead an exiting procession *(Pert:* "going forth"). And if any social or instructional events *(Shesep:* "reception") are to take place following the ceremony, the Sau will direct members to the meeting place. In the meantime, it is important for the ceremonial participants to meet outside of the sanctuary to record the event in the temple book and note any new business that arises from the meeting, such as preparing a schedule for future events.

The last ceremonial act in the ancient temple was the sweeping of the sanctuary prior to its closing. The Sau may perform this symbolic gesture when the room has been vacated, using the ceremonial broom to clear away any dust, footprints, or debris from the sanctuary floor out to the entry before it is closed or sealed until the next ceremony.

Sequence	Name	Meaning	Rite	Performed by
1	Hesi	chants	Hymn	Khener
2	Wehem	repeating	Litany	Kher Heb
3	Gasu	anointings	Anointings	Uab
4	Sekha	considering	Contemplation	Mer
5	Hekaut	magical speech	Invocation	Hem Neter
6	Mau	reflecting	Meditation	Ur Hekau
7	Hotep	offering	Offering	Setem
8	Djefau	divine food	Reversion of Offerings	Hem Ka
9	Menu	dedication	Dedication of the Temple	Maa
10.a	Pert Kheru Neter	god's voice offering	Pronouncement of the Deity	Sentyt
10.b	Tep Ra	mouth of the god	Divination	Sentyt
11.a	Heb	festival	Special Observances	Senu
11.b	Sa Seseneb	healing	Transference of Sa	Senu
12	Temau	completion	Closing	Sau

Table 19—The Liturgical Order

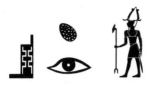

Asar
Season of Aries

Het-Her
Season of Taurus

Djehuti
Season of Gemini

Nebt-Het
Season of Cancer

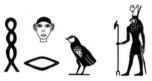

Heru
Season of Leo

Geb
Season of Virgo

Auset
Season of Libra

Anpu
Season of Scorpio

Figure 48—The Iru

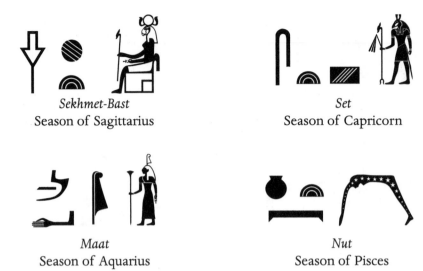

Sekhmet-Bast
Season of Sagittarius

Set
Season of Capricorn

Maat
Season of Aquarius

Nut
Season of Pisces

Figure 48—The Iru

Ceremony of Asar—*Season of Aries*

Hesi: *Hymn to the Neter*

Homage to you, Asar, Lord of Eternity:

Sovereign of all the Neteru, of many names and holy of creations.

You enter the celestial barque and are reborn this day,

Your throne is reestablished in the Two Lands.

Praise be to you, Lord of Maati:[1]

First of the divine brethren who rises in the luminous horizon,

Your beauty is renewed as you travel in the Boat of a Million Years.

Wehem: *Litany of the Neter*

Green God, who lives in eternity.

Foremost of all the Neteru and their Ka's.

Hidden of form in all the temples, whose countenance is venerated.

---

1. For the meaning of this and other terms, see Appendix 3: Spiritual Locales.

Great One contained in the sanctuary of Sekhem.

Chief of the djefau in Iunu

Whose name is commemorated in Maati.

Hidden soul: Lord of Qerert,

Holy One in White Wall,

Soul of Ra, of his very body,

Who is exalted on this day,

Who is Lord of the Great House in Khemenu.

Anedj hra-ek Asar, neb heh, suten neteru ash rennu, djeser kheperu, sheta aru em erperu, shepses ka pu, khent Djedu, ur khert em Sekhem.

Neb hennu em Athi, khent djef em Iunu, neb Sekhau em Maati, ba sheta, neb Qerert, djeser em Ineb Hedj, ba Ra djet-ef djsef hotep em Suten Henen, menkh hennu em Nart, kheper set heset ba-ef neb het aa em Khemenu.

Gasu: Anointings *(Khesu)*

Sekha: Contemplation of the Neter

Asar Un Nefer: he allows me to possess my body.

He makes it possible for me to follow in his dignity

Through the gates of the Duat.

Even as I live upon the Earth,

I come to him, and in my hands I offer truth,

There is no falsehood in my breast.

I set this before him, knowing that it is the food upon which he lives.

Hekaut: Invocation of the Neter

Great one, Lord of Maati:

I have come to behold your beauty.

I know you and I know your names,

And the names of those who exist with you in the Maatet barque.

Your name is *Rekhti Merti Neb Maati*,

In truth I have come so that you will hear me.

I have not oppressed, nor scorned, nor diminished your gifts.

I have seen the eye of Ra when it is full in Iunu,

Therefore let not evil fall upon me where I am,

For I come to you as all your brethren come to you in the Hall of Maat.

May all living ones make offerings to you at your divine appearing,

You, the Lord who is commemorated in heaven and on Earth,

Who is greatly praised and upraised on his throne.

I invoke you: appear in your shrine!

All in the Two Lands will greet with joy

The great brother who appears in his sanctuary.

Prince of the Paut and all of the Neteru,

Stabilizer of truth and true throughout,

Placer of the Sun upon the throne of his father Geb,

Beloved of his mother Nut,

Great One of the twofold strength.

Tall of crown, you enter the Hall of Maat,

You preside over those who await you.

Terp nef nebu neb, Sekhau em pet em ta Ash hy em, Aru nef Ahi an Taui, Em bu ua Ur, Tep en Sennu-ef, Seru en Paut Neteru, Semen Maat Shet Taui eta sa Her Nest-ef aa en at-ef Geb, Merer Mut-ef Nut, Aa pehpeh.

Mau: Meditation on the Neter

Behold the ones who appear in Asar's domain,

The sacred land where he presides over the Ka's.

They await him and his coming.

Power is given to him by Atum, creator of the holy places.

And as he is renewed, all things are renewed.

By his ordinance, I live in the region of the Green Gods.

Hotep: Offering (Khesu)

Djefau: Reversion of Offerings (Khesu)

Menu: Dedication of the Temple to the Neter

Even the revered spirits are overcome by you, Asar,

They honor your name when meeting your majesty.

You roll up into the horizon,
You send air and light from the plumes of your double crown,
The heavens and Earth are penetrated.
I return with blessings and offerings and praises,
And all in your train are granted life, forever.

Pert Kheru Neter: Pronouncement of the Deity

I have come from the city of the Neteru, the territory of primeval time,
The dwelling place of the Ba, the residence of the Ka in the Two Lands.
I reside there as the most holy one, I am Lord of offerings, ruler of Maati.
Even the Neter of the celestial waters, Nun, draws sustenance from me.

Heb: Festival

The Book of Breathings is an appropriate observance for this season.

Temau: Closing of the Ceremony

Homage to you, governor of Amentet and those who reside therein:
Who makes mortals to be born again, who renews his youth.
Who comes in his season and in great beauty,
Who is the lord of greenness in all places.
Heru has opened your mouth on this day,
Rank and dignity have been conferred on all who follow in your train.
I am raised up because you stabilize those who support you,
Firmly fixing with your power the foundations of your estate.
Mighty is Asar in his victory,
Established in this place is his throne.
Mighty is his chamber of renewal,
Eternally abundant are his shrines on Earth.
I rejoice that his sovereignty is renewed,
Glory is brought to his temples and all the places that honor his name.

Ceremony of Het-Her—*Season of Taurus*

Hesi: Hymn to the Neter[2]

O beautiful One, Great Cow, Exalted One:

Mighty magician, splendid lady, queen of the Neteru.

I revere you, give that I may live!

Behold me: Het-Her, mistress of heaven.

See me: Het-Her, shining from your horizon.

Hear me: flaming one from Nun!

Behold me, queen of the Neteru, in all your places:

From sky, from Earth, from Nubia, from Libya, from Manu, from Bakhu.

From each land and place where your magnificence arises.

Behold me and what is in my inmost self, though my mouth speaks not.

My heart is straight, my Ka is in your keeping.

No dark thing finds its place in my breast.

I revere you, queen of all beings,

Give, that I may live!

Wehem: Litany of the Neter

Hail to you: shining as gold, Eye of Ra, his confidant.

Great one, lady of the sky, mistress of all the Neteru,

Whom *Ra Atum Heru Khepri* joins at his beautiful setting.

Lady in the heartland of Manu, who accompanies Ra on his journeys:

I have come bearing truth, I enter in joy

To delight the hearts of those who reside therein.

I approach you to behold your beauty, to be placed among your retinue,

To be under your sycamore tree when Ra dawns at his beginning.

Arit, Akent, Sekhet Ra, Keset, Senmet, Khauit, Madjet, Shetenu Akenu, Khakhat, She Tesher, Per Tennu em Ankh Tauit, Rehesu, Feka, Tep Ahet, Aukat, An Menthu, Maati, Sebti, Kennu, djerutet, Sek, Per Wadjet, Hes, Kenset, Neferu-es, Khekhuit, Antet, Sennut.

---

2. Adapted from a hymn to the goddess inscribed in the Hall of Offerings at Dendera.

Gasu: Anointings (Khesu)

Sekha: Contemplation of the Neter

Beautiful are the rays of the Sun and the Moon,

That unite upon the crown of Het-Her,

They are the lights that shine forth as from the beginning.

Ra accompanies the barque of the Golden One on her journey,

Khons follows in her pathway.

Her feet tread upon the heavenly fields wherein all are born.

I am blessed by my mother as she travels through eternity,

I seek her in the region of dawn,

I am rejuvenated by the luminaries that are joined upon her brow.

Hekaut: Invocation of the Neter

Het-Her: make my face perfect among the Neteru,

Open my eyes, the Sun and the Moon, that I may see each day.

Make ready my place in the holy chamber in Amentet,

Where your light envelopes the darkness

And strengthens my legs to walk with ease through the Duat.

Great Lady of seven times: make me perfect as Ra is to all men and women,

As you go forth unceasingly in the barque of eternity.

*Ta Sent Nefert, Rat Tauit, Ament Het, Sefkhet Aabut, Mehit Tefnut, Ant Hat, Nehemau
Ait, Pakt, Urt Apset, Nebt Hotep, Khent Abtet, Hat Mehit, Ta Netet em Khen Uaa.*

Mau: Meditation on the Neter

O she who dwells in the spacious disc

As it advances toward the sanctuary of Iunu:

In your shrine the divine harmonies emanate,

They cause men and women to utter your praises.

Het-Her speaks the secrets of transformation,

Granting me the power of her seven forms.

Hotep: Offering (Khesu)

Djefau: Reversion of Offerings (Khesu)

Menu: Dedication of the Temple to the Neter

Ra harkens on his eternal journey
As she who dwells on his brow is summoned.
Her throne is made ready for her appearance,
She is given a seat for her manifestations.
The Sun and Moon enter this sanctuary,
They join in peace in the sky of Iunu.

Pert Kheru Neter: Pronouncement of the Deity

I am Nubt, the Golden One in heaven.
I am she who illumines the darkest places.
My power is that which brings light in the Duat.
In my seven forms I exist in all parts of the Two Lands,
I guide those who harken to the day-barque,
I protect those who follow the night-barque.

Heb: Festival

The Festival of the Joyous Union is an appropriate observance for this season.

Temau: Closing of the Ceremony [3]

Het-Her: lady of Amentet, dweller in Weret, lady of Tasert,
Eye of Ra, dweller on his brow, beautiful face in the barque of a million years.
You enter your sanctuary, you are established in peace
For having done what is right and true among the favored.
You go forth in the heavens
Conversing with the Neteru in the divine train.
You make the Sun barque sail on its orderly path in the sky.

---

3. Adapted from chapter 186 of *The Book of Going Forth by Day*.

Ceremony of Djehuti—*Season of Gemini*

Hesi: Hymn to the Neter [4]

Homage to you who records the measures,
Who balances the scale whereon the heart is placed.
Djehuti: self-created, reckoner of the pathway,
Powerful sceptre of the divine serpent Wadjet.
Renewer of forms, giving breath to the weary-hearted,
Bearer of lost testimony in the region of Amentet.
Hail, ibis-head: you who knows all secrets,
Uttering the formulas that dissolve all conflicts.
Djehuti: measurer, counter of stars and Ka spirits,
Member of the Great Council, poise of the eternal balance,
Dweller in the utmost parts of Earth,
Vindicator of Asar on the night of the great battle in Iunu,
All-knowing is your power, great is your word.

Wehem: Litany of the Neter [5]

This is the adoration of Djehuti, son of Ra, the Moon,
Of beautiful risings, lord of appearings, light of the gods:
Hail to you, Moon, Djehuti,
Bull in Khemenu, Dweller in Hesert,
Who makes way for all of the Neteru.
Recording their utterances, knowing all secrets,
Distinguishing one speech from another in this world,
Judge of everyone in the next.
Keen-faced in the barque of eternity,
Courier of mankind who knows every man and woman by their words,
Who makes the deed rise against the doer.
Who contents Ra and advises the sole lord,
Informing him of all things that take place.

---

4. Adapted from the Papyrus Anastasi.

5. Adapted from the text of a Dynasty 18 statue of Horemhab in the New York Metropolitan Museum.

At dawn you summon in heaven, not forgetting yesterday's report.

Wise friend in Iunu, who makes known the wisdom of all the Neteru,

Who knows their utmost and expounds their words.

I praise you, counselor: wise among the Ennead,

Who remembers the fleeting moment, whose words endure forever.

Gasu: Anointings *(Khesu)*

Sekha: Contemplation of the Neter [6]

You come, noble ibis, great spirit who loves Khemenu,

Luminous One, dweller in Iunu and counselor of the Ennead.

You give your counsel, making men great with your endowment of perfect laws.

When Ra speaks, Djehuti writes, and the divine council assents.

Given your word, I walk on the righteous path,

Given your assessment, I am welcomed into the sacred field.

Hekaut: Invocation of the Neter

O you straight plummet of the Scales, repulser of all evil:

Your appearing is divine, your words sound.

Relate to me that which is forgotten, enter the Duat and report the hour.

Divine scribe who changes turmoil to peace, expounder of divine words:

I call upon your wisdom and sound judgment!

Enter this chamber, make safe the bow of my barque

That goes forth into the sacred regions.

Aah Djehuti, Lord of the net

Recorder of divine words in Hesert, lord of Maat in Urit

Judge of the two combatant gods in Per-Ab:

Tekhnu, Shep-es, Asten, Khenti, Mehi, Hab, Aan, Rehehui, Aashep-es, Khemenu, Asten, Khenti, Mehi, Hab Djehuti.

Djehuti Iu aper em peh-ef, kher utu aat em maakheru.

Mau: Meditation on the Neter

Djehuti conveys me to Khemenu, his sacred precinct.

He guards my mouth in speaking.

---

6. Adapted from the Papyrus Sallier.

I enter in the presence of the Lord of the Council, I leave as one justified.

Djehuti brings me water from afar, the Silent One refreshes my thirst.

His well is sealed to him who finds words, it is open to the one who listens.

Hotep: Offering *(Khesu)*

Djefau: Reversion of Offerings *(Khesu)*

Menu: Dedication of the Temple to the Neter

Rehehui: lord of purity who rejects all evil,

To whom falsehoods are an abomination.

Your words bring order to the two banks, your presence makes writing speak,

Your entry in the shrine drives back all untruths.

At your coming forth I am given access to the hidden sounds.

Your place at the prow is established,

And honor is given to you in speaking the spells that utter from your mouth.

Pert Kheru Neter: Pronouncement of the Deity

I am Djehuti, wise scribe, clean of hands: I repulse evil and witness truth.

Favored of Ra, honoring his maker, I am Djehuti, lord of laws.

The learned one proclaims the morrow,

Guiding the prow through sky and Earth, and shadow worlds.

Giving breath to him who is in secret, by the spells that come out of my mouth.

I grant perpetuity as magical protection to your limbs,

Calming wrath and rejoicing within the twin sanctuaries.

I keep your heart alive, uttering words that the gods love.

Heb: Festival

The Invocation of Khons is an appropriate observance for this season.

Temau: Closing of the Ceremony

Maker of eternity, creator of everlastingness:

I am endowed with your power, I am supplied with your book.

Take your place among the Great Council, assume your seat in the West

Where the righteous find contentment.

Shu is empowered to shine upon my body at your word,

He illumines my pathway with the brilliant rays from your appearing.

Ceremony of Nebt-Het—*Season of Cancer*

Hesi: Hymn to the Neter

Hail to you: protectoress, winged one,
Whose name is hidden, whose form is unknown.
You whose wings span the heavens and encompass the Earth
I greet you with rejoicing,
Breathing the wind that comes forth from your feathered arm.
Blessed one of the fountain of Amentet,
Your water provides refreshment, it pours forth onto the fields of Geb.
The Black Land is nourished by your libation,
You restore the form of the Green God.
You are chief mourner of the departed one,
Your lamentations stir life in your beloved brother.
Your favored form brings refreshment to the Ka's in the Duat,
Your weeping is silent, your speech is pure.
Djehuti makes way for you when you enter the hall of Amentet,
He records your mourning chant in the divine book.

Wehem: Litany of the Neter

Sister of the recumbent one, whose vigil never falters,
Your heavenly boat moors in this domain.
O shelter of the roof of heaven, whose crown illumines the darkness,
You bring peace to the place of mourning.
Mistress of the shadow worlds, three times blessed of the Ennead,
Your libations refresh the thirsty.
You to whom the four winds pay homage,
Your name is blessed among the living.
You who stirs the breath of the unmoving one,
You are his protectoress.
Mover of the river, who guides the efflux of Hapi,
Your ministrations restore the anointed one.

Gasu: Anointings (Khesu)

Sekha: Contemplation of the Neter

Nebt-Het is the hidden head, she stands behind the Green God,

She grants her arm to the stricken, she breathes by the sacred disc,

She is the goddess who hides herself.

She brings refreshment to those who are in darkness.

Her name is She-Who-Embraces, daughter of Ra,

The one who gives all pure and good things to Asar.

Hekaut: Invocation of the Neter

Lady of the House of Fire, great one at the altar of offerings:

You refresh every god with your breath,

Your hand guides my barque on the day of sailing upstream.

Extend your arm, lady of the blessed in Amentet!

Hear me, hidden one: take pleasure in the gifts you are offered,

Awaken in peace.

O Lady whose breath is fragrant, to whom all offer libations,

Alight your wings among the living.

Men an Nebt-Het: hap-a Shesheta ari-a, bes sa her Haapi enti am-a sa Asar, sa Haapi,
Asar pu Haapi. Eqna em-a aui her enti Ma-a. Nebt khat urt hekau, ben ra merit kher
seket.

Mau: Meditation on the Neter

The plumes upon the head of the august one are Auset and Nebt-Het.

They go round about the body of Asar,

Providing his offerings, the sisters of the Green God.

Nebt-Het brings refreshment to the silent one,

She anoints her brother, she restores his breath.

Hotep: Offering (Khesu)

Djefau: Reversion of Offerings (Khesu)

Menu: Dedication of the Temple to the Neter

Lady of the sacred vase, dweller within Sennu:
Your house is established as the living ones enter your region.
You are creatrix of new forms, fashioner of the bandalets for the Ka,
Living in the sunrise of the Western Land.
You who enters the sanctuary in Iunu, receive your offerings,
Arise upon the throne established for you.

Pert Kheru Neter: Pronouncement of the Deity

I have come that I may protect him,
My power endows him with strength for millions of years.
I head the bier of the departed one,
Being present also before the great scale,
Assisting the silent to arise as the living.
I am she-who-protects the motionless one,
I provide that which he lacks.
I encircle the Ka of all living things,
I have fashioned the body of the Neteru,
I come forth as your magical protection.

Heb: Festival

The Lotus Ceremony is an appropriate observance for this season.

Temau: Closing of the Ceremony

Sister of the beloved god, who assisted as Auset gave birth,
Who nursed Heru in the hidden marsh,
May you prepare the birthchamber.
May you come forth from the shrine of Iunu in peace,
To preparing libations for the living.
Guardian of the Divine House, chantress of the funeral song:
Alight upon the night-barque, which travels in peace through the Duat.

Ceremony of Heru—*Season of Leo*

Hesi: *Hymn to the Neter*

Son of the silent one, heir to the Great Palace,

Who vanquishes darkness and strife, who rises from the deep:

Take flight to your temple, turn your feathered head toward the North

Where darkness awaits, to be dispelled by your eye.

Son of Auset, who ascends from Earth,

I await the appearance of your glorious rising.

The Neteru in the Two Lands gaze east for your winged image,

All men and women await your coming,

The Aakhu and the living give praise to you.

Wehem: *Litany of the Neter*

Beloved falcon rising from the deep,

Lord of the Great Flood: may you keep me sound.

You are the winged soul of the southern sky,

Djehuti in the northern sky.

O Eldest One: come to Teb, your divine house.

O Youngest One: come to Per Asar, your birth house.

(Chant of Sacred Names)

* *Heru Hekennu*	Heru, son of Bastet
* *Heru Behutet:*	Heru of the Southern Heaven[7]
* *Heru sma Taui:*	Heru, Uniter of the Two Lands[8]
* *Heru em Aakhuti:*	Heru of the Two Horizons
* *Heru Nub:*	Heru the Golden; triumphant of Set[9]
* *Heru an Mut-ef:*	Heru of the Divine Mother[10]
* *Heru Merti:*	Heru of the Two Eyes (Sun and Moon)
* *Ihy*	Beloved (of Hathor)[11]

---

7. His name at the temple of Behutet and as consort of Het-Her.

8. His name at the temple of Dendera.

9. His name as the dual Nubti figure.

10. His name at the temple of Edfu.

11. The son of Heru and Het-Her of Dendera.

* *Heru pa Khart:*	Heru, the Silent One (Divine Child)
* *Heru Shu pa Khart:*	Heru the Great, descendant (inheritor) of Shu
* *Heru Ra pa Khart:*	Heru, descendant (inheritor) of Ra[12]
* *Heru Hennu:*	Heru, the Falcon[13]
* *Heru Khent Peru:*	Heru, Ruler of the Heavens
* *Heru sa Auset:*	Heru, son of Auset
* *Heru sa Asar:*	Heru, son of Asar

Gasu: Anointings *(Khesu)*

Sekha: Contemplation of the Neter

Heru is prince of light, he fills the horizon.

He vanquishes the adversary, he enfolds all in his protection.

Hail to you Heru: you are risen

As a great falcon coming forth from his egg.

You fly to your eastern mountain,

You rise at dawn and in peace.

(Recitation of the Solar Litany)

Homage to you:

O lamp of Iunu and Hememet spirit in Kher Aha,

Unti: Who is more glorious than the gods of the Sheta shrine,

Invocation:

You come in triumph, you appear in glory with your kind eye.

Homage to you: An in Antes, great spirit Heru em Aakhuti,

Who traverses the heights of heaven in spacious strides.

(Invocation)

Homage to you: dweller in Djedu, Un Nefer,

Son of Nut, son of Auset, who is lord of Akhert.

(Invocation)

Homage to you: dominion of the Two Lands,

The Ureret crown is placed upon your head.

---

12. His name at the temple of Hermonthis.

13. His name at the temple of Busiris.

(Invocation)
Homage to you: mighty one in your hour,
Chief, prince, governor of Anrutef, lord of eternity.
(Invocation)
Homage to you: who is founded upon Maat.
Dweller in your boat, foremost in the Sun barque.
(Invocation)
Homage to you: son of the Neteru,
Maker of all things that ascend to heaven,
Heru triumphant, uniter of the Two Lands.
(Invocation)

Hekaut: Invocation of the Neter

The Heru Shemsu[14] appear in their shrine,
The doors of the Divine House are opened,
I greet the appearance of the Two Eyes.
Open Sky, open Earth, open eastern and western gates,
Open starry doors of the horizon,
Open hidden gates of the imperishable region,
Open sanctuaries of Upper and Lower Egypt,
Open pathway of Ra.
Open for the golden falcon who makes flight to his temple.
Open double doors of day and night,
Open for the retinue of the divine son that follows in his train.
Ra Heru em Aakhuti, Heru Tahema, Heru Nedj, Hra Atef-ef, Heru Aah, Heru em Hennu, Heru Tat, Heru em Anpu, Heru Hebennu, Heru sa Auset sa Asar.

Mau: Meditation on the Neter

Falcon who rises from the deep,
Eldest one of the world: you have risen to your divine seat.
Heru em Aakhuti, lord of the two horizons:
You have alighted upon the golden throne,
You have entered your sanctuary in peace.

---

14. Heru Shemsu: "those who follow Horus."

Hotep: Offering (Khesu)

Djefau: Reversion of Offerings (Khesu)

Menu: Dedication of the Temple to the Neter

I repose before the great god,
He who unites the Ennead with his presence.
Heru joins the powerful Sahu,[15]
He is triumphant, presider over the Great House.
The throne of Harakhte is established, he has come.
He counsels the dwellers in the Two Lands:
He rejuvenates those who follow him.
Prince of the Divine House: return to your place among the living.
Golden One in the eastern sky: alight upon your seat.

Pert Kheru Neter: Pronouncement of the Deity

Your form exists on Earth, alive and youthful each day.
Your eyes are opened, your face shining in happiness.
I come, I count all in my presence.
I have enumerated my followers,
I have equipped you with mine eye
And I open this eye that you may behold my presence.
The lord of the Two Horizons is seen when he crosses the sky,
He ascends and the stars perish not,
While all in his company possess eternity.

Heb: Festival

The Anointing into the Temple is an appropriate observance for this season.

Temau: Closing of the Ceremony

You are risen Heru Hennu,
As a great falcon who comes forth from his egg.

---

15. Sahu: the body of ancestral souls residing in the stars.

You are flown and seated upon your throne,

To sit in pleasure among the members of your retinue.

You rest within your sanctuary,

Upon the eastern mountain of your coming into being.

I give praise to you and your illuminations as you cross the sky.

Beautiful falcon of gold: you are raised.

You are a member of the train of Khepri, reborn.

You are presider over the thrones of kings,

Over men and women, and all the Neteru and the Sahu.

You are governor of the two horizons, of sky and Earth.

Welcome in peace beloved son,

As you alight upon the Maatet boat of heaven.

Ceremony of Geb—*Season of Virgo*

Hesi: *Hymn to the Neter*

Homage to you, Geb: who came before all the Neteru,

Whose heirs are seated on the throne of the Two Lands.

I salute you before the great Ben Ben of Iunu

Where you preside as father of all the living.

Hail to you: divine ancestor, prototype of all that exists,

Who brings forth all that nourishes the living,

Who allows the Neteru to feed upon his sacred food and drink.

The body of Geb has joined with the starry sky

And brought forth the divine train of beings,

Who carry the Heka and Nekheka,[16] who wear the crowns,

Who carry out their father's word in their season.

Wehem: *Litany of the Neter*

He who comes in peace, maker of the Great Seat,

He provides libations for the Ennead,

His emanations create natron and incense,

---

16. Heka: crook, Nekheka: flail; the two sceptres of the Royal House.

He is giver of offerings,
Whose firstborn is the Green God, master of his wands.
Plougher of the fields, raiser of Asar,
Consort of the Great Cow, father of the Neteru in Iunu.
Fashioner of the Heka and Nekheka sceptres,
Overseer of the chamber of the throne,
Creator of the sacred trees of balsam.
He sets his sandal upon the head of the adversary,
Bestowing sovereignty to the chief in Amentet,
He came forth from Nun and the Lake of Fire.

Gasu: Anointings (Khesu)

Sekha: Contemplation of the Neter

I am the child of Geb, long of years,
Who sleeps and is reborn each day.[17]
I am an heir of the Earth, dwelling in the fields of my first ancestor.
I awaken from my slumber, rejuvenated as the Neteru each day.
The blood from my divine father's marrow has nourished me,
His steering oar is at the prow of my boat.
On my journey to him I am restored,
I take my place among his descendants.

Hekaut: Invocation of the Neter

Hail to you: Geb, Who strides forth from Iunu,
Urpa Geb, Chief of all divine beings.
You are Lord of the Earth to its utmost limit,
You possess the strength of the Paut.
Behold, you are as every divinity, you are the Ka of all the Neteru.
You reared them, you vivify them in their coming.
Your eye appears from your head as Ur Hekau[18] of the South,

---

17. *The Book of Going Forth by Day*, chapter 87.

18. Ur Hekau: "great magician."

Your eye appears from your head as Ur Hekau of the North.
The Pauti honor you, they place offerings before you.
*Tepiu aui Geb, Taha Geb Qenebti, Sman Tebeh-et Hotep, Kenken Ur, Bennu Smam Ur,
Erpat Geb, Geb Khenti Khat Pest-et, Sef em Tuau.*

Mau: Meditation on the Neter

The great ancestor has given me his hand, I come into being through him.
A wreath of vindication has been placed upon my brow
And I live, beloved of my father who brought forth all life on the first occasion.
He assigns to me his inheritance, his fields are given to me.

Hotep: Offering *(Khesu)*

Djefau: Reversion of Offerings *(Khesu)*

Menu: Dedication of the Temple to the Neter

Geb endures on his throne,
The fields are the places of his manifestations.
He presides in the barque of Ra,
He opens for himself the mouth of the Earth.
His soil is plowed, causing grain to grow.
His strong arm establishes the food on which the living exist.

Pert Kheru Neter: Pronouncement of the Deity

I am the egg that is in the Great Cackler,
I stand watch over the mighty things that come into being,
That which I have caused to open from the Earth thrives.
I germinate as it germinates, I live as it lives, my breath is its breath.

Heb: Festival

The Great Offering Ceremony is an appropriate observance for this season.

Temau: Closing of the Ceremony

The fields of Hotep have been readied
That I may eat therefrom and be restored,

That I may become blessed by my father Geb,
That I may inherit his abundance.
The grain god has granted me sustenance,
And I have been given authority as his heir.
May those beings in the Duat have fear of me,
May they tremble at their gates,
For I am among the blessed dwelling in sunlight.
I have been made from his form and I am restored.
Geb alights upon his throne and I regain my youth.

Ceremony of Auset—*Season of Libra*

Hesi: Hymn to the Neter

Asar takes his sister as his protection,
She drives away his foes, she turns back evil.
The words of power are uttered from her mouth,
She of perfect tongue, of perfect speech.
By divine decree she is the strong one,
Because she avenged her brother.
She sought him unceasingly,
Pursuing him in sorrow, never alighting.
She wept at his bier, she made wind with her wings,
Raising the unmoving one up from his sleep.
She brought forth his seed, creating his heir.
She nursed the youth in solitude,
Unknown is the place where he was raised.
She brought forth him of the mighty hand,
In the house of Geb.
Asar ari en sent-ef, maket-ef seherit kheru sehemet sep shet kheru em khu re-es.
Aquerit nes an uh en metu semenkhet utu metu.
Auset khut nedjet sen-es.
Hehet su atet bakek reret ta pen em hai an khen nes an qemtu-es su arit shut em shut-es
khepert nef em tenhui.
Arit hennu menat sen-es set heset enenu en urt ab khenpet mut-ef.

Arit au-au shetet nekhen em ua-au an
Rekh bu-ef am beset su, a-ef nekhtu em khent het geb.

Wehem: Litany of the Neter

O she of many names, great one who is from the beginning,
Divine one, the only one, the greatest of the Neteru.
Queen of all the Sahu, most beloved of all that lives.
Prototype of all beings, queen of women, the female Ra.
The female Heru, the eye of the Sun, the hidden eye of Ra called Sopdet.
Star-crown of Harakhte, queen of the dekan spirits.
Star who opens the new year, lady of the beginning.
Occupier of the chief place in the barque of heaven.
Maker of the sunrise, the lady of heaven, the holy one of the sky.
She of the beams of gold, the golden one.
The most brilliant Neter, lady of the north wind,
The queen of Earth, the mightiest of the mighty.
Sovereign of the South and the North: chieftaness of the Two Lands.
Lady of the deepest Earth, blazing flame,
Who fills the Duat with all good things!
The great being in the Duat of her brother, in her name of Tanit.
Mother of Heru, mother of the winged one,
Who brought forth her son in secret
So that he would inherit the rank of his father.
Giver of new birth to the god Ka Nekht,
Nurse and protector of her son Heru,
Lady of the divine birth chamber.
Bestower of life, giver of goods to all the Neteru,
Giver of offerings to all the Ka's.
Green goddess, whose greenness is like that of the Earth.
Lady of joy, and gladness, and love, lady of this temple.
Queen of the Great House, the Divine House, and the House of Fire.
Beautiful in appearance, beloved in all lands,
Mighty One, majestic One.
Beautiful of face in Waset, exalted in Iunu, beneficent of Men Nefer.

Mistress of spells, weaver and fuller.
Daughter of Geb, child of the universal lord, daughter of Nut.
First royal wife, consort of her father, whose son is lord of the Earth.
Whose husband is inundation of the Nile,
Who makes the Nile to swell in his season.

Gasu: Anointings *(Khesu)*

Sekha: Contemplation of the Neter

Auset is behind you, she protects your limbs.
As she did for her son, she protects the Heru Shemsu,
Those who followed him from the first occasion.
Her offspring are the living, their lord is sovereign of the Two Lands.
They are born among the Neteru, among the cedars,
They are members of the Paut, the first born.
She is mother of the justified one, he-who-repulses-all-adversaries,
Who makes transformations in heaven and is born each morning.
Her heirs endure forever and ever, they are given life,
They join with the disc eternally.

Hekaut: Invocation of the Neter

Come, you of beautiful forms, the crown is upon your head,
I salute you, arise!
You are upon your throne, you live in your sanctuary.
The words of magic are uttered from your mouth,
They bring life to the motionless,
They dispel all abominations.
Auset Nebuut, Amenit, Menhet, Renpet Sep-et, Hetet, Hurt Thenenet, Ant, Sesheta Heqet, Uadjit Mersekhen. Renpet Nebt Tept, T-hat Techetut, T-het, Shetat.

Mau: Meditation on the Neter

Auset-Sopdet is behind me, she enters this sanctuary,
She makes it holy and divine by her coming.
Her emanations come forth

To vivify all the Neteru and living beings.
She sails forth as a star from her place in heaven,
She travels in the barque of eternity,
She lives and dwells forever in the sacred places.
She illumines the places of her manifestation,
And her sacred day is commemorated from this day forth.

Hotep: Offering *(Khesu)*

Djefau: Reversion of Offerings *(Khesu)*

Menu: Dedication of the Temple to the Neter

May your offerings be pleasant and your Ka satisfied,
Auset-Sopdet, mother of the living.
You are truly mistress of those whose minds are at peace,
Friend of those who steps are just.
May your manifestations be exalted, your words sublime.
May you be strong and powerful in your sanctuary,
May you protect Asar and the souls who reside in his domain.
May you look in favor on those who utter your name,
May all divine offerings be made to you.
Mistress of the barge, goddess whose crown reflects the light of heaven,
Take possession of the sanctuary established for you.

Pert Kheru Neter: Pronouncement of the Deity

You shall not be tired, nor your members weary,
You shall live in eternity and rule through everlastingness.
You become heir to the silent one, as Heru is in his horizon,
You come forth from my womb, a child who lifts his head to see Ra.
You have power over bread and water, power over wind
You have power over all things beautiful and pure.
Your heart is yours, of your true being,
Stable in its place forever and ever.

Heb: Festival

The Lamentations is an appropriate observance for this season.

Temau: Closing of the Ceremony

Auset, speak the secret name of your father Ra,

That the rower of the barque may never cease,

That the power of Khepri may ever sustain me.

Creatrix of the Great Flood, summon the Nile in his cavern,

That the abundance of the Two Lands may be renewed.

Mistress of the living,

Protect and keep safely those who honor you.

Ceremony of Anpu—*Season of Scorpio*

Hesi: Hymn to the Neter

Hail to you, Anpu: watcher of the western gate.

Sole one, whose eyes penetrate the Duat.

You are opener of the ways, keeper of the great door,

Custodian of Amentet,

Esteemed of those who preside over the Sahu of men and women.

I call upon you: take up your staff and admit me into your region.

Thou watchman of the hidden places,

Gatekeeper at the entrance to the Western Land:

Let me enter into the region of silence and learn to speak without words.

When dawn returns, I will awaken as a member of your retinue,

I will follow in your train and stand watch with you,

I will act as your herald.

Western door: open to me,

Staff of Anpu: guide me through the gate.

Wehem: Litany of the Neter

Hail to you, Anpu, jackal face:

Guardian of the Duat, who is Leader of the Divine Train.

(Invocation)
Grant me a path whereon I may journey in peace, for I am righteous.
Homage to you, Ap-Uat: who is the Opener of the Ways.
(Invocation)
Honor to you, Hery Sesheta: who is Upon the Secrets.
(Invocation)
I praise you, Khenty Amentiu: who is Prince of the Western Land.
(Invocation)
Greetings to you, Neb ta Djoser: who is Lord of the Sacred Place.
(Invocation)
Salutation to you, Imiutet: who is Dweller in the Embalming Chamber.
(Invocation)

Gasu: Anointings *(Khesu)*

Sekha: Contemplation of the Neter

I journey onward through the Duat,
Upon the path that leads to the chamber of the Green God,
He who renews all things.
Anpu prepares me for my audience,
My body is washed and bound against all corruption,
My limbs are anointed with libations that preserve and protect my form.
My heart is weighed and found righteous,
My admission is affirmed by the supreme guardian.

Hekaut: Invocation of the Neter

O you who presides in the pavilion of the Neteru,
Keeper of the door that is fastened against the night,
Sojourner of Maat, dwelling in your mountain:
Hasten to the Sacred Land, for I rise.
Rise thou also to my calling.
Anpu, dweller in the chamber of embalmment:
Lay your hands upon the coffin that enfolds me,
Extend your protection to my brow.

Exalt this sanctuary by your appearance,
Lead me on the path of justification.

Anpu ap Uat, Sekhem em pet, Sekhem taui, Her en Anpu, Am Ut, Khent sehet, Tepy dju-ef, Ap Uat Mehet Sekhem, Resu Sekhem Taui, Heb Anep Imiutet.

Mau: Meditation on the Neter

My lips are the lips of Anpu speaking truth,
My tongue is the word of the Great Balance, resounding through Amentet.
All things unknown become known to me,
For Anpu is the horizontal beam that weighs my heart.
My form is commended to his charge,
My Ka is guided by his great staff.
I have washed myself in the water wherein Anpu has washed,
I have performed the rites of purification.
Anpu who is upon his mountain has set all things in order.
My face becomes the face of Anpu, ever watchful in the night.
The god of the coffin leads me through the gates of Amentet
And guides me to the chamber of the Ab.
He opens my mouth and I am made upright in the Duat,
Wherein I speak truth throughout.

Hotep: Offering *(Khesu)*

Djefau: Reversion of Offerings *(Khesu)*

Menu: Dedication of the Temple to the Neter

O you who shroud the dead, fashioner of the coverings for the justified:
May you establish your place in this sanctuary,
Where you will dwell with the Green God,
He who is reborn each day.
May this altar become your western pylon,
To be presided over by the seven guardians in the House of Eternity.

Pert Kheru Neter: Pronouncement of the Deity

You are in your coffins, on your journey,
Upon the path that leads onward toward the Green God.

I have lain my hands upon the bandalets and extend my protection.
I have passed through the infernal regions
To grant you rank and exaltation in the Duat.

Heb: Festival

The Empowerment of the Ushabtiu is an appropriate observance for this season.

Temau: Closing of the Ceremony

I stand within his chamber, in the house of the spirits,
To know truth in the weighing of my heart.
Anpu lives in the region of silence and the southern part of the sky,
He watches for my coming, he guides me with through the Duat
To come in and go out each day.

Ceremony of Sekhmet-Bast—*Season of Sagittarius*

Hesi: Hymn to the Neter

Hail to you, Sekhmet-Bast: Eye of Ra
Pakhet: she who claws, Bastet: she who protects.
Mistress of gates, plume-wearer,
To whom no other of the Neteru is superior.
You are lady of the white and red crowns,
Sole one, exalted by her father.
You are lady of the bright red linen,
Who carries the flint knife of sacrifice.
You are great of magic, presider over the barque of eternity.
You are the sacred one, dawning in the hidden seat of silence.
You are Bastet, aegis of the Great House,
Protectoress, destroyer of the enemies of Ra.

Wehem: Litany of the Neter

Sekhmet-Bast, bright one of the flame:
Who consumes the leavings of evil.
Sekhmet-Bast, protectoress of the fiery breath:

Who dwells in the western part of heaven.
Sekhmet-Bast, lady of the crimson cloth:
Who purges the chamber of transformation.
Sekhmet-Bast, mistress of the sacred eye:
The rays of her father enter the hidden abode.
Sekhmet-Bast, guide of the golden prow:
Who preserves the sanctuary of the Heru Shemsu.

Gasu: Anointings (Khesu)

Sekha: Contemplation of the Neter

She is the hidden fire in the shrine of the Ben Ben,
Her power comes on the day of her appearing.
She awards me a path whereon I am preserved from terror,
She purges my wrongdoing before I enter the divine territory.
She is the shining one, who dawns with the barque of eternity each day,
Her flaming eye dispells all evil.

Hekaut: Invocation of the Neter

Sekhmet-Bast-Pakhet-Bastet,
Beloved of Asheru, lady of great power magic:
Grant me your power, extend to me your protection.
Guardian of the boundaries in the Two Lands, I am among your train.
You who consumes the blood of your father's enemies:
Draw the weapons that cast out what has become corrupt.
*Per Bast, Iuaset, Nut Wadjet, Sekhmet Menhet, Ba Ra Auset, Khut Nebat Shetat, Desher
Irty Imy Het Insi,*
Haq, Khersepser her Pakher, Ser seb kek Remet.

Mau: Meditation on the Neter

The power of the Sekhmet-Bast-Pakhet-Bastet preserves me,
Her flaming eye reflects the dawn of her father within this shrine.
Her flint knife is pure, it removes all abominations,
Her sacred fire has cleansed me of any falsehood,
She leads me to the chamber of purification
Wherein I am renewed.

Hotep: Offering (Khesu)

Djefau: Reversion of Offerings (Khesu)

Menu: Dedication of the Temple to the Neter

I honor the one who preserves from terror,
The mysterious lioness, the sound eye, mistress of the Neteru.
She harbors me from the place of execution,
She establishes me above the field of conflict.
Her redness ascends from the island of fire,
Her magic appears when her altar stone is struck.

Pert Kheru Neter: Pronouncement of the Deity

I am Sekhmet-Bast, the eye of my father,
I cleanse the forms of those who summon me.
I destroy the leavings of evil in the house of silence.
I am Bastet, beloved of Auset and Nebt-Het,
I guard the gate of terror against the adversaries of the Green God.

Heb: Festival

The Festival of Imhotep is an appropriate observance for this season.

Temau: Closing of the Ceremony

Sekhmet-Bast-Pakhet-Bastet: You are the great warmth
That emanates from the brow of your father.
You are smiter of all enemies and destructions.
To those who reside in the sacred precincts
Your light is contained within and without,
Strife and peace are resolved at your appearing.

Ceremony of Set—*Season of Capricorn*

Hesi: Hymn to the Neter

Homage to you, divine ladder,
Ladder of Set which lifted Asar into the heavens.
Your sceptre smites my mouth in the chamber of purification,

I pass through your region to know creation once more.
O mighty one of twofold strength,
Whose kingdom is the northern sky,
You are the great crocodile, the great one
Who consumes my corruption.

Wehem: Litany of the Neter

Homage to you, swallower:
Bringer of night in the day-barque of Ra,
You who are all-powerful within your gate.
Consumer of untruth and the leavings of humanity,
One who is feared, dweller in the hidden cavern.
Divider: who separates contention from he-who-judges in Amentet.
Mediator: who brings both confusion and truth to the arbitrator,
That he may judge from his heart which is righteous.
Enveloper: who commands the serpents of the night barque.
Master of the shadows: who leads them through the gates
On the day of judgment before the lord of the living.

Gasu: Anointings (Khesu)

Sekha: Contemplation of the Neter

The gateway is opened for me, I walk without obstruction,
Whereupon I soar as the primeval one soars, I become Khepri.
Reborn from new soil, I become a Ka and grow as plants grow.
I am the fruit of every Neter, I arise from their exhalations.
I come into being in the hours of night,
I am reborn, I am unfettered throughout my journey.

Hekaut: Invocation of the Neter

Lord of gates, Neter of the funeral mountain,
Set-Amentet, warden in the western region.
Watcher, who travels with the Ka to the natron field,
Who makes way for the divine retinue.
On whose ladder I ascend and enter into the day barque.

Suit Sutekh, Akemu Seku, Seb Ur, Set Nubti, Meskheti, Khepesh, Set Amentet, Set em Maat-f, Set Hra, Apep, Set Heh, Hemet.

Mau: Meditation on the Neter

I am a (son/daughter) of Earth and long of years,
I sleep to be reborn each day.
I have dwelled in the chamber of silence for seventy days,
I have fulfilled my purification.
Death penetrates not my Ka, it passes over my resting place.
I am renewed, rejuvenated throughout eternity.

Hotep: Offering *(Khesu)*

Djefau: Reversion of Offerings *(Khesu)*

Menu: Dedication of the Temple to the Neter

The sons of Heru are present,
They witness the dedication of these vessels
That contain the humours of life:
Qebsenuf brings the sacred fire within the shrine,
Imset makes fumigations that please the Sahu.
Haapi performs ablutions before the house of eternity,
Daumutef endows offerings for the great feast.
The vessels are placed before Set in order,
He is satisfied; my ancestors live.

Pert Kheru Neter: Pronouncement of the Deity

Purified and without fault are the souls who enter the western portal,
They are unbound, their swathings loosed.
Their bodies are arrayed in the wreath of vindication,
They are seated before the lord of risings.
They are counted among the justified,
They unite themselves to all things as Nun.

Heb: Festival

The Festival of Sokar is an appropriate observance for this season.

Temau: Closing of the Ceremony

Possessor of the Ka, liberate the motionless one,
He who has been bathed in natron.
Unswath the coverings that have been placed upon him,
Unlock the chest that has enclosed him.
You who dwells in the region in the north,
The imperishable ones honor you as they turn in the sky.

Ceremony of Maat—*Season of Aquarius*

Hesi: Hymn to the Neter

She who is the image of Ra, Meh-urt,
Lady of the Meten orb who guides the prow of the Sun barque:
I address you, judge of unalterable truth and all that is eternal.
The chamber is illumined by your two lights, Measure and Order.
I walk, following your path inscribed in the sky,
I enter the hall of weighing to await your dispensation.
You are woman of heaven and Earth, the two Duats,
Dispenser of the sacred word in the judgment chamber.

Wehem: Litany of the Neter: Maat[19]

Usekhet nemmat, Hepet shet, Fenti, Am khaibetu, Neha hau, Rerti, Maati-ef em tes, Neba per em khetkhet, Set kesu, Uadj nes, Qerti, Hedj abehu, Am senef, Am beseku, Neb Maat, Tenemi, Aati, Tutu-ef, Uamemti, Maa an-ef, Heri seru, Khemi, Shet kheru, Nekhen, Ser Kheru, Basti, Hra-ef ha-ef, Ta ret, Kenemti, An hotep-ef, Neb hrau, Serekhi, Neb abui, Nefer tem, Tem sep, Ari em ab-ef, Ahi mu, Utu rekhit, Neheb nefert, Neheb kau, Djeser tep, An a-ef.

---

19. The names of the Maati gods and goddesses who are the Assessors in the Hall of Judgment. Their names are the names of the forty-two gates that are passages in Amentet.

Gasu: Anointings *(Khesu)*

Sekha: Contemplation of the Neter

Thou holy and mighty lady of Khemenu:
You preside in the pavilion of Djehuti.
The sistrum of your head drives out evil,
And all that violates the magic of your manifestations.
You are sister of Anpu, mother of the Maati,
You hold the sceptre that established justice for the living.

Hekaut: Invocation of the Neter

Great One, lady of letters, mistress of the house of books,
Keeper of all that is recorded in Amentet:
You are exalted on the throne of Nut, the sky.
Knower of the divine record, dispensator of her father's words,
Lady of scribes, keeper of the sacred lapis:
May my words be pleasing to you,
And my voice truthful in your hearing.
Neb Maat Heri Tep Retui-f, Neb Pehti Thesu Menment [20]
Un Nut, Sefekh Aabut, Sesheta, Sefkhet Aabut, Meh Urt, Mau Taui, Sa Abu djar Khat,
Nehema Uait.

Mau: Meditation on the Neter

In the Hall of Maat all words are weighed, all intent is examined.
The Maati spirits serve truth and its manifestations,
They justify those who enter.
The world of the lotus flower is the region of Maat,
Where honor and order preside.
Here I am renewed and justified in her light.

---

20. The hekau that open the left and right gates of Maat in Amentet.

Hotep: Offering (Khesu)

Djefau: Reversion of Offerings (Khesu)

Menu: Dedication of the Temple to the Neter

The spirits of Maati have entered this chamber.
They have given judgment in accord with the words of Djehuti,
He who is the great reckoner, consort of his sister, the measurer.
The divine retinue is witness, all measures are marked.
Established in truth, my house is set aright.

Pert Kheru Neter: Pronouncement of the Deity

The eye of heaven has given pronouncement:
Assessed without fault is your spirit-soul,
Your deeds have been judged as you set upon my path.
You are bathed in the celestial waters of Nun,
You know the names of the Neteru.
Purified of error, your name shall live
And be recorded among the justified.

Heb: Festival

The Presentation of Maat is an appropriate observance for this season.

Temau: Closing of the Ceremony

O truthful one who presides over all judgments:
Through your gate I pass and am affirmed.
Grant me a path whereon I may know you and your word,
Where I may be guided by Rehehui and his scribes
To read the book of eternity.
I know your seat in the Sektet boat of heaven,
I follow in its course daily.

Ceremony of Nut—*Season of Pisces*

Hesi: Hymn to the Neter

Hail Nut, upon whose head appear the two eyes:

The Sun and Moon who make passage through your vault.

You have taken possession of Heru and become his Urt Hekau,

You have taken possession of Set and become his Urt Hekau.

O Nut, who did decree your own birth in your name of Pet-Iunu[21]

Decree that I should live and that I may not perish.

O Nut, who is risen as queen of the celestial field,

May you take possession of the Neteru and their Ka's,

Of their flesh and their divine food, and of everything that they have.

Grant that I may be without opposition and that I may exist

Under your vault, in the shade of your sycamores.

O Nut, let my life be your life.

Wehem: Litany of the Neter

Your mother comes to you and you move not,

The Great Protectoress comes to you and you move not.

But when Nut bestows her protection upon you, then do you move.

For she has given you your head, she has brought you your bones,

She has collected your flesh, she has brought your heart in your body.

Nut, you live: you speak to those who are before you.

You protect your children from grief,

You purify them with the purifications of the Neteru,

And they come to you with their Ka's.

Ant en Nut, Per Mesten Nut, Per Nedj ma Shu, Het Nut, Per Nut, Naut

Gasu: Anointings (Khesu)

Sekha: Contemplation of the Neter

Behold, I am a lotus that comes forth from the deep,

And Nut is my mother, her water nourishes me.

---

21. Pet Iunu: the name of Nut as "sky of Heliopolis."

The hearts of Geb and Nut are gladdened when their children take form.
I am exalted in the beauty of my mother the nether sky,
I endure in the shelter of her body.

Hekaut: Invocation of the Neter

Your mother Nut spreads herself over you,
In her name, "Coverer of Heaven."
She assists you in becoming as a god,
Without enemy, in the name of Neter.
She takes away from you every evil
In her name defender-from-every-evil.
Great Lady: from the waters of Nun you bring forth life,
You send it on its journey through the heavens,
You welcome its return each time.
Pes shesh nes mut-k Nut her-k em ren-s en shet pet, erta-s un nek en neter an khefti-k em ren-k en neter, khenem-s thu ma khet neb tut em ren-s khenemet tu neb urt thut, ura am mesu-s.

Mau: Meditation on the Neter

Your mother Nut in her name Qersut embraces you.
She brings you dominion over the waters,
Entry to the sacred land of Nun.
She spreads herself above you, she conceals you from harm.
She protects you, the greatest of her children.[22]

Hotep: Offering (Khesu)

Djefau: Reversion of Offerings (Khesu)

Menu: Dedication of the Temple to the Neter

O Nut, you give birth to the stars that proclaim your existence:
May your exalted body encircle this sanctuary,

---

22. Adapted from the Pyramid Texts, Utterance #446.

May you uplift the spirits to whom you have given birth.
Provide me with your nourishment as I ascend to your vault.

Pert Kheru Neter: Pronouncement of the Deity

I am the sky of Heliopolis, wherein all live,
I have risen to take possession of all things in heaven
And to spread over the length of the Two Lands.
I exist without opposition and my life is given to every being,
I grant existence to all whom I have given life.

Heb: Festival

The Book of Hours is an appropriate observance for this season.

Temau: Closing of the Ceremony

Great protectoress, who rests in all places at one time:
At your coming I know the lotus scent that rises from Nun
It appears with the Sun at dawn in the sky.
You enter your sanctuary in splendor, you go forth in beauty.
You are the guide of the sacred land, the body that illumines the Sahu.
Your two eyes are born each day,
They bring sight to all whom you have given birth.

Chapter Six

CEREMONY

. . . the science of the Gods is sacred and useful, and call the ignorance
of things honourable and beautiful darkness, but the knowledge of them
light; and also add, that the ignorance of these things fills men with all
evils, through inerudition and audacity, but the knowledge of them is
the cause of all good.

—Iamblichus: *De Mysteriis* (Chapter X)

Much is noted about the dearth of ceremony in modern times, and the difficulties that complicate our lives when our instincts of joy, loss, and fear find no meaningful outlet for expression. But in ancient Egypt, all events, whether cosmic or mundane, no matter how insignificant or repetitious, brought an opportunity for spiritual acknowledgment and the personal expression of one's relationship with divine powers.

In modern Egypt, a number of festivals survive from ancient times. The Ipet Festival of Thebes, in which the sacred barque of Amun was carried from the Karnak temple to the Luxor sanctuary, is mirrored in the contemporary festival of Abu el Haggag. The portable shine of the Muslim saint, in the shape of a barque, is carried through the streets in an identically festive, city-wide celebration. Similarly, the spring festival of *Shem al Nessim* ("Sniffing the Air") is observed on the Monday following Coptic (Orthodox) Easter. In villages, dancing, singing, games, and storytelling are reminiscent of the ancient *Heb Nefer en Inet,* "the beautiful festival of the Valley."

For the ancient temple, sunrise signaled the appearance of light and entry of the Neter into the terrestrial sphere; at sunset the god withdrew to the darkness of the sanctuary to await renewal the following day. These were solemn occasions that were honored by diurnal rites of welcoming and retirement, to mark the completion of a life-giving principle and the expectation of its return. In the necropolis, the first sliver of light following the New Moon similarly brought a sequence of rites for the dead that culminated with family visitations and special offerings at the Full Moon. The forces symbolized by the increase of Lunar light were believed to pass into the tomb and, ultimately, to the living. And so by presenting goods to those in the supernatural worlds at these times, the powers of increase were returned to the mundane sphere.

The daily observance of the temple and the periodic observances of the necropolis remained essentially unchanged through the millennia in Egypt. But some occasions called for rites outside of the standard ceremonial agenda, such as the investiture of a new monarch or the renewal of a temple. And as the cosmic landscape shifted over time, observances for the panoply of divinities varied as well, so that some observances came into prominence in particular regions while others receded into the background of the cult. These were unique in character and separate from the regulated schedule of events—appearing in unique times or places, fulfilling the exigencies of transition or need.

The Festivals—*Hebu*

The following set of ceremonies fall under the purview of the Neteru who associate with the Solar cosmogony of our liturgy (the Iru). These ceremonies, the *Hebu* (festivals), honor those Neteru by re-creating their powerful acts or commemorating their special powers, allowing us to integrate their attributes and place them within the scope of our everyday lives. This was a practice innate to Egyptian spirituality, and was accessed by individuals on all levels of society through temple drama, processionals, divinations, and public ritual.

The cycle of festivals that follow are appropriately performed at the times that honor the Neteru they summon. They may be performed within the outlined liturgy following the Pert Kheru Neter (pronouncement of the deity) as a "ceremony within a ceremony," a common practice in Egyptian temples. Or, they may be performed as the public ritual of the modern temple, since the introductory material for each explains the context of the rites. The Full Moon is most appropriate for this, as the temple should welcome the public and newcomers periodically, when the astral light is optimum. And while the Iru are ceremonies of a uniform character, the Hebu are specific and may be reserved for the temple's repertoire of special observances that can be offered to its members whenever the necessity arises. They mark important transitional events both in the lives of the gods and in human society—birth, marriage, crisis, and death.

It is important to remember that the Hebu, as well as the Iru in which they are celebrated, are denoted for observance in the seasonal periods of the Northern Hemisphere for modern times. Some were designated in ancient times for other seasons of the year or the Nile flux, but the natural cycle of each environment—geographic and cosmic—should take precedence in scheduling these ceremonial events.

♈ The Book of Breathings

The cycle begins with *The Book of Breathings*, a text that assumes the initiate's physical detachment from the life force and ceremonially restores it through spells that call upon her return to the living. This is a theme that reflects the restoration of life in the Northern Hemisphere at the spring equinox, symbolized by the first Zodiacal sign of Aries. The rhythm of Cardinal Fire is denoted here, the active spark of life that returns with great vitality following the winter quiescence.

The Book of Breathings is an observance that restores hope, bringing new life to conditions that have, by appearance, been in a state of inertia or inactivity. It is recommended for reversing a static situation, an atmosphere of hopelessness, or an impasse in decisions or actions. It is also a powerful affirmation of life when facing transitional events and allows participants to evoke the powers of recuperation, rejuvenation, and the restoration of personal power.

♉ The Festival of the Joyous Union

In the season of Het-Her, the fecundity that is released from the soil in the early spring is celebrated in *The Festival of the Joyous Union*. The energy dynamic of Taurus, the sign of Fixed Earth, is embodied in the image of the fertile goddess, who joins with her consort at the commencement of the growing season. The union of Sun and Moon in her crown symbolizes, among other things, the fusion of the active life principle (the Sun) with the passive soil (the Moon), which together inaugurate the cycle of proliferation in the natural world (the New Moon).

Het-Her's realm of creative expression—art, music, dance, and performance—becomes accessible through this observance. She also gives boon to affairs of the heart and relationships at a distance that await reuniting. The Festival of the Joyous Union conjoins all polarities and encourages the conception of meaningful endeavors, events that bear fruit and continue to proliferate. It ignites the atmosphere of devotion, commitment, and celebration, being an appropriate festival for weddings, engagement, or handfastings.

♊ The Invocation of Khons

The season of Djehuti commences with the ingress of the Sun into Gemini, a Mutable Air sign that brings about the conversion of divine ideas into physical substance and the transmission of the creative word into the realm of manifestation. The ibis god, translator and recorder of divine acts, is scribe of the Akashic record, the cosmic transcription of every thought and deed. In the mundane world, his realm encompasses experiences in earning, education, and written communications. He may be called upon for events that involve publishing and speaking engagements. And as chief prosecutor in the court of the gods, Djehuti gives wise counsel in legal affairs, especially those that involve contracts, financial judgments, and the settlement of moral obligations.

Djehuti is most importantly the master of divination, and is invoked for developing sight in the astral realm. The oracle of the ancient temple was Khons, the mirror image of Djehuti in the Lunar realm as lord of appearances and transitory manifestations. The Invocation of Khons is an observance that evokes insight into conditions that have not yet fully manifested in the material world, allowing the querent to see them objectively beforehand and perhaps alter their course. Khons is also the deity invoked for protection from the denizens of the shadow worlds, being the exorcist *par excellence* in ancient times. His powers may banish nefarious influences and bring clarity to conditions that have been blocked by opposing forces.

♋ The Lotus Ceremony

In the season of Cancer when the Sun reaches its most northerly position in the sky and the summer solstice brings the longest hours of daylight, the powers of Nebt-Het and the mother goddesses she coalesces in the Solar cosmogony manifest in the full flowering of the seed implanted at the spring equinox.

Cancer, the sign of Cardinal Water, raises the image of Nebt-Het—protectoress of the royal throne, nurse to Heru in his youth, and high priestess in the chamber of transformation for her brother, Asar. She fulfilled these roles with fidelity yet remained in the background of high ritual in the temple, ensuring that disturbing forces would not interfere with sacred acts.

The nurturing of youth and induction of neophytes into the sanctuary feature similar intentions—to awaken the high aspirations of the young soul while safeguarding the inexperienced from powerful forces that are benign but unfamiliar. The Lotus Ceremony embodies these intentions, drawing the mother goddess into the sphere of the awakening soul to protect, instruct, and awaken the senses to sacred realities. Through this process Nebt-Het fulfills her task as mentor and nurse to those who enter the divine territory, ensuring that those awakening to spiritual life are dedicated to Maat, the correct path of natural order.

Nebt-Het's realm also encompasses parenthood, one's responsibility to elders in the family, and the improvement of health, especially conditions that concern the diet and nourishment. The Lotus Ceremony is recommended on the initial entering into the temple, coming of age, ensuring a safe childbirth, and purification following birth for both mother and child.

♌ Anointing into the Temple

Midsummer brings the heat of the season, an evocation of the divine fire emanated by the Fixed Fire sign of Leo. It was this power that alighted upon the waters (the previous season of Cancer) in the cosmogenesis to inaugurate the pulse of life in *sep tepi,* "the first time."

On the attainment of spiritual maturity, the powers of creation become conscious, and their use requires the wisdom of the temple to serve the gods and society in the manner they were intended. In ancient Egypt, members of the clergy, whether in part-time service *(phyloi)* or as permanently dedicated servants of the Neter *(hemu),* were anointed into office. Following this event, a "revelation" of the Neter's mysteries was given in the form of entering the sanctuary and circumnavigating the shrine, allowing the innermost chambers of the Divine House to be viewed. Priests of the various temple disciplines—the provisioners, perfumers, librarians, theurgists—would announce their duties and inform newcomers of their responsibilities in those realms, showing the tools, wands, and sceptres of their office.

The season of Leo encourages spiritual elevation, as it is the rhythm of kingship and honor. This is embodied in rites of initiation, and the Anointing into the Temple may be performed as a formal induction into the modern temple's program of service. An important aspect of this observance is the formal recognition of the neophyte's name and recording it in the temple book. Here, the assumption of one's spiritual identity—which may have been presented six months earlier in the season of Maat (Aquarius)—is acknowledged by the Divine House.

The realm of Heru is concerned with the elevation of one's status through work and family duty. This observance may also be performed on an occasion when one faces such challenges in secular life and the responsibilities may appear to be daunting, or when one's name is voluntarily changed and spiritual acknowledgment is sought for the modification.

♍ The Great Offering Ceremony

The growing season attains its peak in the season of Virgo, the sign of Mutable Earth and the rhythm of nature in its harvesting phase. It is at this time, in preparation for the harvest, that ancient societies gave pause to the work of caretaking the Earth in order to celebrate the transformation of their labor and honor the powers in the land.

Geb, lord of the Earth and ancestral father of the Heliopolitan gods, receded into the background of cult observance in the early years of Egyptian history. His powers were subsumed by the dramatic events of his children's lives—the terrestrial four of Asar, Auset, Nebt-Het, and Set. Nevertheless, it was he who endowed his progeny with the "divine inheritance," the red and black lands, and the throne that founded the Royal House. In this season we are reminded of this inheritance, along with our responsibility to cultivate its potential and pass it on to succeeding generations.

The realm of Geb includes matters concerning the enlargement of home and family—projects involving construction, domestic business, family disputes, and the distribution of property through wills and endowments. This observance may be performed for family reunions, memorial services, and group dedications. It is also appropriate for events of thanksgiving and the dedication of a new domicile.

♎ The Lamentations

In the great Osirian mythos, the body of Asar was discovered broken apart in various sacred places along the Nile, where they were collected and taken to Abydos, the ancestral resting place. His two sisters, Auset and Nebt-Het, performed this task with the intent of reassembling and reanimating his form with the support of the gods. This episode in the saga represents the periodic dissolution and descent of the life force into the deepest regions of the Earth, where it will hibernate for a season and return for a cycle of renewal, growth, and fruition once more.

In the Cardinal Air sign of Libra, the relationship between spirit and matter is temporarily sundered, so that each, separate from its complementary half, may become differentiated and regenerated. In human relationships, this season also represents both union and division, the two faces of spiritual experience that arise in the sacred marriage embodied by Auset and Asar.

The Lamentations speak of this division between spirit and matter, as well as the grief caused by the separation and disunity that follows. It also assures us in the season preceding the diminishment of light that its return will restore our wholeness once more.

As *Ur Hekau* ("great of magic"), Auset's realm includes healing from psychic illness and poisoning from any source. She also brings resolution to inequitable circumstances, mends family and friendship disputes, and offers protection in travel to foreign countries. The observance is appropriate for facing loss and separation, and establishing or restoring our commitments to agreements and relationships, as well as ensuring fidelity in marriage.

♏ Empowerment of the Ushabtiu

In the season of Fixed Water, we anticipate the diminishment of light, the inexorable powers of life and death that must be faced in the coming time of hibernation. And while we are reminded of our mortal limitations, the alchemy of nature mirrored in the sign of Scorpio demonstrates how decaying matter may be transmuted into higher substance and life is thereby renewed.

The highest magic may be summoned to work with the natural forces that allow such transitions to occur without loss of one's psychic assets. Those include the wisdom acquired from Earthly experience, benefits accrued from good works, and the reservoir of personal power that is developed from harmonious engagements with the natural world. The ancient Egyptians valued these qualities, as testimonials inscribed in tombs over the millennia reveal. Deeds such as assisting the poor, rebuilding canals along the Nile, and heeding the words of sages are described with pride and as evidence that the soul was qualified for divine rewards.

Such rewards could be delayed or even denied if an individual evaded certain responsibilities on Earth. Yet with the wise application of Heka, even these obstacles could be overcome. The observance of Empowering the Ushabtiu could summon helpful spirits, in the image of the owner, to perform the work and free the soul from the drudgery of the lower worlds. Such "helpers" are essential in realms that pose difficult challenges.

Anpu is master of the shadow worlds, the "opener of the ways." As such, he is the faithful companion of the theurgist, imparting the knowledge to find a path through the limitations and obstacles of the astral realm. He may be called upon to assist in settling the affairs of the departed, and resolving problems with causes that are obscure or complicated. He also provides protection of personal property and psychic defense when entering unknown regions or experiences.

↗ Honoring Imhotep

In the season of Mutable Fire, the rhythm of Sagittarius evokes the healing powers of beings who have served both mortals and the gods. In the Greek tradition, which modern astrology mirrors, the sign represents the centaur Chiron, who taught the physician Asklepios the healing art.

The art of healing in Egypt was a time-honored profession, and modern physicians continue to express amazement at the depth of knowledge and skill their predecessors demonstrate in the medical papyri that have come to light.

The sage Imhotep was known even in ancient times as the pinnacle of human achievement—his mastery included architecture, astronomy, theology, and medicine. Of the latter, his reputation grew through the ages, and by Graeco-Roman times his healing temples throughout Egypt were places of pilgrimage by every traveler in the civilized world. As a physician, he was known as the "son of Sekhmet-Bast," one of the highest honors that could be imparted on the ancient healer.

The realm of Sekhmet-Bast is the healing fire, which purges, seals, and purifies. She is called upon for safe medical treatment, the healing of physical illness, and surgical operations. She also intercedes in serious dissensions, bringing about peace with enemies. Her mediator is Imhotep, the first human being to be deified in the ancient world.

♑ Festival of Sokar

Although associated with the funerary tradition, Sokar truly represents alchemical processes in activity, the entombment of matter in the winter soil and its subsequent transformation. One of his names, "the coffined one," alludes to the phase in the great Osirian mythos when the god was locked in a chest by Set and traveled to sea. Here, the return to the primeval waters and a renewal by emerging from them is symbolized. And death is not the only event that impels this process; incarnation into the physical world is merely the involution of the same powers.

The Festival of Sokar is an acknowledgment of these processes and a reminder of our mortal existence as the darkness of the winter solstice ushers in the isolation of the season. At the same time it generates the expectation of the return to life in the next season, when the hibernating life force awakens in spring.

The powers of Set can be harnessed for use in working constructively with adversaries and superiors. His realm is also entered for resolving financial difficulties and inheritance disputes. The Sokar observance may be performed at midwinter, for events of loss or mourning, and as a remedy to periods of depression. Because of its funerary nature, it is a positive alternative to a memorial service for the departed.

♒ The Presentation of Maat

In the season of Fixed Air, detachment from the physical plane is denoted as the soul approaches the celestial portal. In Aquarius, the goddess Maat requires the fulfillment of social and moral duty by the initiate, and a dedication to the principles of divine harmony. In ancient times, a declaration of those principles was made each time the temple was entered by members of the clergy. And for Pharaoh, who represented human society as a whole in the temple, the periodic rite of presenting Maat was performed to assure the gods that order would continue to be maintained and divine justice would be dispensed by the royal person. The name was given to the goddess as a guarantee of that pledge, therefore name-giving is an appropriate form of offering for this ceremony.

The realm of Maat encompasses all legal circumstances where justice may have been delayed. The inauguration of enterprises is also under her purview, as she was present in her form of Seshat at the dedications of monumental works for the Royal House and temples, and guide for the technical accomplishment of these tasks. She is also the intermediary to her consort Djehuti, the ultimate assessor of human deeds and master of prophetic activities. She may be approached for knowledge through divination and is patroness of apprentices to new professions.

♓ The Book of Hours

In the concluding season of the Solar cycle, the ending of a span of experience is denoted along with the expectation of a beginning. Pisces, the last sign of the Zodiac, draws together all of the powers of the Sun's annual journey and disperses them into the celestial sea, the womb of Nut. It is here, in the realm of Mutable Water, that all souls return to gestate new powers and emerge, reborn, to a new life of challenges and rewards.

The Book of Hours is a reenactment of the vigil maintained by the Neteru, awaiting the reanimation and return of the green god, Asar. It may be observed to alleviate the uncertainty of critical situations, for centering and focusing one's powers in anticipation of formidable events. The realm of Nut is protective; her powers shield the initiate from harmful influences and unseen adversaries.

The Hebu are more than static rituals. They are comprised of words and acts that require the participants to impersonate the gods and re-create divine events in the timeless dimension. When they are performed in the context of drama, they may impart a detachment to the players that is required when working with such profound energies. For the observers, however, considerably intense feelings are also evoked, and this was the aim of ancient dramatic rites.

Sign	Energy Dynamic	Neter	Festival	Service
♈	Cardinal Fire	Asar	*Shai en Sensenu* The Book of Breathings	Restoration
♉	Fixed Earth	Het-Her	*Heb en Sekhen* Feast of the Joyous Union	Wedding, Engagement, Handfasting
♊	Mutable Air	Djehuti	*Wehemu Khonshu Neferhotep* Invocation of Khons	Divination, Exorcism
♋	Cardinal Water	Nebt-Het	*Kheperu em Sesheni* Lotus Ceremony	Birth, Baptismals, Coming of Age
♌	Fixed Fire	Heru	*Khenu Khasyt* Anointing into the Temple	Temple Investiture, Initiation
♍	Mutable Earth	Geb	*Aa Hotep di Nesu* Great Offering Ceremony	Family Resolution, Reunions, Thanksgiving
♎	Cardinal Air	Auset	*Sebehu Djerti* The Lamentations	Grieving, Separations
♏	Fixed Water	Anpu	*Sa em Ushabtiu* Empowerment of the Ushabtiu	Protection, Personal Power
♐	Mutable Fire	Sekhmet-Bast	*Qi en Imhotep* Honoring Imhotep	Healing
♑	Cardinal Earth	Set	*Nen Sokar* Festival of Sokar	Funerary, Commemorative
♒	Fixed Air	Maat	*Hen ek Maat* The Presentation of Maat	Establish Harmony, Reverse Wrongdoing
♓	Mutable Water	Nut	*Shai en Unnut* The Book of Hours	Comfort, Reversal of Peril

Table 20—Order of the Hebu

Shai en Sensenu
The Book of Breathings

Heb en Sekhen
Festival of the Joyous Union

Wehemu Khonshu Neferhotep
Invocation of Khons

Kheperu en Sesheni
Transformation into a Lotus

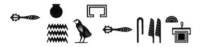

Khenu Khasyt
Anointing into the Temple

Aa Hotep Di Nesu
Great Offering Ceremony

Sebehu Djerti
The Lamentations

Sa em Ushabtiu
Empowerment of the Helpers

Qi en Imhotep
Honoring Imhotep

Nen Sokar
Sokar Festival

Hen Ek Maat
Presentation of Maat

Shai en Unnut
Book of Hours

Figure 49—The Hebu

Shai en Sensenu—The Book of Breathings

This sacred text is also known as *Shai en Wepet Ra er Sensen,* the "Book of Opening the Mouth for Breathing," and Egyptian legend holds that this book was written by the hand of Djehuti himself. Very few copies of it exist, as they were peculiar to a specific time and place in history. All that are known to exist can be traced to a region in Middle Egypt near the ancient city of Per Menu. They were written at the very last stage of Egyptian civilization, in the first century of our era (10–99 C.E.) during the Graeco-Roman period. Moreover, this ritual text appears to have been included solely in the funerary troves of temple priests and priestesses.[1] As such, it implies a ceremony that guarantees a conscious transition into noncorporeal realms.

While this work possesses some of the ritual elements of the *Un Ra* (the Opening of the Mouth ceremony), which animates the lifeless or inanimate, the *Shai en Sensenu* has distinctive features. It is a *conscious* act of reanimation along with entry into a new spiritual reality, the cosmos. It appears to be intended for observance with one already sentient, but it awakens the person into a new realm, where fusion with new powers is possible.

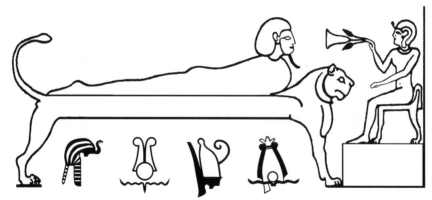

Figure 50—Taiti: The Swathed One

---

1. Epiphanius Wilson, *Egyptian Literature* (New York: The Co-Operative Publication Society, 1901) 385.

The ancient Egyptians recognized that breath is a fundamental attribute of life, and that nature, the gods, and humans depend upon this mechanism in varying forms to exist. But the concept of breathing out or expelling body fluids to infuse life into the inanimate is a concept shared by countless cultures throughout time. Indigenous peoples use an artistic technique that involves chewing the natural materials that produce colors for their rock or sand paintings; in the process they exhale or spit the paint upon the images they draw. They consider these acts to be simulations of the spiritual creation of the universe, and anthropologists believe that this technique has been used from time immemorial—from Neanderthal cave dwellers to Australian Aborigines in the present. In these acts of creating art, the artist becomes both creator and the creation. For the Egyptians, this approach was a fundamental part of the process in giving life, extending it, and renewing it for the recipient. The Book of Breathings fulfills this, and marks the transition to a new life with a full restoration of one's physical and conscious faculties on integrating with cosmic life.

Taiti
"Swathed One,"
the ceremonial image of Asar

Figure 51—Taiti: The Name of Asar Awaiting New Life

Observance

Inscriptions from the island of Philae at the southern frontier of Egypt disclose the sacred tradition of Asar's sanctuary on the neighboring island of Biga, where the holy shrine of Asar existed for thousands of years. Called *Iat Senmut* (the *Abaton* of the Greeks), the shrine received offerings every ten days, at the shifting of the dekanal asterisms in the sky that marked the changing weeks of the year. Here, priests from *Iat Uabet*, Auset's temple on Philae (to the east), journeyed to reenact the visitation of the goddess to the tomb of her fallen husband. The legend at Philae describes 365 altars surrounding the island of Biga, upon which daily offerings of milk and bread were placed. The most solemn conduct was required, and even music was forbidden.

The Egyptians saw the Nile's primeval source at this sacred place, symbolized as a serpent-wound cave that enclosed the god Hapi. His association with Asar is distinctive, as both represent the life-giving powers of the inundation cycle. Hapi embodies the waters of life, and Asar the soil or substance that brings life into being. Their intrinsic relationship was one upon which all depended in the Nile Valley, and their sacred places shared the powers they brought forth.

The Book of Breathings is believed to be in part the ritual recitation of the goddess, as she "created wind" with her wings in the form of a female falcon to cause her husband to breathe. It was reenacted during the ten-days' visit of her priesthood to the Abaton. This would explain why the observance remained undisclosed until the very end of the ancient era, when many of the details of the esoteric tradition reappeared for one last expression of veneration by the faithful.

The Sacred Islands
Iat Senmut
"The mound of breathing," Biga

The Sacred Islands
Iat Uabet
"The pure mound," Philae

Figure 52—The Sacred Islands

This observance is also appropriate for performance during the Lunar eclipse, a period that denotes the diminishment of Asar's powers symbolized by the darkened face of the Moon. The hekau of the ritual allow the Lunar powers of illumination, which take place at the Full Moon (Lunar eclipse), to remain active.

A votive offering to Taiti is made in this ceremony, consisting of water, natron, and incense. Legend also mentions the use of the *erdi tchau,* a flint sceptre whose name means "breath giver."

Dramatis Personae

An important role in rites of transformation is that of the *Iunmutef,* the "pillar of his mother," or representative son of Auset who serves as high priest in the mystical act of restoring his father's sovereignty and the powers of the gods in the temple. As Heru, he protects the "throne of Egypt" (the true meaning of Auset's name) and actively wields the transformative forces of his predecessor in the sacred places—temple and tomb. He "holds steady" the mummy in funerary ceremonies and accompanies the goddess on her important missions for the sake of the fallen god in temple rites. He wears the spotted leopard skin and the sidelock of youth; his role is equivalent to the Setem priest who provides the ritual offerings.

The divine scribe Djehuti provides the recitations and directs the actions of the ritual, just as he endowed the goddess with the divine words that gave breath to her husband at his revival. The ancient rubric states that this role may be assumed by the Kher Heb.

An individual known as *Taiti,* the "swathed one," embodies the ceremonial image of Asar. He also represents all present who may be recipients of the lifegiving infusion of the ritual. This role may be assumed by the Hem Ka, whose patron is Asar.

Nebt-Het stands at the head of the bier while Auset's station is at the feet of Taiti. Much of their work takes place in the metaphysical dimension, as they ritually emulate the passage of divine breath from their stations to the inert form of the swathed one.

Hekau

Djehuti This commences the Book of Breathings,
Made by Auset for her brother Asar:
To give your soul life, to give your body life,
To restore all of your members anew,
That you may reach the horizon of your father the Sun.
That you may ascend to the sky in the orb of the Moon,

And your form may shine in the Orion stars that rest in Nut.
So that this may happen to you
It must be concealed, done in secret;
Let it not be disclosed to anyone's eyes.
It behooves one who is in the Duat and one among the living,
It allows you to live anew in this world, millions of times.

Iunmutef   I come to you, divine chiefs,
Ia kher ten djatdjat aatu,
I bring you the swathed one.
An na ten Taiti.

Nebt-Het   My arms are behind you, they protect your limbs.
I am your sister, beloved of your heart.
I am your protection. Your two sisters restore your limbs.
Wenen iem sa eny seneti sau dja hau-ek.

Auset   My arms are before you, they restore your limbs.
I am your sister, beloved of your heart.
I protect your limbs with my two hands, restoring your form.
Ien-ek senet ek khui i hau ek aui her sau dja djet-ek.

Iunmutef   May you awake at my voice and arise at my speech:
Nehes-ek em kherui pa i-ek em djedi:
May you return to your youthful vigor,
Wehema-ek erpi,
May you be given the sweet air of the north wind.
Iu en-ek tchau nedjen en mehyt.

Djehuti   May life be given you,
That your bones shall knit together and your limbs be firm.
May your muscles be rejuvenated and your spine upright,
That you shall be renewed with the lord of Abydos.

Nebt-Het   You join with the gods of the western mountains,
You are favored at the offering tables.
You receive incense and libations,
You drink the water of rejuvenation.

Auset Every flower is brought to you, every plant
You will pass your time in contentment.
You see the Sun at dawn, the Moon in rising,
You receive favor from the mighty ones in Heliopolis.

Iunmutef Hail swathed one, you are pure.
Aha Taiti, uab-ek.

(incense) Your heart is pure,
Uab ab-ek

(water) Your limbs are purified,
Uab atu-ek.

(natron) You are purified with natron,
Nuk-ek hesmen,
Your form is cleansed.
Uab sekhem-ek.

Auset To you I send winds for your nostrils,
Hu en na ek nifu er fet-ef,
The north wind that comes forth from Atum himself.
Mehit-u en seraui ek pert Atum.
I have restored your lungs.
Sek na sek heti ek.

Nebt-Het I have come for your protection.
Ia una em sa-ek.
Amun gives you breath,
Tu en-ek Amun pa tchau,
Shu gives you the north wind.
Tu en-ek Shu ta menhet.

Djehuti I am the nose of the lord of winds, who makes mortals live.
Nuk fent pu en neb nifu seankh rekhit.
Your soul shall breathe forever and ever
Your form shall be endowed with life on Earth

You shall be in the heart of Ra
Your members shall become the members of the creator.
Water will be poured for you at the 365 offering tables
Those that grow beneath the great trees of Iat Senmut.
Lord of Abydos: your limbs are joined together,
The pain that has afflicted you has been put to an end.

Taiti   Hail Atum, grant to me the sweet breath from your nostrils,
A Atum, tat-ek na nifu pui net em ami sert-ek.
Hail Nut, grant to me the water and air that dwell within you.
A Nut, tat-ek na em mu nifu amet.
I live, I smell the air.
Ankh-a, sesen-a nifu.

Djehuti   You have received the spell of respirations,
That you may breathe with your soul in the lower heaven,
That you may make any transformation at will
Like unto the inhabitants of the West.
Your soul may go wherever it desires,
Living on Earth forever and ever.

Heb en Sekhen—Feast of the Joyous Union

The gods of ancient Egypt knew the pangs of joy brought by love as much as the pain brought by separation. A recognition of the healing power of loving unions between god and goddess, man and woman, and spirits in the kingdom of nature permeate temple ritual, and in some instances formed the basis of great festivals. Many of these events coincided with peaks in the agricultural rhythm of the Nile, one of which took place in the season of Shemut ("deficiency of water"), when the harvest began.

The Feast of the Joyous Union—*Heb en Sekhen* ("festival of the embrace")—was an annual celebration of vast proportion, an enactment of the reunion between Heru and Het-Her. The priesthood from both of their great temples, Heru's seat at Edfu and Het-Her's at Dendera, joined forces to carry the goddess' image on an elaborate barge with hundreds of attendants south to her consort's domain. Legend has it that Kleopatra VII emulated this ritual journey of the goddess to her spouse when she traveled in a golden boat from Alexandria to the encampment of Marcus Antonius at Tarsus in 41 B.C.E. In Plutarch's *Lives,* it is reported that the scented procession wafted a perfume in the air that intoxicated an entire Roman legion.

Figure 53—The Goddess Brings the Consort to Her Priestess

At Edfu, a week-long set of rituals to honor the divine pair melded some of the great temple traditions of Upper Egypt into one marathon ceremony involving the entire populace. To start, an offering of the first fruits of the harvest was made at the temple, followed by the ritual of opening the mouth of the gods' images in the surrounding temples and domiciles. Another important rite was the *Het Behsu,* the "driving of the calves." Indigenous only to the Edfu temple, the symbolic tramping of grain was performed by the four temple calves of Het-Her—each with a coat of black, red, white, and speckled color. This rite ensured the departure of serpents in the harvest grain heaps, just as the reptiles in legend sought to prevent Heru's ascendancy to the throne.

An offering of *maat* ("truth, order") was then made to the gods by the monarch, to allow the year's events to proceed without interference. It was followed by a great revel, the *Heb Teknu* ("festival of intoxication"). Recalling the goddess' drunken rampage to destroy the first race of human beings who defied her father, Ra, the event celebrated her failure to do so by drinking beer, colored by the gods to appear as blood, and thus satiate her rage.

Summer occurs in different months in the Northern and Southern Hemispheres in modern times. For this reason, the Feast of the Joyous Union is appropriately celebrated in late spring and particularly in the season of Taurus, the sign that mirrors the powers of Het-Her and her family. There are also curious parallels between the tradition of drinking the new May wine, the commencement of the wedding season, and the ancient observances in the name of this goddess at this time.

Observance

Marriage ceremony was apparently an informal observance in ancient Egypt. Surprisingly, the legal dimension took far more precedence in secular life, but the spiritual bonds between people were not overlooked, either. Thus, when two individuals pledge a consecrated union, this ceremony allows the formality to assume the profound dimension that the ancients recognized and celebrated.

Nor were the Egyptians arbitrary on same-sex unions. Several tombs depict unrelated men in loving embrace, and it appears that restrictions against such relationships depended on alternating social mores through the ages. In some of the funerary "declarations of innocence," such behavior is alluded to be immoral, though in other versions it is never mentioned.

Certain plants were regarded as appropriate offerings to the gods of erotic experience. One of the funerary pieces in the Tutankhamun collection depicts his wife, Ankhesenamun, presenting mandrake plants, an offering that suggests the virility she arouses in her consort. And at Dendera, offerings to Het-Her include the pomegranate, viewed as a symbol of the vulva by the ancients. Lettuce was considered an aphrodisiac, as well as the lotus flower. Offerings that emulate these symbolic gifts are appropriate to this ceremony.

The life-bestowing sounds of sistra and menat necklace rattles form an important segment of this ceremony, honoring in part the rhythmic powers of Het-Her. The written record of the festival of intoxication also mentions that red beer, dyed with pomegranate juice and red hibiscus flowers, was dispensed by the temples in brilliant blue faience cups. These are the colors of the one who was called "Mistress of Turquoise." Collars of fragrant blossoms, woven to represent the *Usekh,* the collar of the goddess that bestows her life-giving breath, were worn in these celebrations. And ancient travelers reported that the air was filled with clouds of myrrh incense throughout the event.

At Dendera, the union of the gods took place at the New Moon, in the eighth hour (proceeding from dawn). The couple may return to the temple on the fifth day to make an offering, as legend says that Ihy, the child of Heru and Het-Her, was conceived on the fourth night of their union. His powers to bring peace to the marriage are evoked by this gesture.

Dramatis Personae

The Setem performs the initial offering on behalf of the couple. Accompanying the pair are the *Shebtiu,* the nine ancestor gods of the Edfu temple, who receive the first offerings and preside as attendants and witnesses to the ceremony. One or more individuals may represent this honored body, who also take the role of the immediate ancestors of the couple.

A female Khener, whose patron is Het-Her, assumes the form of the goddess. In this ceremony, she presides as "Mistress of Virgins," one of the goddess' names. In this role she provides husbands for her favorite priestesses, thus eliminating the role of "best man" in Western wedding observances. Here, it is the goddess who brings the consort to her priestess, who has first invoked her in the sanctuary.

Hekau

I. The Offering

Setem   I offer pure things, giving the beer of truth,

              Iu wabu, di henqet en maat,

              Giving the divine food of everlastingness,

              Di en djefa en neheh,

              To the ancestral spirits in the sacred land.

              En heri djadjat ta djeser.

II. Invocation to Het-Her [2]

Bride   Homage to you, Het-Her in Heliopolis!

              Your crown is of brilliant gold, your brow is electrum.

              When you shine, all rejoice in your light,

              All living beings and every god.

              Come, mistress of the Neteru,

              Make your face gracious to me on this day.

              (The sistra and menat are sounded.)

Shebtiu   Spirits of the eastern sky, gods who rule the western shores,

              All who rejoice at the sight of the golden one,

              Who love to see her beauty risen.

              Tell her that we rejoice at her coming,

              That our hands are open to her, that we invoke her.

III. Appearance of the Goddess and Consort

Setem   Het-Her, Lady of the sycamore:

              Receive this offering on the day of your appearing,

              And from it may we be rewarded by your goodness.

              We are illumined by the light that comes forth from your crown,

              We are rejuvenated by the rays of your dekan stars.

---

2. Adapted from an inscription at the Abydos temple of Seti I.

We follow in your pathway into the lightland of Manu,

To the abode of generations wherein we were born.

(Red beer is offered by the Setem to all present.)

IV. Pledges

Bride   Come in peace, beautiful one,

Iui em hotep amit.

I have come to you with a heart of love.

I-kua kher ten em ab merut,

May your life be devoted to the honor of your beloved.

Ankh ek qendet em tu-ek senenti tu em meri-ek.

Consort   I am he who will arouse you with endless music,

Every day, at every hour,

To your Ka, wherever it may be.

May you be at peace with these sounds,

May you go forth in happiness,

May you rejoice in gladness with Heru,

Your consort who loves you.

(The sistra and menat are sounded.)

V. Blessing of the Couple[3]

Shebtiu   Het-Her, lady of the living, dweller in the heavenly barque,

Het-Her, nebet ankhiu, amit uaa en pet,

Golden one, eye of Ra who is upon his brow,

Nubet, maat Ra amit hat-ef,

Beautiful face in the barque of a million years:

Neferet em uaa en heh:

Grant the seat of peace for this right and true act,

Tat auset hotep en ari maat

For the favored ones before you.

Em khennut en hesiu her-ek.

Khener   I am the coiled one, the divine eye:

Nuk mehnyt neteret,

---

3. Adaptation of chapter 186 of *The Book of Going Forth by Day.*

I come to the august beings.
Per-i en shepses.
Beloved ones: life is yours in very great peace.
Meriu: iu ankh en-ek em hotep nefer uret.

V. Censing of the Couple

Setem   The revered goddess protects your limbs,
Au shepset em sa en hau-ek,
Seed is within you, to make that which is becoming.
Mu am-ek, en ari unnut.

Bride   I am protection behind him.
Nuk sa ha-ef.

Consort   I am protection behind her.
Nuk sa ha-es.

Wehemu Khonshu Neferhotep— Invocation of Khons

Khons, patron of divination and exorcism, is the Neter who bridges the divinatory powers of Djehuti (in the season of Gemini) and the reflective, healing powers of Nebt-Het (in the following season of Cancer). In the Egyptian calendar, he is regent of the ninth Solar month *Pa en Khonshu* (Pachons) and in sacred astronomy, the Neter of the *neomenia*—the first New Moon of the New Year.

At his exclusive domain at Karnak, he was known as *Khons-Djehuti Neferhotep*, "he who vanquishes the powers of darkness." A legend at this Theban temple discloses the circumstances of the god's banishment of a possessing spirit in the New Kingdom. The story tells of a princess Bentreshy, the sister of Raneferu, one of the queens of Rameses II. The girl's brother, the prince of Bekhten, sent an appeal to Egypt for the assistance of Pharaoh's magician-priests in delivering her from the illness. The oracle of Khons was approached on the matter, and the Neter consented to help after the oracular consultation. Subsequently, the priests of the temple undertook a journey to the distant kingdom in the company of a small statue in which the great statue of Neter at the temple had charged its spirit into the smaller one. It was brought to confront the demon, and "the Neter thereby made peace with it." A great shrine to Khons was established in Bekhten afterward.

In addition to his divinatory powers, Khons has a special association with the placenta, which the Egyptians believed was the body's twin, its undeveloped mirror image. As such, this deity represents unmanifest life, that which is "becoming." He is also patron of the royal Ka, its protector and custodian. He embodies the potentiality of the royal soul, all that once existed and all that shall be. He is past and future, the unrealized culmination of royal power. From this symbolism, it is obvious why the Neter held sway over oracular activities and the astral world.

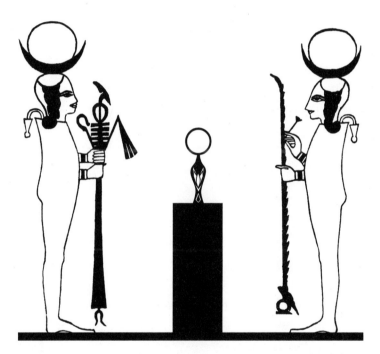

Figure 54—Images of Khonshu Neferhotep: Khons, Neter of Lunar powers, endows the royal sceptres that grant sovereignty over the myriad realms of transitory phenomena. He is also chronocrator of linear time, of phases and transitions from the visible to the invisible worlds. In his aspect as Khonshu Neferhotep, he is exorcist and peacemaker.

Observance

The spell for invoking Djehuti is initially recited, to protect the ceremonial proceedings from invading spirits. This draws the essential functions of both gods to exorcise malevolent influences. An offering to the image of Djehuti is then made in the form of scribal instruments: writing paper, pen, and ink. These are received by the Kher Heb, who is now prepared to record any phenomena, auditory or otherwise, that may arise from the ceremony.

Khons is then approached to provide responses to questions or conditions that the temple may authorize for answers. The mode of divination is left up to the Sentyt, who should choose her most proficient medium. However, the method of choice is the scrying bowl or mirror, an honored tradition in the Egyptian temple. The bowl may be filled with water from a vase, and temple oil is sprinkled on it to create a reflective surface. The bowl should also be generously censed before it is examined. Temple mirrors were fashioned of copper and kept covered in wooden boxes; they were likewise anointed and censed before use.

The atmosphere of divination should be one of reverence, though it is tempting for those new to the process to have unrealistic expectations or impatience for not receiving information in a manner they can easily understand. The ancient oracles were never hurried, nor were they expected to demonstrate their powers for frivolous purposes. Entering the realms of divine insight should be undertaken with appreciation for its benefits, and for the observers, respect for the stamina required to consummate it successfully.

Dramatis Personae

The Kher Heb, whose patron is Djehuti, officiates in this ceremony. She is assisted by the Sentyt, whose patron is Maat, consort of Djehuti. Together, they invoke the gods of divination and interpret the phenomena that arise from these acts. To preserve the integrity of the ceremony, all results from the divination should be disclosed after its conclusion.

Hekau

I. *Spell Invoking Djehuti*[4]

Kher Heb   Come to me, Djehuti, noble ibis,

Who issues forth from Khmennu,

Letter writer of the Ennead, great one who dwells in Iunu.

Come to me, provide me with your counsel,

Make me skillful in your calling.

Better is your livelihood than all others,

It allows men and women to become great.

Those who master it are found fit to hold office,

Many are such whom you have supported.

They are now among the Great Council,

They are strong and affluent through your help.

You are the sole one who provides counsel,

Fate and destiny emanate from you.

Come to me, lend me your wisdom,

For I am a servant of your house.

I will disclose your honorable acts wherever I may be,

And the multitudes will say, "Great are the deeds of Djehuti."

They will come, bringing their children to assign them your calling,

It is a great work that pleases the Neteru.

They are happy who perform it.

Sentyt   I am your palette Djehuti,

Nuk mesetchi-ek,

I have brought you your ink jar.

Se ari na nek pesek.

Lord of speech, lord of purifications, lord of the justified,

Neb djed, neb uabu, neb maakheru,

Who knows the balance,

Rekh merkhet,

---

4. Adapted from Papyrus Anastasi.

Annalist of gods and men, he who makes whole the eye,

Nekheb genut en neteru nar-et, shuja uadjat,

He who hears, Djehuti, lord of laws: come to me.

Sheten, Djehuti, neb hapu: iem en-i.

(The offering to Djehuti is presented.)

Kher Heb   I am the keeper of the book,

Of that which is, and of that which shall be.

Nuk ari sapu en enti, unen.

I am yesterday, I know tomorrow.

Nuk sef, ekh kua tuau.

II. Spell Invoking Khons

Sentyt   Divine one, come into being in the temple of the brilliant Moon.

Neteri, peri en het iah sabati.

Sublime of magic: join your image with Djehuti

Heb menekh hekau: chenem seshemu-ef her Djehuti

In the eastern horizon of the sky.

Im akhet iabetet net pet.

Lord of Thebes, child of the hidden one: come to me.

Neb Waset, mes es amun: iem en-i.

Kher Heb   I come forth that you may see.

Per kua her maa-ek.

Sentyt   Glorious one: come to the mouth of my vessel,

Imy ba: en-i heru emen netet en asey,

And tell me in truth everything that I shall inquire of.

En mehu, wehen metet maat.

(The divination proceeds and is recorded.)

Kheperu em Sesheni—The Lotus Ceremony

The *kheperu em sesheni,* "transformation of the lotus," is the name of a spell in *The Book of Going Forth by Day.* It endows the initiate with the power to become a divine youth, as Nefertum arose from the primeval waters in the beginning of time.

Figure 55—The Lotus Ceremony

Inscriptions show that the extract or tincture of the Egyptian blue lotus was made by infusing wine with the flower, which was then drunk in ceremony and celebration. Recent investigations into the properties of this plant disclose remarkable facts about the manner in which it was used in ancient times. The phytosterol signature of the lotus flower includes three bioflavonoids (primarily responsible for the color in plants but containing powerful antioxidant properties). These are found in many known herbs; their physiological effects closely resemble—but are more concentrated than—ginseng and gingko biloba (especially the latter). Effects include the stimulation of blood flow and aphrodisiac qualities. Well-known for their expertise in herbal medicine in the ancient world, the Egyptians valued the blue lotus for its beauty, perfume, and the sense of well-being it promoted. In symbolism, the flower represents health, enhanced sexuality, and rebirth.

All of these qualities reflect episodes in human experience of creative awakening, both spiritual and physical. At adolescence, when the creative force becomes conscious, ancient societies established rites of passage into this wondrous and powerful sphere. Instruction in the proper use of these powers was conveyed, often in ceremonies that reenacted the mysteries of the primeval creation—the emergence of new life from the waters of the celestial ocean.

Similarly, the life-giving acts of partuition and nursing evoked other meaningful observances to ancient people—rites that recognized that the forces that brought all life into being are also innate to human beings. The so-called "purification" for new mothers in such times was in reality an acknowledgment of this power to bring life, symbolized by anointing and baptismal ceremonies of mother and child that once more mirrored the primordial genesis.

Both *The Book of Going Forth by Day* and the Pyramid Texts feature episodes of the soul entering a divine state and assuming the form of a lotus. In these texts, one ascends from the Earth, and a sacred island is reached in a timeless realm where the gods of creation—Nun, Ra, and Khepera—exist in repose. Upon this ascent, the initiate comes to realize the essential bond between human and divine life that defines the meaning and purpose of the new existence that has been entered. As a result, these very powers may be awakened within, and one's potential for their expression may be realized.

Observance

The Lotus ceremony consists of a purification and dedication, a sequence of ritual bathing, censing, and anointing that is followed with a pledge by temple mentors to guide the soul through the new territory. All are symbolic acts, though in high ritual the purifications were performed in the outer court of the temple, and the dedication took place in the Hall of Appearings, immediately outside of the sanctuary. The initiate may approach the inner sanctum, but entry is reserved for events associated with the next cycle in Leo, in celebration of the Anointing into the Temple.

Depending on resources, the temple may elect to perform either the Gasu Nedj ("small anointing") or Gasu Ur ("great anointing"). The initiate receives new raiment (a temple gown or shawl), and an image of Nefertum or a single lily flower is placed in his or her hands. In the *mammisi* ("birth houses") of the great temples, reliefs show mothers and their children bringing fragrant flowers and herbs as offerings to the god of the locale who appears as the Divine Child. Likewise, the initiate may bring a floral offering that will be presented at the conclusion of the ceremony, on approaching the sanctuary.

Dramatis Personae

The initiate possesses the central role in this ceremony, which is the assumption of Nefertum's image and the Solar powers that accompany this Neter.

The Senu and Uab perform the purifications, and the Hem Neter, whose patron is Nebt-Het, officiates at the dedication. If the ceremony is performed for a coming of age, the parents perform the purification. If it is done on behalf of a new mother and child, the temple will perform the purifications for both and the mother will read the initiate's recitations.

Hekau

I. The Ceremonial Bathing

Uab   O thou lotus, who came into being in Manu:
          May you awaken in the sacred region,
          May you be given a seat there,
          Beside the Neteru who dwell in the horizon.
          May you receive every feast that is offered there,
          On the tables of offering where we will place sacred food
          For those who ascend to eternity.

II. The Anointing

Senu   O thou lotus, Nefertum who dwells in the lightland:
          How fragrant is your odor.
          It is the flame that ascends from the horizon,
          It is the heavenly boat that moors you in the sacred regions.

III. Donning of the Raiment

Uab   Hail to you, who comes forth from the womb
          Herak-a, per em khet
          Your mother Nut gives you birth.
          Mut-ek mes entu.

IV. Gift of the Lotus

Senu   Nefertum, thou great lotus who dwells in Manu:
          Nefertum, nekheb ur khenti en Manu:
          May you awake in beauty.
          Res-ek nefer her tep.
          (The lotus is placed in the initiate's hands.)

Hem Neter Child of the morning, who ascends in the lotus flower.

Ihy en duait, aub per em sesheni,

Beautiful one, you appear in the lightland,

Nefer-tcha, khai-ek em ta aakhut,

You illumine the Two Lands with your rays,

Sehedj-ek taui em satu-ek.

We are joined by your beauty.

Tema-em en neferu-ek.

Uab Welcome in peace.

Iau seper ti em hotep.

Senu Welcome in peace.

Iau seper ti em hotep.

Hem Neter As the primeval being who brought forth the primeval ones,

Em pauti mesiu pautiu tepiu,

Maat appears on your forehead.

Iu Maat kai ti er iat-ek.

Your mother Nut protects you each day.

Chenem tu mut-ek Nut er-au nub.

V. Presentation of the Offering

Initiate I am the plant that comes forth from Nun,

Nuk uneb per em Nu

My mother is Nut.

Mut-a pu Nut.

I am the pure lotus who rises to the god of light,

Nuk sesheni aub per em khu neteri,

I exist as the breath of Ra.

Un-i em as em Ra.

Hem Neter O you primeval ones, take to yourselves this lotus

Who came into being in the beginning,

Who drives away the storm though knows it not.

May your heir shine as a stripling in the newborn sky.

Initiate   Os you gods who are present, grant me your arms.

Amiu bah imma na aaui ten.

I will come into existence among you.

Kheper-na am ten.

Khenu Khasyt—Anointing into the Temple

Egypt's priestly tradition originated in times that elude historical documentation, but legend attributes the ancestral body of the temple to the *Heru Shemsu,* the "followers of Heru." This mystic fraternity was believed to have brought the ceremonial agenda for both temple and tomb to Egypt from an undisclosed motherland, and continued to preserve it through the flawless and unchanging practices of ancient theurgy for the thousands of years that followed. Thus, it is appropriate that upon entering the temple these ancestral beings are recalled and the sacred duty of Heru, son of the gods and soul of the Royal House, is acknowledged as the ideal officiant in the Divine House.

Figure 56—Seti Anointing Min in the Temple: Seti I anoints the image of Min Kaumutef in the Festival of Min Going Forth. Temple of Seti I, Abydos (Dynasty 19).

The Egyptian priest or priestess was anointed into office, a ceremony that entailed the first enactment of the daily ritual: bathing, anointing, censing, and the declaration of purity. In some temples, a fast was observed before this event, though it may have only proscribed certain foods—those considered offensive to the Neter of the temple—over an unknown period of time. The candidate was then formally presented in the temple by the sponsor, often a relative or a higher-grade cleric. The event culminated with entry into the sanctuary, to receive "sight of the Neter," which may have been the first of many or, in some temples, the only opportunity allowed, as one cleric was designated solely to perform the daily ritual of "unveiling the face of the god." A company of sanctuary priests may have acknowledged the consecration by showing the implements of their service in a procession where they were announced or introduced by the Hem Neter. In some temples, the revelation of the Neter's mysteries took place, and this may have taken the form of a ritual, drama, or seclusion in the most sacred area of the temple.

Observance

This ceremony may be preceded by instruction in the temple purification (Gasu Nedj or Gasu Ur) and the donning of the priestly apparel outside of the sanctuary. The candidate brings a generous offering to the temple and should choose a *ren neter* ("divine name") beforehand, preferably in the season of Maat. This will be acknowledged by the priestly body and recorded in the temple book. The candidate is then given "instruction" in the form of exemplary ritual acts. For the lustration, the head is bowed.

There were few vows or pledges made in the Egyptian temple other than to follow the rules of the Divine House being entered. Such promises are in reality only reminders of one's personal and collective dedication, and for the enlightened, they are no longer required when service to the gods becomes a natural exercise in conscious living.

The candidate now enters the "sacred territory" of the sanctuary and is promised protection by the temple in the form of a litany originally recited by Djehuti when he restored the eye of Heru. Here, the adze sceptre is touched upon each member of the body indicated by the recitation. This is another reminder of Heru's role in the maintenance of order as it is enacted by the temple priest and the protection that is received by performing it. It is also a transference of power—when one's faculties are restored, the act is perpetuated through subsequent temple duties performed by the clergy that restore the powers of the gods in the sanctuary.

In conclusion, the ritual gesture closely associated with the Heru Shemsu is given by the temple body in unison—the Henu salutation. It is depicted in both temple and tomb in the concluding scenes of initiation, and in historical annals as part of the rites of victory. The gesture is as follows: The candidate falls on the right knee with the left foot balanced flat on the floor (the right foot is at a ninety-degree angle to the floor). The left arm is raised in salutation with bent elbow. The right arm is extended forward with palm upward in offering, then brought to the chest as it closes, under the heart. The right arm is then re-extended forward with palm upward and the gesture is repeated three times. The recitation "Given life, power, and stability" *(Di ankh, uas, djed)* is spoken as the right hand meets the heart.

Figure 57—The Henu Gesture: The legend of the Heru Shemsu speaks of two priestly castes, the "souls of Pe" and the "souls of Nekhen." The latter, originating in Upper Egypt, possessed the wolf or hound as their emblem. Their sacred precinct at Nekheb was the Per Ur ("exalted house"), a name that is supposed to be the root of the Greek term *pharaoh*. They bestowed the white crown on the king, which was protected by the vulture Nekhebet. The members of these two houses were collectively referred to at times as the "Souls of Heliopolis," and were believed by the Egyptians to have been the body from which the Solar priests at the Heliopolis temple descended.

Dramatis Personae

In the high ritual of the temple, especially for initiating the new monarch into the mysteries of the god's house, a figure emerges who assumes the role of protector, sponsor, and initiator—the *Sameref* ("kinsman, friend").[5] This is a ceremonial role associated with Heru, and her function is similar to that of sponsor in Masonic ceremonies. This role may be assumed by the Maa, whose patron is Heru.

The Uab assists in the candidate's first purification, and accompanies the candidate to the sanctuary. The Kher Heb performs the name entering, and the Setem provides the ceremonial substances of salt, water, bread, and the Hotep tray of offerings, which the candidate will present to the god of the temple.

Hekau

I. Namegiving

Kher Heb   May your name be given to you in the great double sanctuary,
                Erta-ek ren-ek em per ur,
                And may you remember your name in the House of Fire
                Sekha-ek ren-ek em pa Nezer
                On the night of counting years and months.
                En gereh pui en ap renpet en tennut abedju.
                You are with the divine ones,
                Net-ek ami puiu,
                Your seat is upon the eastern side of heaven.
                Hemes-ek her kes abti en pet.
                (The name is written in the temple book.)
                You come before the Neter, appareled in light.
                You enter his/her house, you perform his/her work,
                In your name of *(title).*

II. Instruction

Maa   (Name) Remember how natron is chewed.
           (Salt is administered to the tongue.)
           (Name) Remember how censing is performed in the god's domain.
           (The candidate is censed.)

---

5. *Samer-es:* the feminine form.

(Name) Remember how water is poured from the vase at dawn.

(Water is poured into a vessel and the initiate is lustrated.)

(Name) Remember how bread is prepared

On the day when the head is lustrated.

(Bread is placed in the hand of the initiate.)

(Name) Remember how divine offerings are brought to the gods.

(The Hotep offering tray is presented to the candidate.)

Remember how the pillars are erected,

And how the offering tables are carved.

Remember how the temple is purified,

And how the Divine House is rejuvenated.

Remember how the temple is regulated,

And the observance of days.

Remember the conduct in the god's house.

(Name) Remember and perpetuate these things.[6]

Candidate Homage to you, Heru of the two horizons:

Anedj hra-ek Heru em aakhuti:

Lord of transformations, who created himself.

Neb Khepera, pu kheper djesef.

Doubly beautiful at your appearance in the horizon.

Neferui: uben-ek em akhet.

Lord of the perch: your light illumines the Two Lands,

Neb djeba: se hedj-ek taui,

The gods rejoice when they see you as sovereign of heaven.

Em satu ek neteru nebu em haaui maa sen tu em suten en pet.

(The Hotep tray is presented to the gods.)

III. Protection

Kher Heb I am Djehuti, I come from heaven to protect Heru,

To drive away all poisons that may afflict him/her.

You shall be stable,

You are a son/daughter of Geb, lord of the two eyes,

Residing within the powers of the gods.

Your nose is given to you:

---

6. Adapted from *Admonitions of a Sage*, Dynasty 6.

You shall not inhale the fiery wind.
Your inmost is given to you:
Your strength is great to banish the adversaries of Asar.
Your arms are given to you:
You receive the rank of the green god.
Ptah has balanced your mouth on the day you are reborn.
Your heart is given to you: the *Aten* disc is your protection.
Your right eye is as Shu, your left eye is as Tefnut,
They are the children of Ra.
Your belly is given to you: the children of the gods are in it,
They shall not receive the venom of the scorpion.
Your legs are given to you: Set shall not prevail against you.
Your virility is given to you:
It will provide food for your children in the course of each day.
The soles of your feet are given to you:
You will rule the south and the north, the east and the west.
(The candidate performs the Henu salutation. The assembly follows suit.)

Aa Hotep di Nesu—Great Offering Ceremony

What sort of offering is appropriate to honor the Lord of Offerings? This is the season of the Neter who sustains all living things, and impels them to bring forth the fruit of their own nature as well.

At Edfu, scenes at the rear of the Pylon gateway depict an important temple ceremony, the *Offering to the Shebtiu* ("ancestors"). These beings were believed to be the founders of the temple in antiquity and ever present in the Divine House as guiding spirits. Tradition also said that they were buried in the temple necropolis.

Every temple in Egypt accommodated such events, which were regarded as essential periodic remembrances in the scope of spiritual life. Acknowledgment of the temple's tradition, as well as those who inaugurated and preserved it, was an important dimension of ancient spirituality and was commemorated at regular times to maintain that memory. Along with these rites, the forebears of the community and the Royal House were remembered, as they were also recognized to be part of the spiritual continuity of the temple.

Figure 58—The Offering Procession

The Great Offering Ceremony serves this purpose in the season of Geb, father of the Heliopolitan quaternary of Asar, Auset, Set, and Nebt-Het, and Neter of ancestral origins. The inheritance of Geb, which was often alluded to in the legendary accounts, is the harvest of the land, symbolized by the gathering of the Earth's fruits in the sign of Virgo. But his inheritance is more profound and extensive than cultivated crops. As the divine predecessor, he endows his children with the means to elevate themselves to regions beyond the Earthly sphere. The throne that he endows is the terrestrial sovereignty of the Royal House and the dormant vitality of temporal power, which his firstborn, Asar, assumed and was passed on to Heru and every monarch afterward.

Observance

The Great Offering Ceremony begins with an honor to Geb, the ancestral father. Eight libations are presented, each representing the endowments from the other eight members of the Heliopolitan Ennead, of which Geb is the spiritual father. These libations are the traditional offerings of bread, beer, wine, water, fowl, natron, incense, and sacred oil. A special set of vases, four red (containing the consumables: beer, wine, bread, fowl) and four white (containing the purifications: incense, water, oil, natron), was used in ancient times for this presentation. In the modern temple, these vases may be presented at the altar symbolically (their names may be written in hieroglyphs on the vases) on their own tray. The names of those who are to be remembered are written and also placed on the tray of vases. For the memorial service, photographs may be included.

Symbolic offerings were considered as real and appeasing as material ones in ancient Egypt. The *pert kheru* ("voice offerings") are another example of the power of vocal evocation in Egyptian theurgy. Incriptions on many tombs will address visitors and passersby to read the invocation for providing the deceased with goods, thereby fulfilling the ancient custom of bringing them to the tomb should the descendants and Ka priests fail to do so.

The second part of the ceremony honors the ancestral body, those who have passed on. The Hotep tray(s) that contain the actual food and votive offerings are here proffered. Distribution of these offerings will take place at the conclusion of the ceremony in a communal meal.

In conclusion, the traditional *Hotep Di Nesu* ("royal offering") is given for those who are to be specifically remembered. Here, the Setem assumes the role of Heru, son of Asar, who initially offered sustenance to his deceased father in order to restore his life. Following this theme, the ritual was always performed in the name of the king, who was descendant and representative of Heru; hence the title. As such, the rite was deemed the most powerful that could be offered in a sacred environment.

The version given here is adapted from a Dynasty 12 inscription in the tomb of Senusert, and it should be noted that it is also a spell that appeases the restless spirits of the necropolis, who may be disturbed by those entering their places of rest.

The final recitation extends the benefits of Geb to all who are present.

Saabut
The four purification jars

Nemset
The four offering jars

Irep
Wine

Menket
Linen

Mu
Water

Merhet
Oil

Henket
Beer

Seneter
Incense

Biuk
Grain

Wadju
Herbs

Figure 59—Hotepu—The Traditional Offerings

Hesa
Milk

Semu
Vegetables

Ta
Bread

Hebsu
Clothing

Hotepi
Flowers

Hesmen
Natron

Aped
Fowl

Neshem
Meat

Figure 59—Hotepu—The Traditional Offerings

Dramatis Personae

The Hem Neter and the Setem, whose patron is Geb, officiate in this event. They are assisted by the Uab, who may bring the Hotep trays into the sanctuary when it begins, present them at the altar, and remove them to another area in the sanctuary when the recitations are concluded. For the memorial service, members of the family may present the trays to the Uab.

Hekau

I. Presentation to the Lord of Offerings[7]

Hem Neter An invocation offering for the revered great ancestor Geb,
      Father of the gods:
      Pert kheru en imaki urpa Geb, it neteru:
      Your *sekhem* is nigh upon you,
      You are established, chief of all powers, Bull of Nut
      Who throws out his one hand to heaven and his other toward
      Earth.
      The eight libations are presented to you,
      Before your altar of tchehent.[8]
      The nemset, the saabut are brought forth
      From the Divine House.
      They are given to you, O Geb, who arises in peace.
      (The offering vases are presented.)

Setem Lord of Offerings, greatly esteemed one:
      Behold, we have brought you these offerings,
      That you may live thereby and we may live thereby.
      Be gracious to us,
      Avert any anger that is in your heart against us.

II. Presentation to the Ancestors

Hem Neter O you who provide abundance,
      Who take provisions from the fields,
      Give unto them that they may be satisfied,
      Let them have abundance in the Field of Offerings, *Sekhet Hetepet*
      Let them have peace in the Field of Reeds, *Sekhet Iaru.*

Setem To my forebears who existed before me:
      En itui kheperu en hati:

---

7. Adapted from chapter 14 of *The Book of Going Forth by Day.*

8. Tchehent: crystal.

Thousands of bread, linen garments, wine, and fowl,
Khau em ta, menket, arep, aped,
Thousands of divine offerings, all things good and pure
Khau hotep neteri, khet neferet uabet
Given in their memory . . . (names)
Di en ka . . . (names)
(The Hotep trays are presented.)

Hem Neter O Geb, chief of the Neteru, grant to me and my family,
My children, my brethren, my father, my mother,
Those who serve me and my dependents:
Remove them from the acts of Set
And the numbering by any god or goddess,
From any spirits male or female.
(Silent remembrance.)

III. Hotep Di Nesu—Royal Offering

Setem A royal boon given in the name of Asar, lord of Busiris,
Hotep di nesu Asar ren net, neb djedu,
Neter of greatness, sovereign in Abedju.
Neter ay-a neb abedju,
(Name) is given invocation offerings and refreshment
(Name) Di-ef pert kheru em et henket
(Name) is given all things good and pure on which the Neteru live.
(Name) Di ef khet het nebet neferet uabet ankhet neter em,
In the name of the revered one (Name), the justified.
En ka en imakhi (Name) maakheru.

Hem Neter From the cavern of Hapi refreshment is given, *(water is offered)*
From the breast of Nut sustenance is given, *(beer is offered)*
From the house of Geb strength is given, *(bread is offered)*
From the fields of Hotep an offering is given, *(wine is offered)*
From the estate of Nefertum libation is given. *(oil is offered)*
May the lord Geb be gracious to you, may he extend love to you
Geb hesy-ef tu, mery-ef tu
May he grant you prosperity, may he overthrow your enemies.
Se uadj-ef tu, sekher-ef khefiu ek.

Sebehu Djerti—The Lamentations

The passage of the Sun across the sky through the seasons has throughout the ages marked episodes of profound consequence in nature that alter the course of human activity and in turn, the awareness of spiritual realities. When the orb of the Sun approaches the constellation of Libra at dawn, the season of fall begins and ushers in a short period of equal light and darkness, followed by a lengthening of the night that heralds the dark of winter.

Figure 60—An Osirian Mourning Scene: All observances for the dead in ancient Egypt were re-creations of the Osirian funeral. At the same time, the departure of vital force in the land was also regarded as the death of the god, though the expectation of his return was closely woven into his rituals. The two mourning sisters, Auset (right) and Nebt-Het (left), were always present at the funerary scene—an allusion to their role in reviving the departed soul.

In concert with these cosmic events, the cycle of mysteries commenced in ancient times. The departure of agricultural powers that comes with the autumnal equinox in the Northern Hemisphere is a signal of both regret and preparation, a reminder of the diminishing flux of life that must be honored and preserved for the longed-for renewal of the next spring. But these mysteries were not only an acknowledgment of the change in the celestial current. They were also an opportunity to descend, as the Sun descends in the southern horizon in the latter half of the year, to the realm of dark powers that confine the body but renew the soul in the darkness of the season.

Within a vast repertoire of ceremonies that comprised the mysteries of Asar celebrated annually throughout Egypt, *The Lamentations* emerge as the most powerful and the most poignant. It is at this stage in the great saga of the god's life, death, and renewal that his sisters Auset and Nebt-Het have lovingly reassembled his broken body and realize the loss that his absence represents to themselves and to all of Egypt. Their laments convey the grief of this event, as well as the sorrowful hope that by calling his soul back into the world of life, he will return restored and whole to them. This observance is a metaphor of both the season and human mortality; it evokes our power to withdraw into the invisible sky, surrender to its powers, and thereby ourselves find the means to becoming whole and restored.

The Lamentations contrast sharply with the Book of Breathings (associated with the spring equinox in the opposite season of Aries), which was also a part of the mystery rites of Asar. In the latter, the restoration of Asar takes place and his visage transforms from black (hibernation) to green (germination). But now, following the course of nature, the god who brings life must withdraw for a time and seek his own creative source in the world beyond nature.

It is the two sister goddesses (*djerti:* female hawks) who now assume the powers of nature in the mystery cycle that commences in the fall and concludes in the spring. Auset and Nebt-Het furnish the rites, the invocations, and the vigils that will ensure a return of the creative forces. At the same time, they are the vehicles for those forces to come forth in their time. Nebt-Het is "the lord's house," and Auset is "the throne." Together, they establish the framework through which divine powers return to life in the phenomenal world.

The Lamentations were performed throughout all of Egypt to inaugurate the ceremonies comprising Asar's mysteries, but the most commanding event took place at Abydos, where weeks of observances occurred to honor the death, restoration, and renewal of the god. The entire city, including the necropolis and all the temples in the region, reenacted the funeral of Asar and his interment in the sacred soil of the ancient burial ground. Statues in his image of grain, clay, and earth were assembled and mystically infused with his powers to ensure the fertility of the Two Lands in the next cycle of growing and harvest.

Observance

According to a Ptolemaic papyrus of *The Lamentations,* the performance took place on the 25th of Choiach, a date that corresponds to the Sokar Festival in the Lower Kingdom (a few days before the winter solstice). In ancient Egypt, this was the time of year that Orion receded from the night sky and did not return to visibility for approximately three months. And while it was performed throughout Egypt to coincide with the implantation of seed in the renewed land following inundation, its premier observance took place in Abydos. Here at the seat of Asar's mysteries, priestesses resided in the temple precinct solely to perform this annual rite and retire for the remainder of the year.

The ritual text specifies that *The Lamentations* are to be performed in the third and eighth hours of the day, which would be counted following dawn (the first hour).

Dramatis Personae

Two priestesses assume the key roles of this observance: Auset and Nebt-Het. The ancient rubric specifies that they possess beautiful bodies, and have written on their arms the names of Auset and Nebt-Het (it is possible that the priestesses who performed these rites had the names permanently tattooed on their arms).

The Ur Hekau, whose patron is Auset, invokes the ancient spells, and a Setem priest assumes the role of her son Heru by performing the offering. The Setem prepares a clay jar filled with water and a small loaf of bread for each priestess. It is said that the jar is to be held in the right hand, the bread in the left, and the priestesses' heads are bowed during the recitations.

An image of Asar may be placed upon the altar to receive the offering. If it is performed for one who is absent, the name may be inscribed upon the image or an object belonging to that person may be substituted. In addition, the precious materials indicated in the concluding recitation—gold, silver, lapis lazuli, alabaster, turquoise, and myrrh incense—may be presented to the image. These should all be fabricated in uniform size and shape and placed upon the Hotep tray.

Hekau

Ur Hekau　This is the rite that is recited in every place where Asar is honored.
It establishes the body, it causes the Ba to enter the sky.
It makes the Ka rejoice and gives it breath.
It makes the hearts of Auset and Nebt-Het glad,
It places Heru upon the throne of his father.

Auset　Come to your house, brother, for your foes exist not.
You who came forth in Iunu, enter your domain.
It has been long since I've seen you, my heart mourns for you.
My eyes seek you, will they ever behold you again?
Come to your beloved, your sister who loves you.
Weary-hearted one, behold me and those who weep for you.
Leave us not, hear my voice,
For I am Auset, your sister whom you loved on Earth.

Nebt-Het　Good majesty, come to your house, for your foes exist not.
Your sisters call upon you, they are beside you at your bier.
Gods and men weep for you, they seek you out.
See us, speak to us, banish the pain from our hearts!
We live by your countenance, make our hearts happy to see our
　　lord.
Your adversary has fallen, he shall not exist.
I am with you, your bodyguard for eternity,
For I am Nebt-Het, your sister whom you loved on Earth.

Ur Hekau　The court of gods is in your favor,
Those who dwell in the Two Lands perform your rites.
Your two sisters bring libation, Heru presents your offerings
While his sons keep watch over your body.
All pour water to refresh your Ka.
Come to your courtiers, part not from us!

Auset　You cross the heavenly fields, the Sebau fiend has fallen,
Your image in the sky rises and sets each day.
I am Sopdet who follows you, I do not depart from you.
Your noble face nourishes gods and men, all live by it.

Nebt-Het Come to us, powerful bull who strides the heavens,
Lover of women, companion of men.
The son you have engendered is before us,
We guard him each day, we leave him not.

Heru You will come forth from your cavern in your season,
You will pour out the seed of your Ba.
I will make abundant offerings in your name,
Gods and men will do likewise.

Auset Come to your beloved wife,
Beautiful youth, pilot of time, who grows in his hour.
I cry out to you, my voice penetrates heaven,
Hear me, come in peace, come in your true form,
We will embrace you.

Nebt-Het Mighty sovereign, come to your house triumphant!
Come to Djedu, your pillar
Come to Djedet, the place of your Ba.
Come to your mother in Saut, drink deeply from her breast,
Divine son, return to your seat in Teb.

Auset You who grows young, whose eyes are glorious,
Because you are gone I weep,
Your absence causes the Earth to be watered by my tears.
You are avenged, you are established in your house.
Beautiful soul, repeating of births, come in peace.
Ba nefer, wehem mesut, iui em hotep.

Nebt-Het None is more mighty than the heir of Geb
He is the stable one, the dweller in solitude.
Come brother, your loved ones await you,
Vanquish the sorrow from our houses.
Beautiful soul, repeating of births, come in peace.
Ba nefer, wehem mesut, iui em hotep.

Heru   Your mother Nut covers you, she brings life to your body.

You are endowed with your Ba, you are established.

You enter the fields of turquoise, you hair is lapis lazuli.

Your skin is alabaster, your bones are silver.

You emanate myrrh, you are raised as gold.

You are established.

(The Hotep tray is offered.)

Ur Hekau   O you gods in the heavens and you spirits on Earth,

O you beings in the Duat, and those in the primeval territory:

Seek him, the unmoving one, who grows young,

Whose life springs up for us from nothingness.

(The bread and water are offered.)

Heka Ushabtiu—Empowerment of the Ushabtiu

The *ushabti* (also called "shabti") is as fascinating as it is ubiquitous in the funerary lore of ancient Egypt. Innumerable ushabtis have been found in tombs, and in some periods 365 of them were placed with the deceased so that a helping spirit would be available for each day of the year.

Chapter 6 of *The Book of Going Forth by Day* gives the formula for empowering the *ushabtiu* with life and assuming the identity of the owner. The spirits are then directed to perform any work that they may be called upon to do. The cultivation of fields, irrigation of land, and transportation of sand from the eastern to the western zones of the sacred regions were all readily accomplished by these attendant spirits.

The spell is nearly identical with others used to empower or give life to the tools of the temple magician. Believed to have an identity of their own, the wands, sceptres, crowns, and even portions of fabric infused with the powers of the gods were regarded as essential instruments of transformation.

Situla

The ceremonial container that is carried in processions to the sanctuary. It may hold incense, or liquid offerings of milk, water, and wine. Closely associated with the observances of Auset and Het-Her, it represents the womb of life.

Sistrum

The sceptre of Het-Her produces the sacred rhythm that invites vital, protective forces. As Neter of music and dance, her instruments re-create the harmony of divine life. It is used at the commencement of ceremonies to ward off nefarious forces and protect the sacred precinct.

Nekheka

The right-handed royal sceptre is the flail with three loose streamers, representing Hu, the creative manifestation. Originally an ancient agricultural tool of the Lower Kingdom, it was used to separate the grain from its chaff at harvest. It conveys the powers of justice and well-being.

Ankh

In nearly every example of Egyptian iconography, the gods are depicted holding the ankh emblem in the right hand, the symbol of "life." In this context, it represents the life force of the deity who possesses it. This force is modified by the nature of the god or goddess, yet always represents an infusion of the god's power that bestows new vitality upon the recipient.

Djeset

Flint is a substance considered by the Egyptians to contain the sacred fire of purification. Its use was limited to certain priestly specialists in the funerary, healing, and sorcery disciplines. The flint knife is carried by Sekhmet, the "Red Goddess" who was solely privileged to shed blood; her temples were renowned surgical centers in the ancient world.

Figure 61—Tools and Sceptres of the Temple Magician

Heka

The crook—originally the shepherd's staff—is one of the sceptres of royalty, representing the divine pattern (Maat) that guides humanity. In the left hand it extends Sia, the innate wisdom awakened in the monarch.

Sekhem

As a hieroglyphic sign, this sceptre represents authority and the power it brings. It is also known as the *Kherep*, the "wand of the master." It often accompanies the royal insignia of crook and flail, denoting the active influence given the monarch by the gods.

Uas

Carried exclusively by Sekhmet and male deities in the left hand. The shaft represents the electromagnetic flux first emanated by Ptah. It is believed by some to have been fabricated from the mummified remains of the bull's penis and scrotum, symbolizing the virile power of the male creator gods.

Figure 61—Tools and Sceptres of the Temple Magician

Objects charged with power have always been associated with acts of theurgy, and a wide variety of implements are depicted on inscriptions depicting the priestly art in temple and tomb. Each Neter possesses a sceptre that both represents and transmits its power, though they are often found interchangeably. And in the sacred anatomy, each of the subtle bodies possesses a power that is raised by a sceptre. A morning hymn inscribed in the sanctuary of the Edfu temple describes the regalia and sceptres of the god as they are presented in the morning service. It also specifies the hand into which each sceptre is placed.

Observance

An invocation to Anpu is initially made to ensure that protective influences will be drawn into the objects to be empowered. Certain sceptres should be inscribed with the names of their protective deities beforehand. For example, the flint knife belongs to Sekhmet-Bast, the Heka and Nekheka belong to Asar, and the sistrum is associated with Auset and Het-Her. Following this, the Invocation of the Five Elements should be performed for these instruments.

In effect, the ritual infusion of all amulets, talismans, and ritual regalia may be included in this act.

Dramatis Personae

The Sau, whose patron is Anpu, officiates in this ceremony. She may be assisted by the Ur Hekau, who answers for the empowered figures.

Hekau

I. Heri Heka Anpu—Invocation to Anpu

Ur Hekau   I am the pure magic in the belly of Ra: gods, be far from me!

Un-i hekau pui uab imi er khet ra, neteru heri tiueni er-i!

Sau   Praise to you, Anpu: come to me,

Heri Anpu: iem en-i,

Thou chief of mysteries in the shadow world.

Ep heri ep ser, ep heri sesheta.

Come to this Earth,

En pe heny en pehu,

Show yourself to me on this day.

Netek es en-i her maat neb.

Come to me, come to me!

Iem en-i, Iem en-i.

II. Empowerment of the Figures

Sau   O thou ushabtiu, your faces have been opened!

I ushabtiu ipen, ari apet ari heseb!

If (Name) calls upon you to perform work in the domain of the Neteru,

Ir (Name) arit kat nebet arit em Neter Khert,

You will answer.

Setu en set.

If any obstacles have been placed before him/her,

Ebet am em se er khert-ef/es,
You are charged to do those tasks.
Er serut ent sekhet er semehet uteb.
Obey the one who has created you, obey not his/her enemies.
Madjen-ek kheper er-ek, ni madjen kheftiu-ef/es.

Ur Hekau   Here am I. I have come for your protection.
Maku-a. Ia una em sa-ek.
I am here when you call.
Maku-a ka-ek.

Qi en Imhotep—Honoring Imhotep

Ceremonies associated with Sekhmet-Bast remain elusive in modern times. This is surely testimony to the powerful magic of this goddess, which was so exclusive that it could only be wielded by those dedicated entirely to her service.

Figure 62—Images of Imhotep

One known rite exclusive to Sekhmet-Bast is an extensive litany, recited in an event known as "the ritual of appeasing the Eye." The name is a reference to the terrifying power of the goddess' fiery gaze that could annihilate the enemies of her father, Ra. Three hundred and sixty-five recitations, each elucidating her destructive powers, were spoken annually to the same number of her images, each standing for one day in the Solar year.

Enigmatically, the same quantity of stunningly powerful black granite statues of the goddess have been discovered at several sites, which were undoubtedly meant to represent her power over each of the days. Such groups of statuary have been discovered at the southern sector of the Karnak within the precinct of Mut, and at the mortuary temple of Amunhotep III on the west bank of Thebes. The purpose of the rite was to appease the goddess each day and ensure the protection of the monarch thereby. She is also connected to the dekanoi; the recitations were meant to prevent the dekan spirits in the celestial realm from bringing pestilence on their days of rising throughout the year.

Conversely, the healing powers of the goddess were recognized and honored. Her priesthood was renowned throughout the ancient world for its skill in surgery, medical treatment, and psychic healing, particularly exorcism. The most esteemed of her Senu was Imhotep ("he comes in peace"), the Old Kingdom sage whose accomplishments in architecture and the sciences were only exceeded by his healing powers. Throughout the ages, he was regarded as a miracle worker, and temples dedicated to his service extend nearly the full span of Egyptian history—thousands of years.

Imhotep is the intercessor to Sekhmet-Bast, the Neter whose powerful nature was never approached—even by royalty—except by her dedicated priesthood. Imhotep's sanctuaries include the upper terrace at Hatchepsut's house of eternity, the modern Deir el Bahri on the western bank of Thebes. A healing sanctuary in his name is also present at Philae, preceding the eastern pylon of Auset's temple. Other places where he is honored include the necropolis of Saqqara, where his legendary tomb has yet to be unearthed and where Graeco-Roman historians spoke of a vast healing center dedicated to his apotheosis, called the Asklepieion.

At Karnak, the Roman temple of Ptah features a unique dedication to Imhotep and another deified healer who lived more than a thousand years later, Amunhotep, son of Hapu. Also a magician and architect, the two have been equated in provocative ways in the Egyptian pantheon, and there is reason to believe that they were viewed as one and the same soul. At this temple, the two doorposts praise each of them, alluding to their similarities of talent and recognition by the gods. It is from this site that the hymn to Imhotep is adapted to this ceremony.

Observance

A votive offering honoring Imhotep should be prepared; it may include the traditional medicine jar, flint knife, and linen bandage roll on a Hotep tray. This, along with incense and water, is offered to the god of healing. An image of Imhotep, in his well-recognized guise as a simple scribe, may be brought forward to receive the offerings.

For those who may be in need of healing, an offering to Imhotep is appropriate. This may be placed on the tray along with the name of the donor inscribed on or near the offering. It may either be returned to the donor or received as a gift to the temple at the discretion of the officiants.

Dramatis Personae

The Senu, whose patron is Sekhmet-Bast, recites the great hymn to Imhotep. She is assisted by the Hem Ka, who oversees the extension of benefits to those who serve and request favor of the Divine House.

Hekau

Senu   Good physician, son of Ptah:
             Senu nefer, sa Ptah:
             Hail to you kindhearted god,
             Enter your house.
             Come to your domains in Waset and Men Nefer
             So that your servants may welcome you in gladness!
             May you inhale the incense.
             (The image is censed.)
             When your servants bring this libation,
             May you refresh your form.

(Water is poured into a vessel and placed before the image.)
Allow this place become your favored domain,
Let it be more splendid to you than other places.
Here you will see the Neteru in their seasonal feasts,
And your seat will be joined to theirs.
May you endow life in the Palace of Endowing Life,
And may it join your house in Manu.

Hem Ka   Lord of Memphis, powerful in Thebes:
Neb ineb hedj, user en Waset:
You catch the north wind that is southbound by your house.
You see the Sun shining in rays of gold
At the doors of the palace called Regent of Illumination,
You view the gods' houses from the four sides of your house.

Senu   You receive the offerings that come from their altars.
May you receive what is presented here.
(The Hotep tray is presented.)
Your Hem Kau offer to you all good things
All that you may require each day:
Wine, beer, milk, burnt offerings at nightfall.

Hem Ka   May your Ka descend from heaven to your house every day
At the welcoming voice of your priestly singer.
May you hear the chantings of your steward
As he/she sets gifts before your Ka.

Senu   Men applaud you, women worship you.
One and all exalt in your kindness,
For you heal them, you revive them,
You renew your father's creation.

Hem Ka   They bring you their donations, bear to you their gifts,
Proffer to you their goods,
That you may eat the offering loaves and swallow the beer
With your brothers the elder gods.
You feed the worthy spirits with your surpluses.

Senu The learned ones praise the gods for you,
Foremost of them is your brother who loves you,
Amunhotep, son of Hapu, the one whom you love.
He joins with you, he parts not from you;
Your forms become a single body,
Your souls receive the things you love.

Nen Sokar—Festival of Sokar

The Festival of Sokar, Neter of the Memphite necropolis and a form of Asar in hibernation, is an expression of the hope for returning light in the darkest period of winter. It is also an acknowledgment of the powers that the season brings—inertia, decay, consolidation, and confinement—the realm of Set.

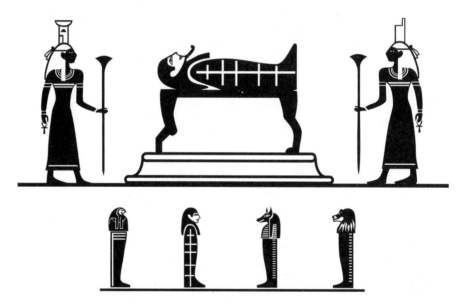

Figure 63—The Sokar Bed: The Sokar bed represents the fallen Asar in his quiescent state before reanimation. His two sisters stand watch, with Nebt-Het at the head and Auset at the feet of the bier. The four elemental genii (from left), Qebsenuf, Imset, Daumutef, and Haapi also stand watch, bringing the creative forces of Fire, Air, Earth, and Water into the chamber of renewal.

The Festival of Sokar took place near the winter solstice, in the Solar month of Choiach. This is the time of year when Orion—the constellation associated with Asar in his triumphant manifestation—begins to fade from view in the night sky, signaling the descent of the constellation into the *Duat* (besides the metaphysical meaning of "shadow world," the term is used in Egyptian astronomy to designate the unseen sky below the horizon). This was also the time in ancient Egypt when the waters of inundation had receded and the next season's crops had been seeded into the soil. Hence, expectations were high that the seed's implantation would have no hindrances and germinate after its period of hibernation.

The embedding of Asar in the deepest regions of the Earth is a metaphor of this "implantation" of seed into the soil—both events evoke the forces of creation and procreation. In this phase the god is Sokar, the life force in latency. Hence, images at Abydos, Dendera, and Philae depict him on his bier of hibernation, ithyphallic (responding to the creative force within the Earth), autoerotic (bringing forth his innate creative powers), and copulating with Auset who appears in the form of a falcon (generating the future seed in the conception of Heru).

At the winter solstice, the day hours are shortest in the Northern Hemisphere and the fields are temporarily bereft of life. It is a time of year that invites introspection and remembrance of those who have passed into the Western Land; hence, the melancholy and isolation of the season. But it is an opportunity to honor the existence of those gone before us, and recall the inexorable connection between the living and the dead. With this, we are able to realize our endowment of life and go forward and participate in life-manifesting events that will come, just as our ancestors will reappear in the theater of active existence after their cycle of "hibernation" is complete.

One of the surviving customs of ancient Egypt continues in the distant oases of the Western Desert today. Relatives of the deceased visit the tombs periodically to pour water and grain around the perimeter. They say it is done to bring the birds to the tomb, but the custom undoubtedly stems from the ancient belief that the Ba (in the form of a bird) will return to the tomb if it is provided offerings.[9] This return is essential—the living depend on the reservoir of experience

9. Zahi Hawass, *The Valley of the Golden Mummies* (New York: Harry N. Abrams, 2000) 114.

and wisdom of their ancestors to cope with certain realities, while the dead are reminded that their lives continue to influence the living.

Observance

At Abydos, elaborate ceremonies took place during this season that included the fabrication of statues in the image of Asar, which were carefully wrapped and enshrined for a process of alchemical transformation that was provoked by the recitation of invocations and spells. These were kept in the Sokar chapel for the duration of the year.

The observance begins with a reenactment of the journey to the four funerary cities of the Lower Kingdom, the cortege of Asar that visited Sais, Buto, Mendes, and Heliopolis. This journey is an emulation of the soul's transfiguration, from the departure of the body in Sais (west), the feeding of the Ka in Buto (north), the joining of the Ka and Ba in Mendes (east), to its exaltation in the celestial worlds in Heliopolis (south).

Returning to the northernmost part of the temple, the region of Set and the unmoving force in creation, the polestars are invoked. The action then moves east, where the implantation of seed into the soil of the Sokar bed and the watering rite is performed. Life-giving light is then welcomed into the ritual space. In ancient times, the sacred images were brought from the crypts of the temple to the roof chapels, exposed to the Sun on their sacred days, and symbolically germinated by the cosmic powers.

If there is a Sokar bed from the previous year's festival, it is embalmed in linen, anointed with cypress oil, and placed in a coffin. It is then symbolically buried in the western necropolis of the temple.

The materials used in this rite are water, grain, incense from a tree gum (frankincense, copal, storax), oil extracted from an evergreen source (cedar, cypress, pine), and a Sokar bed. The latter may be an oblong, coffin-shaped tray of stone or clay. In the ancient temple, the bed was fabricated in the reclining image of Asar. The grain may be corn, barley, or the type of wheat known as spelt.

A commemorative feast is traditionally held at the conclusion of this observance, in memory of the departed and with the expectation that Sokar will rise from the soil in the sprouting seed to provide an abundant life harvest once again.

Dramatis Personae

The Temple of Seti I at Abydos features a Sokar chapel, where the monarch makes offerings to Ptah and Geb, the creators who provide the earthly form with its essential qualities—the matrix from the former, the substance from the latter. They should be present in statuary or pictorial form. Inscriptions also show the king burning incense and making libations of water and sacred oil before Sokar, who in recumbent form upon a lion-headed couch is attended by Auset, Nebt-Het, and the four elemental genii. An image of Sokar is not necessary, as the soil itself represents his latent powers.

Besides these deities, Taurt is present as the reciter at the northern station of the sanctuary. She is Neter of partuition, and chieftainess of the circumpolar stars. Her association with Set brings the forces of the solstice into creative process, allowing the inert substance of Sokar to transmute and come into being with greater power. She is accompanied by the four "sons" of Heru, who reside in the stars of Ursa Minor (the Little Dipper). In addition, protective deities in the forms of lizards and snakes ward away nefarious forces and evoke fertile powers into the theater of transformation.

The Mer, whose patron is Set, officiates as Pharaoh's representative—the living Heru—performing all ritual action, particularly the exposure of the Sokar bed to sunlight. The four sons—Imset (incense), Daumutef (soil), Qebsenuf (oil), and Haapi (water)—attend the rite, providing the ritual substances. Besides coming into the sanctuary as the provisioners, they embalm the former Sokar bed, and they then retreat. On temple reliefs, they are depicted beneath the Sokar bed, an allusion to their elemental nature. Alternately, one person may perform the service of the four genii.

Another attendant, the grain god Nepri, presents the sprouting seeds on a Hotep tray, which will be implanted in the Sokar bed by the living Heru. The goddesses may optionally be represented. The observance begins with a procession entering the sanctuary, carrying the implements of the rite. It moves from west to north, to east and south, as the Kher Heb recites the hekau of the funerary journey and the implements are offered at each station.

Hekau

Mer   I make an offering of bread in Sais.

(West)   *Ari-a hotep tau em Saut.*

       I come into existence in Buto.

(North)   *Kheper-a em Pe.*

       I become vigorous in Mendes.

(West)   *Uat-a em Djedet.*

       I rise up in Heliopolis.

(South)   *Un-a em Iunu.*

Taurt   O never-setting stars, the chanters are before you

       Au akhemu seku, shemau her hat ek

       Gather together the flesh and bone that comes forth from Ptah,

       Sehu aui pert Ptah,

       The efflux that proceeds from Geb.

       Ash shu pert Geb.

Daumutef   Lord of the necropolis, I have collected your bones,

       I have gathered together for you your limbs.

       Neb Neter Khert temt-a kesu ek saq-a ek at-ek.

       (The soil is poured into the Sokar bed.)

Nepri   You are the plant that springs forth from Nun.

       Nut-ek weneb per em Nu.

       (The seeds are implanted in the soil.)

Haapi   You are watered and purified.

       Nut-ek uab tura.

       (The soil is watered.)

Imset   Your soul lives, your seed germinates,

       Ankh ba-ek ertu ahai-ek,

       You renew your youth upon Earth among the living.

       Unnut a tep ta em ma ankhiu.

       (The Sokar bed is fumigated with incense.)

Qebsenuf   The Earth becomes green through you,
Uadj nek taui,
The never-resting stars praise you.
Akhemu urtchu tua tu.
(The Sokar bed is anointed with oil.)

Nepri   Behold the splendors of heaven's disc,
You renew yourself each day.
As samau aten nu en pet, maui hru neb.
(The Sokar bed is exposed to the Sun. The four genii may now embalm
the former Sokar bed and place it in the western station of the temple.)

Taurt   May I see the birth of your Ba, its illumination as Orion
Maa na mesiut bak ba-ek em sahu
In the southern sky with your divine sister Sopdet at your side.
Em pet resyet senet-ek neterit sopdet em sa-ek.

Mer   I come into being,
Kheper na,
I am strong upon the Earth, before Ra.
Nuk ut-a tep ta kher Ra.
I eat bread, I drink beer.
Au an taum sura na heqet.
(An offering of bread and beer is made at the altar.)
I have come, I am here.
I-kua, maka.

Hen ek Maat—The Presentation of Maat

An effective religious practice must yield a positive framework for living, a moral code that benefits both the practitioner and her environment. In ancient Egypt, this was achieved through the Presentation of Maat by the living pharaoh, a covenant periodically made with the Neter of divine order. This ceremony was also a pledge to maintain and uphold truth and order with all the powers granted to the royal person by the gods. Its guarantee was the offering of the name, considered by the ancients to be the most powerful possession of a person.

Figure 64—Dedication of the Name: Maat, in her aspect as the divine scribe Seshat, records the name of Rameses II for eternity. The name will be placed in the sacred Persea tree of Heliopolis, under the protection of Djehuti.

The Declaration of Innocence, comprised of forty-two pledges of morality, is another pact made with the gods by the temple servant. An abbreviated version of it is inscribed on the inner doorjamb of the pronaos in the temple of Horus at Edfu, where priests who entered for the daily ritual recited the text as the final act of ritual purity before performing their duty.[10] Coincidentally, it is the forty-second act of the morning service. It is therefore appropriate for the temple body to formally announce and renew these moral precepts periodically. New entrants to the temple may also perform this rite as their initial act of intent before proceeding to the Anointing into the Temple in the season of Heru (Leo).

---

10. Barbara Watterson, *The Temple of Horus at Edfu* (Stroud, Gloucestershire: Tempus, 1998) 82.

The forty-two Maati goddesses are emanations of Maat's expression; each represents an aspect of divine conduct that must be mastered in life. In the inner life, these deities pass judgment on the conduct of the initiate, and forty-two declarations were recited to each of these judges by the sojourning soul to assure final passage into the heavenly fields.

Observance

A Declaration of Innocence precedes the Presentation of Maat. Understandably, these precepts are impossible for any individual to fulfill at one time, and it should be remembered that they are meant as guidelines to the ideal existence— living in harmony with divine beings. The ancients struggled to comply with these morals as much as the modern person, and their recitation may, if only for the short-term, endow the recipient with a reflection of their benefits. Acknowledgment of the celebrant's pledge is made in the form of an anointing with temple oil on the nostrils.

In the next segment, the name, written on paper or a small plaque, is presented by hand to the image of Maat or the altar in the sanctuary. A white feather is given to the celebrant as acknowledgment that the name has been recorded in the temple book.

Dramatis Personae

The Sentyt, whose patron is Maat, presides over the ceremony and carries the image of the goddess. She is assisted by the Kher Heb (under the patronage of Djehuti), who reads the invocations to the forty-two Maati. The candidate responds with the forty-two declarations.

Hekau

I. Declaration of Innocence[11]

Kher Heb   1) Hear me, Usekh Nemmat, who comes forth from Iunu:

Candidate   I have not committed evil.

2) Hear me, Hepet Shet, who comes forth from Kher Aha:
I have not robbed.

---

11. Adaptation from the Papyrus Nu.

3) Hear me, Fenti, who comes forth from Khemenu:

I have not done wrong in place of what is right.

4) Hear me, Am Khaibit, who comes forth from Qerert:

I have not committed thefts.

5) Hear me, Neha Her, who comes forth from Rostau:

I have not slain men or women.

6) Hear me, Ruti, who comes forth from the two horizons
    Shu-Tefnut:

I have not diminished the bushel.

7) Hear me, Ariti-ef Shet, who comes forth from Sekhem:

I have not defrauded.

8) Hear me, Neba, who comes forth and retreats:

I have not profaned sacred property.

9) Hear me, Set Qesu, who comes forth from Henensu:

I have not spoken falsehood.

10) Hear me, Khemi, who comes forth from the hidden sanctuary:

I have not robbed.

11) Hear me, Uadj Nesert, who comes forth from Het Ka Ptah:

I have not cursed god or man.

12) Hear me, Her-ef Ha-ef,[12] who comes forth from Tephet Djat:

I have not stolen food.

13) Hear me, Qereti, who comes forth from Ament:

I have not uttered slanders.

14) Hear me, Taret, who comes forth from the night:

I have not betrayed my heart.

15) Hear me, Hedj Abehu, who comes forth from Shedyet:

I have not trespassed.

16) Hear me, Unem Snef, who comes forth from the slaughter
    block chamber:

I have not slain sacred animals.

17) Hear me, Unem Besku, who comes forth from the Mabet
    chamber:

I have not destroyed lands.

---

12. Ferryman of Ra and Asar.

18) Hear me, Neb Maat, who comes forth from the city of Maati:
I have not revealed secrets.

19) Hear me, Thenemi, who comes forth from Per Bast:
I have not spoken unwisely.

20) Hear me, Anti, who comes forth from Iunu:
I have not been wroth without cause.

21) Hear me, Tutut-ef, who comes forth from the nome of
Anjety:[13]
I have not been lustful.

22) Hear me, Uamemti, who comes forth from the chamber of
slaughter:
I have not defiled myself.

23) Hear me, Ma Antef, who comes forth from Per Menu:
I have not lain with one who is pledged to another.

24) Hear me, Heru Serui, who comes forth from Nehat:
I have terrorized no one.

25) Hear me, Neb Sekhem, who comes forth from Gerui:
I have not spoken harshly.

26) Hear me, Shet Kheru, who comes forth from Ruit:
I have not ignored the admonitions of the law.

27) Hear me, Nekhen, who comes forth from Heka Andj:
I have made no one weep.

28) Hear me, Kenemti, who comes forth from Kenmet:
I have reviled no one.

29) Hear me, An Hotep-ef, who comes forth from Saut:
I have not acted with violence.

30) Hear me, Ser Khru, who comes forth from Unti:
I have not rushed to judgment.

31) Hear me, Neb Heru, who comes forth from Nedjef-et:
I have not attacked the teachings of the gods.

32) Hear me, Serekhi, who comes forth from Ut-henet:
I have not gossiped.

33) Hear me, Neb Abui, who comes forth from Saut:
I have not countenanced evil.

---

13. Anjety: the ninth nome of Lower Egypt.

34) Hear me, Nefertum, who comes forth from Het Ka Ptah:

I have not spoken treasonably of my lord.

35) Hear me, Atum Sep, who comes forth from Djedu:

I have not polluted water.

36) Hear me, Ari-em Ab-ef, who comes forth from Tebu:

I have not raised my voice.

37) Hear me, Ihy, who comes forth from Nu:

I have not blasphemed my god.

38) Hear me, Uadj Rekhyt, who comes forth from Saut:

I have not been arrogant.

39) Hear me, Neheb Neferet, who comes forth from his temple:

I have not been prideful.

40) Hear me, Neheb Kau, who comes forth from his sanctuary:

I have not gained except by my own effort.

41) Hear me, Djeser Tep, who comes forth from his shrine:

The local gods have not been cursed by me.

42) Hear me, Ana-ef, who comes forth from Augeret:

I have not mocked the gods of my forebears.

Sentyt   Behold (Name) true of voice, clothed with pure raiment,

An (Name) maakheru, unekh-ef hebes uabet,

Shod with white sandals,

Tchab em tebtu hedj eti,

Anointed with sublime oil:

Urhu em tepet ent anta.

Performing Maat is breath for your nostrils.

Tau pu en fened-ek iret maat.

(Temple oil is brushed on each nostril.)

II. Presentation of Maat

Kher Heb   Homage to you, gods who dwell in the chamber of truth

Anedj hrau ten, neteru am usekhet tchen ent Maati

Without evil in your bodies.

At ker em khat ten.

We feed upon truth, we live in truth.

Sam-en em maat, ankh-en em maat.

Candidate Homage to you, lady of truth,

Anedj hra-ek nebet maat,

She to whom the Ennead extend their arms:

Setchat pesjet aui-sen her-es:

I am pure, I have been purified in the southern pool.

Ab kua, ab na em seshetyt.

I have committed no faults, I have not erred,

Enen asfet-a. ene khebent-a,

I have not done evil, nor have I borne false witness,

En tu-a enen meteru-a,

I come forward to make a declaration of truth.

I-na aa er semeteret maat.

I present truth, I present my name.

Henek-i maat, henek-i ren.

(The name is presented to the Kher Heb and is held before the image of Maat.)

Kher Heb Maat is come, that she may be with you.

Maat is in every place of yours, that you may rest upon her.

Sentyt I am here before you, and you are given:

Em-ek ui em bah-ek, her di en-ek:

Power over the waters, divine food, the lifetime of Ra, eternity.

Uas tep nu, hotepu djefau, ankh en Ra, neheh.

(The Shuti feather is presented to the candidate.)

Shai en Unnut—The Book of Hours

In the tombs of Egypt, the cosmic landscape was depicted with representations of the gods and their realms governing the funerary space. The lower levels would show Geb, lord of the Earth, in company with the nome spirits of Egypt and the nature spirits who embodied animal and plant life.

Figure 65—Offerings of the Hours

The ceilings of the inner chambers depicted the firmament, with the various stages of celestial life and the divinities who inhabit the sky realm. Nut encompasses this region, and in many tombs her terrain is divided into linear time, represented by sacred hours.

The Book of Gates, an enigmatic sacred text inscribed on the alabaster sarcophagus of Seti I, is also featured on the walls of the corridor leading to the Osireion at Abydos. The latter was regarded in antiquity as the entry into the royal chamber of initiation, and its function continues to evade scholarly evaluation. Believed to be of very ancient origin, the text discloses the Solar journey of the soul through cosmic regions that culminates in a celestial rebirth through Nut, the sky goddess. Each hour of the Solar journey is described as a gate that is passed into by the conscious soul. In each, the meeting with a divine serpent is encountered, a symbol of the protective deities who guard the Sun god in his nightly journey through the *Duat,* the invisible sky.

Observance

This ceremony recapitulates, on an hourly basis, the annual Solar journey through the monthly mansions of the Zodiac, the constellational "houses" where the Neteru's powers reside. The Book of Hours compresses this cyclic event into one night what the Sun accomplishes in the sky through the year. The ceremony also reenacts the *sejeryt* (vigil) that the gods kept over the body of Asar, as it became renewed by the mystic processes performed by Auset and her retinue.

An offering and recitation will be made at each hour, following the Solar journey of twelve night hours that proceeds at dusk (the first hour). This symbolizes the twelvefold Solar cycle that is coming to a close, the conclusion of the Sun's journey through the twelve seasons before the spring equinox. The ancient rite included a comprehensive recitation of all divine forces throughout the hours—the protective deities in the nomes, temples, celestial regions, and the shadow worlds. Calling upon these diverse powers serves the purpose of "drawing together" the regions of the land, the houses of the gods, and the dimensions of creation through which the Neteru express their powers. The hymns and litanies of the Solar liturgy may also be recited throughout the hours in the sequence of the Solar year.

Dramatis Personae

All members of the temple should assist in the offerings and recitations that are to be performed. Those whose patron deities are associated with the hours may perform the recitations. For example, the first hour, governed by Asar, may be performed by the Hem Ka, and the second hour, governed by Het-Her, may be performed by the Khener.

In the ancient temples, incubation sleep was a profound means of communicating with divine forces. Attendant priests stood watch with and observed sleeping visitors in the temple, recording words spoken, dreams, and visions that took place in the night hours. In this instance, where the ceremony will last through the night in the dark hours of winter in the Northern Hemisphere, the arrangement of such an observance is appropriate.

Hekau

Company   He who illumines the Duat with the rays from his eyes,

Sehedj duat em setiut irty-ef,

He has gone far from us.

Djer hert-ef er en.

Come now, let us weep for Asar.

Em mi rem-en Asar.

O you divine beings of the southern and northern sky:

Neteru pet resyt pet mehtyt:

The vigil of the god begins,

Sejeryt neter net shaa-ef,

You shall justify the Foremost of the Westerners.

Se maakheru Kentiamentiu.

I. Hour One

Hem Ka   Hail to you, Imset, Daumutef, Qebsenuf, Haapi,

In Saut and Iunu, in Djedet and Pe and in Abedju:

Let him be established among the resplendent ones,

Uau su ami em khu,
May the Duat be opened to him.
Unu en-ef duat.
(Offering: water)

II. Hour Two

Khener   Hail to you, Het-Her in Behdet, in Bakhet, in Iunu, in Khemenu,
In Tjebu, in Iunyt, in Teb, and in your seat at Iat Uabet:
Let him be established among the resplendent ones,
Uau su ami em khu,
May the Duat be opened to him.
Unu en-ef duat.
(Offering: flowers and herbs)

III. Hour Three

Kher Heb   Hail to you, Djehuti in Henensu and Khemenu:
Let him be established among the resplendent ones,
Uau su ami em khu,
May the Duat be opened to him.
Unu en-ef duat.
(Offering: fowl)

IV. Hour Four

Hem Neter   Hail to you, Nebt-Het in Het Sekhem and Iat Uabet:
Let him be established among the resplendent ones,
Uau su ami em khu,
May the Duat be opened to him.
Unu en-ef duat.
(Offering: bandages and linen)

V. Hour Five

Maa   Hail to you, Heru in Teb, in Ineb Hedj and Nubet:
Let him be established among the resplendent ones,
Uau su ami em khu,
May the Duat be opened to him.
Unu en-ef duat.
(Offering: wine)

VI. *Hour Six*

Setem   Hail to you, Geb in Kher Aha, in Kemet and Nekhen:

Let him be established among the resplendent ones,

Uau su ami em khu,

May the Duat be opened to him.

Unu en-ef duat.

(Offering: bread)

VII. *Hour Seven*

Ur Hekau   Hail to you, Auset in Djedu, in Iat Uabet,

In Hebet and Iunu:

Let him be established among the resplendent ones,

Uau su ami em khu,

May the Duat be opened to him.

Unu en-ef duat.

(Offering: incense)

VIII. *Hour Eight*

Sau   Hail to you, Anpu in Zawty, in Iuny and Kher Aha:

Let him be established among the resplendent ones,

Uau su ami em khu,

May the Duat be opened to him.

Unu en-ef duat.

(Offering: anointing oils)

IX. *Hour Nine*

Senu   Hail to you, Sekhmet-Bast in Saut, in Waset, in Per Bast and Nekheb:

Let him be established among the resplendent ones,

Uau su ami em khu,

May the Duat be opened to him.

Unu en-ef duat.

(Offering: beer)

X. *Hour Ten*

Mer   Hail to you, Set in Djanet, in Abu and Iunyt Ta Senet:
             Let him be established among the resplendent ones,
             Uau su ami em khu,
             May the Duat be opened to him.
             Unu en-ef duat.
             (*Offering: meat*)

XI. *Hour Eleven*

Sentyt   Hail to you, Maat in Bahut, in Per Khemenu and Iunyt:
             Let him be established among the resplendent ones,
             Uau su ami em khu,
             May the Duat be opened to him.
             Unu en-ef duat.
             (*Offering: grain*)

XII. *Hour Twelve*

Uab   Hail to you, Nut in Manu, in Rostau, in Ament:
             Let him be established among the resplendent ones,
             Uau su ami em khu,
             May the Duat be opened to him.
             Unu en-ef duat.
             (*Offering: milk*)

XIII. *Completion*

Company   Circler, guide of the two lands,
             Deben seshemu taui,
             Good steering oar of the western sky:
             Hemu nefer en pet imentyt:
             Mother of the living: extend your arm to the awakened ones.
             Mut em ankhiu: aut-es em nehsu.

Chapter Seven

TRANSFORMATION

May your flesh be born to life,
And may your life encompass more
Than the life of the stars as they exist.
                                    —Pyramid Texts: Utterance #723

Chaos—whether actual or symbolic—is never fully resolved; it is a cyclic oc-currence that requires cyclic resolution, as the Egyptian legends instruct us. Thus, the essential aim of ritual is to return to the primeval unity and order of the upper worlds, to banish the uncertainties brought by the mundane flux, and to ratify the intrinsic harmony between the visible and invisible realms. This must be done cyclically, in unison with conditions that may bring the worlds to-gether in harmony.

The liturgy allows us to be placed within this scheme of synchronous events, at its center. In the process, we rediscover all of the dimensions in which we exist, and become familiar with the divine powers in those dimensions. This is what the creation accomplished and what we in the mundane sphere seek—an act of communicating with our spiritual face.

While the ceremonies in the liturgy convey a deep reverence for, and ac-knowledgment of, the powers of the Neteru, they are not in any sense a pro-gramme of worship. Egyptian ritual assumes equal ranking among the three kingdoms in the universe—the *akhiu* (nature spirits), the *ankhiu* (living human beings), and the *neteru* (gods). For human beings, it is the application of Heka (one's creative force) in concert with Sia (innate intelligence) and Maat (organization) that powers the liturgy. Its ultimate purpose is to access Sa (the constituting, universal energy) for coming into conscious participation with all the worlds of creation.

Hesi—Hymns

Egyptian ceremony features hymns in every instance, initially opening the rites to reflection on the divine qualities of the Neteru. These forms of praise allow us to see the gods in the manner that the ancients viewed them, and to understand the unique qualities that distinguish each of them.

The opening hymn for each of the Iru may be recited daily during the period that it honors. For example, during the season of Auset, the Hymn to Auset given in the Iru for the cycle of Libra may be read each morning or used as the seed for one's daily meditation.

Alternately, the repertoire for a personal Khesu may include the recitation of familiar hymns that begin or conclude the day. Egyptian literature is filled with such poetic works, and those that reflect the Solar cosmogony are included here.

Praise of Khepri[1]

Praise be to you, who comes into existence each day,
Iau en-ek kheper Ra nub,
Who gives birth to himself each morning,
Mes es su tenu duait,
Who comes forth from the womb of his mother without cessation.
Per em khet mut-ef nen abu.
The two halves of Egypt together bow before you,
Iu en-ek iterty em kesu,
Giving praise at your rising.

---

1. Adapted from an inscription in the tomb of Horemhab, Saqqara.

Di sen en-ek iau en weben-ek.

The land is made luminous with the splendor of your body,

Set hen en-ek ta em iamu hau-ek,

Being divine in the heavens, you are the beneficent Neter,

Neteri ti em sekhem imy pet, neter menheh,

The ruler of eternity, lord of light,

Nesu en heh, nub shesep,

Great of appearance in your Barque of Dawn,

Heka hedjut heri neset-ef em mesketet,

Prince of radiance in the Barque of the Dusk.

Ay-a khau em mai en djet,

Divine youth, heir to eternity,

Hu en neteri iuau en heh,

Who has begotten himself and given birth to himself.

Utet su mes su djes-ef.

The Pauti acclaim you, the Neteru are jubilant on your behalf,

Dua tu pesdjet aya-et. henu en-ek pesdjet nedjset,

For you are Khepri in the morning, Ra at noon, Atum in the evening,

Nuk-ef Khepera em tuauu, Ra en ahau-ef, Atum amit masheru,

And they adore you in your beautiful forms.

Dua seten tu em iru-ek nefer.

Praise of Ra

Homage to you, Ra, great circler, glorious being:

Anedj hra-ek Ra, shenu ur, khu khi:

Maker of all that exists, creator of what shall be,

Ari enti-es, qemam unenet,

Foremost of all beings.

Khent sa kheperu.

Father of fathers, mother of mothers,

Tef em tefu, Mut em mut.

Becoming young in your time.

Renep et ra tcha.

O god of life, lord of love:

Neter ankh, neb meret:

All people live when you shine,

Ankh hra nebu pesed-ek,

Those who follow you sing your praises.

Hai nek ami tchet-ek.

You rule all the gods,

Heq-ef neteru nebu,

You go forth over heaven and Earth each day,

Dja-ek heret ta ra neb,

You receive the opening of the heart in your shrine.

Seshep-ek aut ab em khen kara-ek.

You stride over the heaven in peace,

Nema-ek hert em hotepiu,

Your enemies are overthrown.

Sekher khefta-ek.

May you be at peace with me,

Hotep-ek na,

May I advance upon this Earth and see your beauty.

Udja-a tep ta maa-a neferu-ek.

Aakhu—Protection

The ancient Egyptians did not hesitate to employ any reasonable means to deflect the adversarial powers of nature and certain of the gods. Spells of protection and prophylactic rites were given to the human race by these very same deities, to ensure the maintenance of Maat through the ages despite the occasional disruptions of powerful forces.

Amulets (objects containing natural powers) and talismans (manufactured objects) were used in daily life for every possible type of protection. For the Egyptians, however, such distinctions were not so clear-cut. Precious metals and stones were used in the construction of sacred objects, thus combining the forces inherent in the natural forms of divine beings with manufactured articles. Carnelian, jasper, lapis lazuli, steatite, hematite, gold, copper, and rare woods were the materials of choice, though even the impoverished could possess powerful objects made from faïence and glass. And images of the Neteru and their sigils or icons were equally powerful.

Objects can be infused with Heka, to evoke transformation continuously, or solely for a specific purpose or time of need. For the ancients, many so-called inanimate objects were believed to possess intelligence—being fetishes in the true sense of the term—in that they were seen to embody a spiritual force that continuously accumulated and transmitted its own Heka. An example is the nome standards that were always present at the temple. Some were believed to have originated in great antiquity, while others were "reincarnations" of the power of the region that protected the territory and maintained its power.

Djehut Unnu
Ibis

Ten
The Shrine

Nefer Ament
Western Harpoon

Nefer Abet
Eastern Harpoon

Figure 66—Nome Standards: The forty-two nome standards provided more than a symbolic designation of their regions. They were viewed as living entities, possessing the powers of their origin and the soul of the land itself. In the Upper Kingdom (above), *Djehut Unnu* brought the powers of Hermopolis where it was placed, and *Ten* encompassed the spirit from Edfu to Esna. In the Lower Kingdom (below), *Nefer Ament* represented the powers of the northwestern Delta along the Rosetta branch of the Nile, while *Nefer Abet* possessed the spirit of the eastern Delta near the Bitter Lakes.

Temple priests often oversaw the preparation of objects charged with Heka to serve specific purposes. Such items were produced in great quantity at the temples and distributed as souvenirs—though still sacred—of pilgrimages by the faithful to the Divine House. These were infused in special ceremonies with the Heka of the temple's deity. Examples include the miniature cat figures from the temple of Bastet worn as protective jewelry, and the Menat collars of Het-Her that ensure breath.

Images of the Neteru who are closely associated with high magic also possess amuletic power—figures of Djehuti can make the spoken word effective to the gods, while those of Selqit may banish physical or psychic poisons.

Nile water and soil from the sacred precincts possess Heka, as revealed by the worn stones, walls, wells, and courtyards of the temples that are visible today. Diminished by the hands of pilgrims taking dust on their journeys home through the ages, they are testimony to the enduring belief in the powers of sacred places. Objects crafted by the human hand, such as written spells on papyrus and linen, are also talismanic because they contain the signs and images of the Neteru, considered sacred in themselves.

All these apotropaic devices possess Heka that can be transmitted to the owner. They may purify, influence special conditions, or deflect adversarial forces. They transmit their power by being worn, burnt, or placed in strategic locations. The magical Harris papyrus describes the manufacture of images of Hapi in the time of Rameses III, fashioned in precious stone and metal. These were inscribed with spells invoking a plentiful inundation, and were cast into the Nile as offerings to the Neter.

The creation and use of amulets is an honorable and often necessary function of the temple. The names of the Neteru, inscribed upon papyrus or cippi (plaques of clay, stone, or wood), along with their associated talismanic figures, offer considerable psychic protection. They may be empowered during the Iru of the Neter to which they belong, separately, or in a special observance of the Ushabtiu ceremony. For those that were regarded as the highest magic, the hekau are included here.

Uadjat

The right eye of Heru is the reconstituted power of the god and the restored order of the universe. Its presentation in the form of offerings at temple and tomb provide the spiritual substance that restores the powers of the soul that are divided by illness or demise.

Heru Merti

The "eyes of Heru" were worn together by a select few—royal persons and the priesthood. The right eye represents the Sun, the left eye the Moon. In the great myth of the battle between Heru and Set, the former was said to have lost his right eye, which was restored by Djehuti, lord of the Moon. The legend also alludes to the Solar Eclipse, believed to be caused by Set.

Khepri

The Neter of cyclic return assumes the image of the scarabaeus sacer beetle, which is rolled in its egg by the parent toward the Sun in the chrysalis stage prior to emerging as a benevolent, winged creature. Its life cycle is a metaphor of the transformative processes in nature that are engendered by the Sun, which quickens the life force on Earth.

Djed Pillar

One interpretation is that this figure represents the acacia tree trunk that concealed the body of Asar after it was cast in the Nile. Another is that the four segments represent the four regions of his spinal column that were dismembered by Set: the cervical, thoracic, lumbar, and sacral. Rejoined in this form, it endows stability, strength, endurance, and permanence.

Figure 67—Amulets

Menat

The beaded necklace with counterpoise is an amulet of Het-Her, bringing protection to the back of the neck where the forces of the astral and physical worlds meet.

Shaken in temple ceremonies to produce rhythmic sounds, the Menat was also believed to arouse the goddess. Thus, it ensures renewal of the sexual instincts, promising physical well-being and fecundity in the female, and virility in the male.

Ba Bird

The man-headed hawk is the amulet of the soul, granting protection against nefarious forces in the shadow worlds. It also invites clairvoyant vision, as it signifies the astral body in flight. Chapter 139 of *The Book of Going Forth* empowers the amulet of the Ba, which is placed on the breast so that the soul may visit its body in the tomb. This is why it may be worn by both the living and the dead—its purpose is to bind soul and body.

Frog

The African matlametlo arises from the sand in the Sudan after rainfall, as if spontaneously appearing from the barren land. Thus, the frog in ancient times embodied the primeval forces of Huh and Hauhet, who propagated in the cosmic waters to impel the creation. The frog also symbolizes the powers of rebirth inherent in the goddess Qerert, the mirror image of Hauhet on Earth.

Figure 67—Amulets

Thet

The "buckle" or knot of Auset represents the womb of the goddess, she who incubates the latent seed of Heru Ur. It is worn to protect the female generative organs. The knot is colored red, symbolizing the blood she shed after learning the secret name of Ra—a metaphor of the menses and its power of rejuvenation.

Sedge and Bee

The sedge plant (nesut) and the bee (bity) are pharaonic emblems. A legend tells that when Ra wept at the death of Asar, his tears fell to Earth and became bees. The bee's function in nature is pollination, an allusion to the king's potency to germinate divine life in his subjects. The sedge plant provides a rich mulch in the Nile Valley that optimizes fertilization, symbolizing the king's embodiment of the alchemical ferment that quickens organic vitality in the land.

Papyrus Stalk

The Wadj ("verdant") ensures the power to grow and flourish. Often carried by the female Neteru, it represents the nourishment received from spiritual sources that translates to fecundity in nature, the body, and society.

Spell 159 of *The Book of Going Forth* specifies that the amulet be fabricated of green feldspar and placed at the throat of the initiate. The spell also promises that the amulet will "knit the spine together."

Figure 67—Amulets

Seal of the Necropolis
The image of Anpu, guardian of the ancient cemetery,
surmounts the symbolic nine captives.

Figure 67—Amulets

Uadjat—The Eye of Heru

The "eye of Heru" represents the innate wholeness that exists among the cosmic
and mundane worlds. In the celestial sphere, it symbolizes the all-pervading
power of light embodied by the two Solar Neteru—Ra (the physical Sun) and
Heru (the spiritual Sun). Derived from the word *udja,* "to be sound," the image
represents all that is vibrant, restored, and perfect. Chapter 167 of *The Book of
Going Forth by Day* discloses one of the restored eye legends—that of Ra, which
was torn out by the Apep demon and recovered by Djehuti. In Heru's combat
with Set, Djehuti once more restores the eye of the former after a prolonged battle between the gods of cosmic proportion. In both scenarios, the "Sound Eye"
symbolizes the magic that restores a vital function to the initiate or deceased. As
an amulet, it is the prototype of the mystic charm of later ages that dispels the
Evil Eye.

The amulet of the eye may be inscribed upon any material or it may be painted or written on any object that requires continued vitality and protection from adversarial forces.

Hekau

Djehuti restored the eye of Heru, he made peace with it.

Inen Djehuti uadjat, iu-es hotep en-ef.

He is sound, it is sound, and I am sound.

Udja-ef, udja-nes, udja-a.

I repose in the pupil of the eye,

Hemes-a em djesert,

"Seer of millions of years" is my name.

Maa heh en renpet ren-a.

Thet—The Knot of Auset

The *Thet* ("knot or buckle of Auset") is a frequently encountered amulet of great power. Usually worn around the neck, it represents the Neter's generative organs, and invites protection from female illnesses. It also encourages the fortitude and perseverance she displayed in her search for Asar and through the trials imposed by Set to contravene the ascent of Heru to Egypt's throne. Colored red, it symbolizes the blood of the goddess that was shed when she learned the words of power from Ra, the Sun. It is probable that the blood also refers to the menses, which is shed to renew and prepare the womb for the new life she is heralded for bringing forth from death.

In Chapter 156 of *The Book of Going Forth by Day*, a formula is given for empowering the knot of Auset, an amulet that brings the goddess to the initiate for protection. This amulet was also popularly worn, ensuring the health of the womb, safe delivery in childbirth, and the reversal of diseases in the female organs.

The rite is quite simple, the rubric stating that the recitation is to be said over the Thet and that it should be fabricated of red jasper. It should be dipped in jasmine water (one of the goddess' flowers), inlaid in a heart of sycamore, and placed on the neck. When completed, "the power of Auset comes to protect him, and her son Heru will rejoice to see it. No way will be blocked to him, he will have one hand toward heaven and one hand toward Earth." The brevity of this spell makes it easy to memorize, but by no means reduces its effectiveness to the user.

Hekau

The blood of Auset, the magical words of Auset,
Senef en Auset, hekau en Auset,
The emanations of Auset are my protection,
Khut en Auset, ut ati sa er betaui pu,
They destroy what is my abomination.
Hedj sen net betu-a.
Auset says to me: I have come to be your protector.
Djet in-i Auset: Ia un-a em sau-ek.

Khepri—The Scarabaeus

Certain creatures in nature embody the actions of the Neteru. The scarabaeus sacer beetle, indigenous to the Nile Valley, epitomizes the actions of Khepri, the Solar principle in its daily rhythm of coming forth from the eastern horizon. The scarab's motion of continuously rolling its eggs toward the rising Sun each day was seen as the powerful, transformative aspect of light, as when the chrysalis of the insect transforms from cocoon to winged beetle. Khepri is a creature of water and fire, as he has an association with both remote, cosmic life (the watery world of Manu) and Earthly life in the rhythms of the Nile (water) and the Sun (fire). In the funerary tradition, his presence assures the awakening of the deceased in the afterlife as the myriad number of funerary scarabaei testify.

The scarab is a potent amulet for protection in magical operations if worn close to the heart. It is best anointed with personal or temple oil during the recitation of its empowerment to be effective to the wearer. The rite should be performed at dawn, in the waxing hemicycle of the Moon. At the conclusion, the Praise of Khepri may be recited.

Hekau

I am that which comes into being, in the form of Khepri.

Nuk pu Kheper, em Khepri.

I become the creator of what comes into being,

Kheper na kheper kheperu,

And that which has come into being.

Kheper kheperu neb em khet.

After my coming into being, many were the things

Kheper-a ashet Kheperu

That came forth into being from my mouth.

Em per em ra-a.

Un Iertet—Protection in the Necropolis

Certain places are known to be reserved for only those whose abilities can match the potent forces that are consecrated there. In ancient Egypt, the tomb was regarded as such a place, where all of the Heka that could be evoked on behalf of the transformation of the deceased was concentrated. On entering these places, the individual faces both protective and adversarial influences. The sigil of the necropolis embodies just this—nine bound captives, each representing one of the ancient countries hostile to Egypt (nine is also the number of all possibilities), surmounted by Anpu in his jackal form. Placed at the entrance to the tomb, this talisman ensured that the powers of the divine watcher would protect the contents within.

To shield oneself from these conditions, which may be encountered inadvertently or as the result of misapplication of Heka, a formula of protection contravenes the effects. The *Un Iertet* spell ("opening the tomb") is given in Chapter 67 of *The Book of Going Forth by Day*. It allows the soul's release from the confines of the tomb, but it was also recommended to the ancient Egyptians as a spell that may offer protection to one living, who enters the tomb and may leave it without the hindrances of the shadow world to which one is exposed.

Hekau

I. Declaration

This portal is opened for those in the shadow worlds,
And those who are living shall be unhampered.
Shu moves through this portal as I move through it.
I enter the cavern of Geb and receive his sanction.
I take hold of the lashings of he who has charge of the mooring posts.
I will go down to my seat in the Sektet barque of Ra,
I will not suffer nor be deprived of my seat
On that which takes me over the waterway of the lake.

II. Invocation

The place where my soul dwells is opened.
Unnut untha en ba-a ami-es.
Open to me!
Un na!
You will not enclose my soul, you will not fetter my shadow.
An khena ten ba an saa ten khaibit-a.
A way will be open for my soul and my shadow.
Un uat en ba-a en khaibit-a.
Those beings of hidden places who fetter the limbs of Asar
En setau auset sau at Asar,
Who fetter souls and spirits,
Sau baiu khu,
Who block the shadows of the dead,
Khetemi her khaibit mitmitu,
Who intend evil toward me,
Ariu tut er-a,
May they not do evil to me.
An arit sen tet er-a.
May their paths turn away from me.
Asebi uatu na en.
You will open a way!
Aba-ek!

Peseg Neter—Execration

The ancient Egyptians did not view anger, grief, loss, or vengeance as strictly negative emotions. In the divine legends, the gods experienced betrayals and injustice, and at times were deprived of their beloved consorts, progeny, and even their well-being when adversarial forces altered the natural order. Such events were known to happen even in celestial realms, and the next course of action required great strength, personal trial, and sacrifice. In these cases, the gods demonstrate that the exercise of one's powerful Heka is called upon to right such errors, so that Maat may govern the world once more. One means to effecting this is the expression of the deep emotions that result from catastrophic events, and in this respect theurgy provides the time-honored vehicle.

Figure 68—Slaying Apep: Apep, the serpent of darkness, presents a continual threat to Maat and the Solar powers. In the temple, its defeat was celebrated each day with execration rites, and in the tomb the use of Heka allowed the sojourner to meet the Solar barque without hindrance.

Peseg neter ("divine curse") texts from many periods and sources in Egyptian history exist. They are found in the early Pyramid and Coffin Texts, in the temple and funerary works of the Middle and New Kingdoms, down to the Graeco-Roman and early Christian eras. In all cases the criteria are implied but never specified in detail; it is left to the practitioner to define the circumstances under which the casting of the divine curse is performed. The enemies of the nation, personal adversaries, and intangible ones—such as disease, a poor river flood, or a tormenting spirit—were all eligible for execration.

Observance

The texts are written to accompany certain actions that will allow the execration to go forth to the person or cause of the misfortune. The number four is significant, so that certain phrases are repeated, or images of the adversary are struck or smashed four times.

Typically, the consumption of sacred substance that is inherent in Egyptian magical practice plays a considerable role in the effectiveness of execration rites. Recalling that symbiosis is a primary means to bringing about balance and neutralizing overpowering forces in theurgy, the ingestion of food was employed in nearly every aspect of Egyptian ritual for equalizing volatile powers in and around the initiate. For example, in the Pyramid Texts the enigmatic "cannibal" passages speak of the divine beings encountered as the royal person ascends to the sky. Through they may prevent him from taking his celestial seat, these beings become his food; it is then transmuted into power that makes him godlike:

> *He lives on the essence of every Neter,*
> *He consumes their bodies*
> *Even those who arrive with bodies full of Heka.*
> —Pyramid Texts: Utterance #273

Set is the great divider and separator, as indicated by his forked tail in some representations. On Earth, he breaks apart that which is united and sunders the harmony in nature. In the heavens, he separates the gods from human beings and blocks the way to restoring the natural unity between them. But Egyptian theurgy does not call for such separation, as the legend of Heru and Set's extended combat relates. In order to bring peace, the gods melded into the Nubti figure, so that even the adversary could find redemption. Rites of execration assume this occurrence, as the officiant symbolically consumes the adversary and performs the mystic symbiosis.

The rite that follows has been adapted from the text of the Edfu mystery drama, in which the divine son Heru slays his father's adversary with the acclaim of the gods. In a concluding scene of the play, a cake made in the image of Set (a hippopotamus) was dissected and eaten through the recitations. After the performance of this drama in ancient times, an extensive recitation of *The Legend of the Winged Disc* was made, which recounted the supremacy of Heru and his victory over his enemies. The text includes instructions for placing a winged scarab upon the breast of Pharaoh (who assumes the role of Heru) for protection against danger; to reprise this ritual action it is suggested that the officiant of this rite likewise wear a scarab over the heart. At the conclusion of this rite, all implements should be completely removed from the sanctuary and cleaned; any remaining cake is placed in an area where it will be consumed by night animals, evoking the desert jackal of the Egyptian desert.

Other observances of this genre, such as *The Book of Overthrowing Apep*, employed red clay pots (Set's color) that were smashed during the recitations. This was a rite performed daily in the temple of Amun at Karnak to ensure the subjugation of the dark forces that prevent the light of Ra from animating the world.

In part of the royal coronation, mention was made of Pharaoh's enemies being similarly vanquished. Sandals, inscribed with Egypt's national foes on the soles, were donned by the monarch and trod upon in a ritual dance, perhaps a precursor to the saying "dancing on one's grave."

Dramatis Personae

The performance of execration should be confined to private circumstances and not employed as a ritual display. The emotional power that is focused in this rite is strictly a personal expression, as many ancient texts written by their owners reveal. Thus, the only participants should be the individual performing the rite, who impersonates Heru the avenger of his father, and a witness or recorder.

It is important for the participant to maintain a calm and authoritative demeanor. The adversary Set was known as "the raging one," and any association with malice and other destructive emotions nullifies the power of this rite.

Hekau

Heru   I have not forgotten the night of the flood, the hour of turmoil,
For this, Sekhmet-Bast brings him who was rebellious to me.
Djehuti protects me, for I have overthrown my enemy.
I am Harakhte, the triumphant one, my inheritance is mine.
(*The cake is brought to the offering table.*)
You will not exist, nor will your soul,
You will not exist, nor will your body.
You will not exist, nor will your flesh,
You will not exist, nor will your bones.
You will not exist, nor will your Heka.
You will not exist, and the place where you are will not exist.
Set is annihilated!
(*The cake is cut into *four portions and placed in offering dishes.*)
My enemy has fallen, he who was hostile to me is dismembered.
*His foreleg is consigned to Djedu for my father, Asar,
*His ribs are sent to Sekhem for Heru Ur,
*His shoulder is conveyed to Zawty for the great brother Apuat.
*His thigh is given to Khnum in Abu,
So that the followers of the gods will increase.
(*A portion of each offering is eaten.*)
His bones are given to cats, his fat to worms,
His flesh to the harpooners who desire to taste him.
Heru has overthrown his enemy,
He comes in victory, he appears in glory.
His two eyes open, they illumine the Two Lands,
The fire that emanates from him ignites his enemies.
Heru makes powerless the ones whose hearts are against him,
He makes an end of those who trespass against him.
The enemy, he is bound by the two hands of Aker,
Seba, au-ef her sau her aaui en Aker,
So that he shall not have his hands or feet,

An un aaui-ef an retui-ef

He is chained to one place

Satet ef en auset ua ma

While Ra inflicts his punishment upon him.

Hu Ra sedjebu-ef.

I have stabbed the heart of Set, the fiend has fallen,

Heseq-a an pen en Suti, sabau kher,

His name will not be among the living.

Enen ren-ef emem ankhiu.

My enemies are overthrown.

Sekher khefta-i.

Un Ra—The Opening of the Mouth

The ceremony of the Opening of the Mouth is undoubtedly the most ancient of Egyptian rituals documented, yet it is also the most obscure and enigmatic. Its performance can be traced to archaic times, as the instruments used in the observance have been found in graves from the first two dynasties.

It is known that the ceremony was performed as both an empowering and healing act, one that was intended to reanimate the vital force of its recipient and at the same time inaugurate new powers. Whether it was performed in the temple or tomb, upon a living recipient or inanimate object, its purpose was the same: reimbodiment of the vital nature into a newly formed or restored body with intact senses. The ritual was performed for living human beings, the deceased and their tombs, the images of gods, and temple buildings. We also know that it was performed to reverse illness and restore vitality to the sick, or in times of crisis. Even sacred images inscribed on the walls of temples and tombs received this ritual, in order to allow their magical functions to "come to life" and become operative. The ceremony of the Opening of the Mouth is a renewal, a rebirth, and a restoration in one event. It is an act of creation and the supreme act of reaffirming life. As such, it is a powerful observance that affects all who participate on very deep levels. And though each of the players may assume but a subsidiary role derived from Egypt's legendary tradition of embuing life by the gods to the lifeless, the forces that are invoked in the process have a commanding and personal effect on all who are present.

Figure 69—Opening of the Mouth Funerary Scene: From the Papyrus of Hunefer, Dynasty 19 (1310 B.C.E.).

Many ask why this powerful observance possesses such a curious name, and in this we must look to Egyptian culture for an explanation. On the physical level, we know that agriculture and its continuum governed the daily life of the ancients. The connotations of the Nile's rhythm, the planting and harvesting of crops, and the intrinsic bond between the land and its keepers created a unique environment. This participation of human beings with nature's renewing powers brought insights into the spiritual powers imbued in food—through the processes of growth, harvesting, ingesting, and recycling those elements back to nature and in returning the body—literally or metaphorically—back to the Earth.

Death, illness, and the quiescent period prior to birth all have the commonality of halted or undeveloped bodily functions. And so in a spiritual landscape where food represents the end result of spiritual and material powers that culminate in the sublime manifestation of nature, those functions become critical. We also cannot overlook the supreme importance the Egyptians placed on the spoken word, especially in the context of exercising Heka. Without this function, entry into the realm of the gods would be hindered. And once accomplished, absorption of divine powers could only be possible with all the functions of the spiritual body intact. Thus, the ceremony of the Opening of the Mouth fulfilled the exigencies of both mortal and immortal existence.

But in order to further explore the profound cosmological basis of this ritual act, an examination of the legendary and symbolic elements that constitute the tradition must also be examined.

The Heru Shemsu

In the sacred literature, occasional reference is made to the *Heru Shemsu* ("followers of Heru"), a group of beings associated with Egypt's Royal House and temple tradition. The name alludes to those who "follow" or succeed Heru, but whether this refers to the past or present is not expressed. The Heru Shemsu are first mentioned in the Dynasty 5 pyramid texts of Pepi I. Inscriptions show the king assuming the forms of various deities, and he is told that he has both satisfied and joined the body of his ancestors by these acts. Then, he is informed that before he ascends to celestial regions, he will be purified and receive the opening of the mouth ceremony by "the followers of Heru."

It is believed that this enigmatic fraternity was in fact a priestly caste that traced its origins to predynastic times. They instituted certain temple traditions to perpetuate the great mystery of fusing the royal Ba and Ka to create the Akh, the luminous body that would become the celestial vehicle for the ascended royal person. The mission of this caste passed into the functions of the royal priesthood, who initiated the monarch into the sacred mysteries of the throne in order to guide Egyptian society to live in Maat and assume his or her place among the gods. An elaborate cycle of ceremonies and the investiture of crowns on the assumption of the throne was performed by this body, in order to awaken in the royal person the powers of the ancient demigods.

The Heru Shemsu descended from two legendary houses, the foremost being the "souls of Pe," originating in Lower Egypt and possessing the falcon as their cultic image. They governed two sacred precincts at the ancient capital of Buto:

the *Per Nezer* (House of Fire) and the *Per Nu* (House of Water). From them, the red crown and the Wadjet cobra were bestowed on Pharaoh. The second house was the "souls of Nekhen" and was said to have originated in Upper Egypt, possessing the wolf or hound as their emblem. Their sacred precinct at Nekheb was the *Per Ur* (Exalted House), a name that is supposed to be the root of the Greek term *pharaoh*. They bestowed the white crown on the king, which was protected by the vulture Nekhebet. The members of these two houses were collectively referred to at times as the "Souls of Heliopolis" and commanded the dual shrines seen in many temples and royal estates, such as Djoser's vast *Heb Sed* complex at Saqqara. In turn, they were believed by the Egyptians to have been the body from which the Solar priests at the Heliopolis temple of the Sun descended.

The legendary authority of the Heru Shemsu extended into several areas of sacred duty. In the tomb, the ancient role was assumed by the *Sameref*, the "kinsman" or "friend." It was this priest who performed the intimate, exclusive rite of opening the mouth for the deceased, and with this fulfilled the mission of the elite body who passed on the sacred act that Heru performed for his father to restore his powers. In the temple, the Sameref's role was fulfilled by the priest who conducted the daily Opening of the Mouth ceremony for the gods, empowering the divine forces of the temple to animate the sacred space.

The powers of the Heru Shemsu were not viewed as remote forces, but as vital agents that could be spiritually accessed for transformation. They were seen to reside in the polar region of the sky, a place where the most powerful deities exist and the source of Sa for our phenomenal world is centered. But it is also the region of Set, and only the highest magic can penetrate the supreme constraints he governs there.

Akhemu Seku—The Imperishable Ones

Fundamentally, the body of Egyptian ritual may be seen as reenactments of the cosmological truths that comprised the great temple traditions of Heliopolis, Memphis, Hermopolis, and Thebes. The visible aspect of the sky was regarded as harboring two realms of powerful divine influences, embodied as stars in the *Akhemu Urtchu* ("never resting ones") that continuously revolve from east to west over the horizons, and the *Akhemu Seku* ("imperishable ones") that remain stationary at the pole.

Neter	Cosmic Station	Nome Spirit(s)
Nun	Milky Way	Wadj Wer
Naunet	Galactic Center	Mehet Weret
Huh	Dubhe (Ursa Major)	Tatenen
Hauhet	Merak (Ursa Major)	Heqet
Kuk	Phact (Ursa Major)	Mehen
Kauket	Megrez (Ursa Major)	Wadjet
Djehuti	Gemini	Aah
Maat	Aquarius	Seshat, Heret Kau
Sopdet	Sirius	Sopdu
Ra	Sun	Bakha
Khepri	Pluto	Heh
Ptah	Mercury, Vulcan	Herybakef
Sekhmet-Bast	Sagittarius	Paket
Nefertum	Arcturus	Herishef
Khnum	Saturn	Banebdjedet
Neit	Chiron	Hatmehyt, Taiyet
Heka	Bungula	Nehebukau
Atum	Solar Apex	Iusaas
Shu	Uranus	Weneg
Tefnut	Neptune	Satet
Nut	Pisces	Hesat
Geb	Virgo	Aker
Asar	Aries, Orion/Canopus	Anher
Auset	Libra/Sirius	Meskhenet, Selqit
Set	Capricorn	Ash
Nebt-Het	Cancer	Renunet
Het-Her	Taurus, Pleiades	Bat
Younger Heru	Leo/Regulus	Mont
Ihy	Mars	Aahes

Table 21—The Forty-Two Neteru, Cosmic and Terrestrial

Neter	Cosmic Station	Nome Spirit(s)
Heru Ur	Polaris	Khenty Irty
Anpu	Scorpio	Ap Uat
Sokar	Earth	Andjety
Amun	Jupiter	Kaumutef
Mut	Venus	Nekhebet
Khons	Moon	Min
Imset	Kochab (Ursa Minor)	Res Hati
Haapi	Phecda (Ursa Minor)	Kesefemtep
Daumutef	Yildun (Ursa Minor)	Imyut, Nemty
Qebsenuf	Alifa (Ursa Minor)	Baba
Taurt	Draconis	Ipy
Hapi	Aldebaran	Nepri
Apep	Ursa Major	Sobekh

Table 21—The Forty-Two Neteru, Cosmic and Terrestrial

Egyptian legend speaks of the polar region of the sky as a sacred domain, a place inhabited by cosmic powers that is concealed from the terrestrial world by the domination of Set. At the same time, it is the destination of the ascended soul, the door through which celestial life may be accessed and one may know eternal existence:

> *The sky has opened for me,*
> *I am a living one, a son of Sopdet.*
> *My house in the sky will never perish,*
> *My throne on Earth will never be plundered.*
> —Pyramid Texts: Utterance #302

Knowledge of such realms was essential, and to guide the soul toward this ideal experience the region was carefully described in sacred texts and inscriptions in sacred places. Such an example is found in the tomb of Pharaoh Seti I in the Valley of the Kings, where the polar region of the sky is depicted on the ceiling to provide the monarch with a map to divine territory.

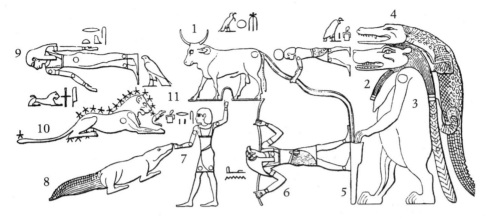

Figure 70—The Polar Region of the Sky: Ceiling of the Tomb of Seti in the Valley of the Kings, Dynasty 19.

(1) The constellation we know as the Great Bear (Ursa Major or Arktos) was associated with Set, but the symbolism of the constellation was not strictly adverse. Known as *Meshtiu* ("the bull"), in some periods it was depicted with only two bull's horns, and in others as the bull's foreleg. Ursa Major contains the Big Dipper, symbolized in Seti's ceiling by the adze upon which it stands.

(2) The hippopotamus is a form of Taurt, Neter of proliferation. Her name in this context is *Hesamut* ("fierce mother"), and the remaining stars that comprise her body are the constellation Draco. Hesamut is guardian and dispensator of Sa (the fifth element, the Quintessence), indicated by the "mooring post" upon which her hand rests.

(3) The star on her shoulder is *Thuban* (α Draconis), the polestar of Seti's epoch. This star possesses its own identity—it is associated with Hotepsekhus, the cobra goddess who is eye of Ra and who "leads" the *Djatdjat* (the four ancestral spirits) who are the first of the Heru Shemsu. They in turn are the cosmic forms of the four genii who provide the elemental forces to manifest life.

(4) The crocodile that rests upon Hesamut's shoulders is *Apep*, and contains the stars of the Little Bear (Ursa Minor), which we see as the Little Dipper. It is comprised of the four asterisms that embody the four genii:

Imset (Kochab), Haapi, (Phecda), Daumutef (Yildun), and Qebsenuf (Alifa). They are the four Djatdjat of the Divine House.

(5) *Ak* ("the eye") is the mooring post of a boat, representing Dubhe (α Ursa Major), another polestar that was sometimes depicted as the hieroglyph Sa. A cord or tether runs from this marker to (1) Meshtiu.

(6) *An* is a form of Heru the Warrior, representing *Sah,* the constellation Orion.

(7) *Meskheti* ("the harpooner") faces (8) *Hotep Redwy* ("restful of feet"), an epithet of Sobekh, shown as a large crocodile with a straight tail. Meskheti has a spear that he drives into Sobekh.

(9) *Selqit,* the scorpion goddess who is an emanation of Auset in her role as healer and banisher of poisons, stands watch over the southern constellations.

(10) *Ru Neteri* ("divine lion") is surrounded by eighteen stars and represents Leo Minor, which lies above the Zodiacal constellation Leo Major. The star at the end of his tail represents Denebola.

(11) *Sak* is a small asterism in the form of a crocodile with a bent tail next to Meskheti's head. It is known as the "plunderer" and "capturer."

As simplistic as these images may appear on the surface, they assume vital roles in the performance of the Opening of the Mouth ceremony, which is a restoration of powers that may become lost when passing through this region of the sky. Whether it is the ascension of the soul after death or through the process of a life-affirming initiation, and whether it is the descent of a divine force into the manifest world or the embodiment of a sacred place—all must face the inexorable powers that separate the cosmic realms from sentient life.

Sa Seseneb—The Mystic Embrace

From written and graphic representations, the consummation of the daily ritual in the temple shows the royal person (or the designated priestly representative of the monarch) in the role of Sameref embracing the sacred image of the god and receiving its vital force, becoming "charged" with divine power. In turn, those in the immediate environment were embraced, so that in the metaphysical sense the power obtained from the divine source was passed on to them. Some inscriptions, such as ones in the Ramesside temple of Khons at Karnak, tell of secondary images of the deity receiving this charge, to carry its power out into the world. In the instance of the princess of Bekhten, such an image was used to contravene the destructive powers of a demon.

This act, the *Sa Seseneb* ("mystic embrace"), alludes to a divine attribute, one that was initially bestowed by the demiurge Atum. When he poured Sa, his life force, into his first creations—Shu and Tefnut—the cosmic landscape came into being. Subsequent to that event, it is maintained with the indivisible energy of this substance, bringing and restoring life to its recipients. Sa, the fluid of life, was believed by the Egyptians to protect the bodies and souls of human beings, animals, the home, and temple. Protection of the body is assured through the wearing of the Sa amulet, and a house can be protected by placing Sa images in wall niches, outside the house, or buried with the amulets facing the directions from which psychic attack is expected. But its ultimate function is disclosed in certain temple inscriptions, where those regarded to be in possession of Sa (the gods, royal persons, and certain priests) could transfer it. This was accomplished by embracing another and then "making passes" with the hands placed on one's back, from the nape of the neck to the lower vertebrae. The Sa could also be received by a person from a god by taking its image in one's arms, a ceremony that was part of the temple's daily ritual and certain rites requiring healing and exorcism.

The evocation of Sa—its reception, transference, and maintenance—is the primary intention of the Opening of the Mouth ceremony. Here, the spiritual power received from this act is directed to what was regarded by the Egyptians as the highest magic and the sublime goal of all theurgy.

Observance

This ceremony is performed when the psychic fabrication of a body or vehicle for performing life-giving acts is accomplished. In temple tradition, it begins with the daily ritual, regarded as the birth of Solar forces each day at dawn. In this context, the act awakens the Neter to its new reality on Earth and endows the divine presence with the physical senses to accept the morning offering and transmute it into divine food, as well as to breathe, speak, and transfer its power to the living.

As a dedication ceremony for the temple or sacred space, it becomes the formal consecration of the building, called "handing over the house to its lord." In this instance, the chamber becomes a living entity, capable of divine embodiment when the Neter is evoked.

As a healing, the Opening of the Mouth transfers vital energy when it has been unnaturally diminished in the recipient. And as an initiation, the ritual provides awakening in a reverse manner—the initiate consciously enters the Duat (shadow worlds) and awakens to this new spiritual reality with all Earthly functions and senses restored through the ritual.

In this liturgy, reception of the Opening of the Mouth signals an event of completion as well as the beginning of a new life plan. Throughout the Solar cycle, the construction of the light body (Akh) has progressed as the Solar force, symbolized by Ra, moves over the visible sky in the constellations through the year. In this rite, the Akh's conscious embodiment by the soul becomes possible. The vital nature of the initiate enters the light body, thus merging the Ba (personal soul) and the Ka (living vitality) to fuse and create the Akh (light body).

The Opening of the Mouth must be performed at the most opportune cosmic time, at the ingress of the Sun into a new constellation, the New Moon, or a solstice, when the terrestrial force is high. Contrary to popular belief, the equinoxes are periods of balance, when there is neither high nor low flux in the psychic environment.

The ceremony begins with a formal sprinkling of water upon the recipient, followed by an elaborate censing. The first act performed is the "separation," a symbolic birthing gesture of cutting the umbilical cord with the *pesheskef.* First, the recipient is presented with the bandalet, a length of fine linen that has been tied around the brow. Inscriptions often show the mummy with the bandalet around the chest, and for consecrating space a perimeter ribbon is erected (this is undoubtedly the origin of ribbon-cutting ceremonies for inauguration of businesses). Legend places the origin of this sacred cloth at the loom of the goddess Taiyet (a form of Neit), who weaves the bandages that restore or awaken the body's powers when they are wrapped within them. After the cord is cut, the pesheskef is held to the face of the recipient to announce its independence.

Seb Ur
Ceremonial adze also known as
Meshtiu (a name of Ursa Major),
taken by Heru from Set to restore
Asar's functions.

Pesheskef
The flint birthing blade that cuts
the umbilical cord.

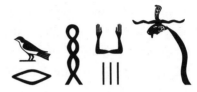

Neterui
Sceptres of iron of the North and
South that "make firm" the mouth.

Ur Hekau
"Mighty of enchantments" sceptre
that transmits Sa, the fluid of life.

Duwen-a
The ritual instrument that "opens."

Bandalet presented in the Ceremony
of the Opening of the Mouth.

Ha-tches
The first offering that brings vitality
from the four kingdoms of nature.

Figure 71—Sceptres for the Opening of the Mouth

For the healing or initiation ceremony, Sopdet now appears, and the initiate presents the petition for entering the realm of the gods. The opening of the mouth then proceeds, with the presentation of the *Duwen-a* (which opens the mouth), the *Neterui* (which makes firm the jaws), and the *Seb Ur* (which smites the face and restores the functions). Sopdet transmits vitality with the *Ur Hekau* sceptre, and the first offering from the *Ha-tches* flasks are made.

The Ha-tches represent four symbolic offerings from nature—liquid, solid, sacrificial, and living nourishments (water, bread, meat or fowl, and plants). They symbolize the endowment or the restoration of the vitality of the one receiving the ceremony. In the funerary environment, they restore the limbs, organs, and fluids of the recipient in the afterlife. In the healing service, they are the means to bringing Heka into the body of the afflicted. And for consecrated spaces or objects, the offerings provide the vitality that will empower them to become animate.

Dramatis Personae

The Sameref plays the central role in this observance, as chief of the Heru Shemsu who will open the mouth of the one who seeks life, emulating the archaic time when Heru opened the mouth of his father and restored his senses. The ancient texts speak of this officiant as the "loyal friend or kinsman" of the initiate. The role is associated with Djehuti and may be filled by the Kher Heb.

Another enigmatic figure who appears for this observance is the *Sekhen Akh* ("reviver, raiser of the Akh"). Believed to be a function of the Hem Ka,[2] this priest has an association with Heru Ur of the Initiatory Triad. Indeed, this officiant may have a connection to the mysterious *Heru Dunawy* ("he of the outstretched talons"), who appears rarely but at the coronation ceremony of kingship, as depicted in some Karnak inscriptions.

A clue to this priest's ritual duty is depicted in some New Kingdom star charts, as the falcon-headed polar deity who opposes Set (in his form as *Meshtiu*, Ursa Major). Here he is "the uplifter" and gives name to one of the mouth-opening instruments, the *duwen* ("to stretch"). In ancient times, the high priest of Letopolis was regarded as the premier "opener of the mouth" in state ceremonies. The interesting connection here is that the city was capital of the second nome of the Lower Kingdom, "the foreleg," and its highest cleric possessed the power to subdue this image in the sky—Meshtiu, "the foreleg" in the polar region.

---

2. Henri Frankfort, *Kingship and the Gods* (Chicago, Ill.: University of Chicago Press, 1978) 377.

Shemsu
Elders, ancestors, followers

Samer-ef
"His beloved son,"
the kinsman or friend

Sekhen Akh
"Raiser, reviver of the spirit"

Figure 72—Names of the Officiants

A third important figure is presented at this ceremony, primarily for initiation and healing observances. Sopdet is the all-important link between the living and celestial life, she who brings the soul to fruition and presides over births in all dimensions.

Four witnesses, who represent the Djatdjat, the original Heru Shemsu, are also present with the ceremonial instruments and offerings. Imset, Daumutef, Qebsenuf, and Haapi possess the sceptres that effect the restoration of the senses and personal power of the recipient.

Figure 73—The Libation of the Opening of the Mouth

Hekau

Sameref   I come to you, divine chiefs, mighty ones
Ia kher ten djatdjat aatu,
In heaven, in the Two Lands, and the shadow world of the sky:
Amu pet, em Taui, em Neter Khert:
I bring you one justified,
An na ten maa kheru,
That you may grant him (her) to be with you each day.
Amma un-ef (es) hena ten hru neb.

Sekhen Akh I come to you, lords of Rostau, those who follow Heru,
Ia kher ten nebu Rostau, Heru shemsu,
In the Western Land, in the Field of Offerings,
Amu Ament, em Sekhet Hetepet,
I bring you the justified one,
An na ten maa kheru,

That you may grant him (her) to be with you each day.

Amma un-ef (es) hena ten hru neb.

I. Pouring of Water

Sameref   You are pure, your Ka is pure.

Aha uab-ek, uab ka-ek,

Your soul is pure and your power is pure.

Uab ba-ek uab sekhem-ek.

You will live for millions of years.

Ankh-ek er heh en heh.

II. Censing of the Recipient

Sekhen Akh Your soul is pure among the gods.

Uab ba-ek am neteru.

You rise up

Khes khu

Your essence is in heaven, your body is on Earth.

Mu-ek er pet, khat-ek er ta.

III. The Separation

Sameref   May your soul not be restrained,

Em khena ba-ek,

May your shadow not be restrained.

Sauti khaibit-ek.

That which was separated is now restored.

Tesh pu en-ek tcheba iger.

(The Bandalet is presented and tied to the recipient's brow.)

Sekhen Akh May the way be opened for your soul and your shadow,

Un uat em ba-ek en khaibit-ek,

That you may see the great gods.

Maa-ek neteru aa.

(The Bandalet is severed.)

Recipient   I honor you, lady of radiance

Anedj hra-ek, nebet seshepet

At the head of the Great House of night and darkness.

Khenti het heret net keku samau.

Sopdet   I am the woman who lights the abyss.

Nuk hem seshep meti.

The darkness is doubly lightened,

Kekiu het sep sen,

I have overthrown those who destroy.

Sekher na ashemi.

I have compassion for those in the darkness,

Tua na amu kekiu,

I stand upright those who are prostrate,

Se aha na aakebi,

For those who are ashamed, for those who are despondent.

En amen nu her du sen, en bakai sen.

Recipient   There is no falsehood within me.

Enen isefet em khet-i.

I have come to you, I am pure,

Ina kher-ek, ab kua,

Give to me my mouth that I may speak with it.

Ta-ek na re-a djedu-a.

IV. Opening the Mouth

Sekhen Akh May your mouth be opened, may your mouth be unlocked.

Unnu er-ek wepu er-ek

May you rise in the horizon of heaven.

Weben-ek em akhet net pet.

On the high mound of Nun.

En set Nun uret.

(*Presentation of the Duwen-a.*)

Daumutef   That which was loosened is now made firm.

Sefekhi pu en-ek imem iger.

I have bound together your head and your limbs.

Khesu-ek tep at-ek.

(*Presentation of the Neterui.*)

Imset   By the iron adze possessed by Shu,

En Shu em nut-ef tui eny et bia et eny pet nety,

With which he opened the mouths of the gods,

Wep en-ef er eny neteru em-es,

Lift up your head into the horizon.

Seres-ek tep-ek er akhet.

(The smiting of the face with the Seb Ur.)

Haapi   Hail, sycamore tree of Nut:

A nehet tui ent Nut:

Grant to him (her) the water and air that are within you.

Di-ef (es) em mu nifu amet.

(The mouth is moistened with water.)

Qebsenuf   May he (she) never perish

An sek-ef (es)

And may his (her) body never see corruption.

An hetem-ef (es) en djet en djetta.

(Presentation of the first offering.)

Sopdet   May he (she) behold his (her) body,

Maa-ef (es) khat-ef (es)

May he (she) repose in his (her) glorified frame.

Hotep-ef (es) her sah-ef (es),

(Presentation of the Ur Hekau.)

Sekhen Akh You have made your transformations.

Ari na, kheperu-a.

Firstborn of Geb: you are exalted.

Sensu en Geb: Hai-ek.

Go in peace.

Khep em hotep.

If this ceremony is performed as the final consecration of the temple, the opening of the mouth inscription should be permanently placed outside the entry chamber.

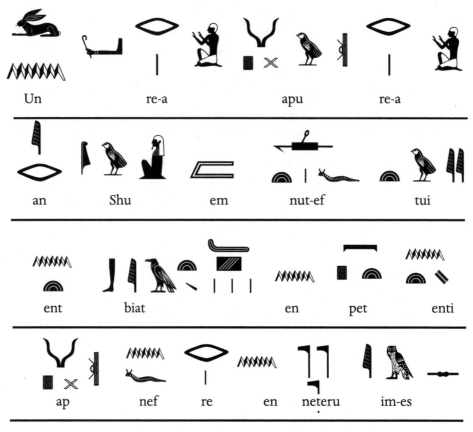

Un	re-a		apu	re-a	

an	Shu	em	nut-ef	tui	

ent	biat	en	pet	enti	

ap	nef	re	en	neteru	im-es

My mouth is opened. It is unlocked by Shu's celestial weapon of iron.
It is opened by that which opened the mouths of the gods.

Figure 74—Inscription for Opening the Mouth of the Temple

Hru Setem—Daily Practice

Many who are drawn to the enigmatic philosophy and religion of Egypt question whether a statement of belief or faith exists in these realms. Faced with a proliferation of divine images and the intricate ceremonial protocol of temple and tomb, it is difficult to discern the essential creed of ancient Egypt. Are there precepts that have prevailed through the great epochs of time and cultural expression and that state the timeless, spiritual message of the ancients?

There is a quantity of literature that articulates many of the attitudes and beliefs of Egyptian spirituality. The wisdom writings of the sages is an example of this. They present the proper conduct and disposition for the spiritual life as the ancients envisioned it. In addition, the temple inscriptions acclaim the names and powers of the Neteru, infusing the visitor with a profound inspiration of the sacred. The metaphysical concepts of the funerary texts are also enlightening, as they define the psychic terrain that is entered beyond the physical world, whether by the living or the dead.

It is in one of these sacred texts that Egypt's esoteric philosophy is profoundly expressed. It has, since its decipherment, been recognized by many scholars and theologians as a distillation of ancient spirituality. For some, it evokes an epiphany similar to the Lotus Sutra in the Buddhist scriptures or the Revelation of St. John in the New Testament. It is in part an eloquent and complete expression of the concepts that comprise Egyptian religious thought, and overall it clarifies the meaning of those concepts to the individual soul.

Observance

Chapter 17 of *The Book of Going Forth by Day* is a Middle Kingdom text whose ideas stem from the oldest religious writings of Egypt. One legend ascribes it to the writing of Djehuti himself; it is alluded to by Clement of Alexandria[3] to be one of the Hermetic books. Its literary form is unique—it is comprised of remarks made by the Sun god, statements of cosmological reality couched in the legends of the gods. Appended to these statements are commentaries that elaborate on the mysteries enumerated. Throughout, the Solar cosmology of Heliopolis dominates the passages, and the functions of the Neteru in relation to the enhancement of the individual soul are discussed.

A New Kingdom version of this text is found in elaborate form in the tomb of Tutankhamun. Inscribed on the gold leaf panels of the innermost shrine surrounding the king's sarcophagus, its close proximity to the body alludes to its importance in elevating the soul to divine regions.

The inclusion of this text in funerary works, like many spells and hymns of the genre, is not an indication of its exclusive use by the dead, but instead reflects the typically Egyptian intent to equip the soul with all the worldly wisdom that

---

3. Clement of Alexandria: A Graeco-Roman theologian (150–215 C.E.) and Christian apologist who wrote of forty-two books authored by Hermes Trismegistus, the deity regarded in his time as patron of the ancient wisdom.

has been accumulated in life for active use in the next. As such, it states at the inception—like the spells and hymns that are bound together with it—that it is intended for use by the living, to "excellently equip the soul" and become the Akh, the resplendent body of light.

In pursuit of this aim, the recitation of this chapter serves as the foundation for a daily spiritual practice. As it articulates the concepts that constitute the liturgy and ceremony of Egypt's sacred tradition, it serves as an important everyday reminder of that tradition and the reasons for practicing it. It also discloses the ultimate aim of Sacred Science—the means to acquiring divine qualities, the fusion of the Ba and the Ka, and the ascension of the individual into the realm of the gods.

Dramatis Personae

The text may be read by the individual as a morning or evening observance, when time for reflection or meditation is available. For gatherings, it may be recited by the Kher Heb or one serving as lector, while the group assumes meditative repose.

Hesi er Sahu em Pert—The Praises and Glorifications of Going Forth

It is good for one to recite this while upon the Earth, for then all the words of Atum come to pass. Here begin the praises and glorifications of coming out from and going into the shadow worlds, of going forth by day in all the forms of existence that the Ka shall undertake, and of appearing as a living soul:

Ha em setjes sekhu pert haiyt em Neter Khert khut em Amentet nefert, pert em hru em khepera neb meri-ef, pert em ba ankhi:

I, the Living One, declare upon arriving in the haven of rest:

"I am Atum in rising. I am the Only One. I came into existence in Nun. I am Ra, who rose in the beginning, the ruler of this creation."

Who speaks? It is Ra, who at the beginning rose in the city of Henensu, crowned as a king at his coronation. The Pillars of Shu were not yet created when he was upon the steps of him who dwells in Khemenu.

"I am the Great God who created himself, who made his names to become the Company of the Gods."

Who speaks? It is Ra, the creator of the names of his limbs, which came into being in the form of the gods who are in his company.

"I am he who cannot be repulsed among the gods."

Who speaks? It is Atum, the dweller in his disk, and Ra when he rises in the eastern horizon of the sky.

"I am Yesterday, I know Today."

Who speaks? Yesterday is Asar, and Today is Ra, when he shall destroy the enemies of Neberdjer, the lord to the uttermost limit. Then he shall establish as prince and ruler his son Heru.

It may also be said that Today is Ra, on the day when we commemorate the festival of the meeting of the dead Asar with his father, and when the battle of the gods was fought in which Asar, the Lord of Amentet, was the leader.

What is this? Amentet is the creation of the souls of the gods; it came into being when Asar was leader in Set-Amentet.

It may also be said that it is the Amentet that Ra has given to me; when any god comes he must rise up and fight for it.

"I know the god who dwells therein."

Who speaks? It is Asar. It may also be said that his name is Ra, and that the god who dwells in Amentet is the creative organ of Ra; thus he had union with himself.

"I am the Bennu bird that is in Iunu. I am the keeper of the Tablet of Destiny, of the things that have been made, and of the things that shall be made."

Who speaks? It is Asar. It may also be said that it is the inert body of Asar, and yet others say that it is his remains. The things that have been made and the things that shall be made become the inert body of Asar.

It may also be said that the things that have been made are Eternity, and the things that shall be made are Everlastingness, and that Eternity is the Day, and Everlastingness the Night.

"I am Menu in his coming forth, may his two plumes be set on my head for me."

Who speaks? Menu is Heru, the advocate of his father, Asar, and his coming forth means his birth. The two plumes on his head are Auset and Nebt-Het when these goddesses go forth and set themselves thereon, and when they act as his protectors, and when they provide that which his head lacks.

It may also be said that the two plumes are the two powerful uraei that are upon the head of their father Atum. Others say that the two plumes that are upon the head of Menu are his two eyes.

"I, the Living One, whose word is true, a giver of all the offerings that are made to the gods, rise up and come into his city."

What is this city? It is the horizon of my father, Atum.

"I have made an end of my shortcomings, and I have put away my faults."

What is this? It is the cutting of the navel string of the body of I, the Living One, whose word is true before all the gods, and all my faults are driven out.

What is this? It is the purification of Asar on the day of his birth.

"I am purified in my great double nest, which is in Henensu on the day of the offerings. They are for the followers of the great god who dwells therein."

What is the great double nest? The name of one nest is Millions of Years, and Great Green Sea is the name of the other. They are also known as Lake of Natron and Lake of Salt. And concerning the great god who dwells there, it is Ra himself.

"I pass over the way, I know the head of the Island of Maati."

What is this? It is Rostau, the gate to the south of Nerutef, and it is the northern gate of the Hidden Domain, the tomb of the god. And concerning the Island of Maati, it is Abedju. It is the way by which my father Atum travels when he goes forth to Sekhet Iaru. It is the source of the gods' food, those who are in their shrines.

The Djeseret Gate is the gate of the Pillars of Shu; it is the northern gate of the Duat. The Djeseret Gate is the two leaves of the door through which Atum passes when he goes forth to the eastern horizon of the sky.

"O you gods who are in the presence of Asar, grant to me your arms, for I am the god who will come into being among you."

Who are these gods? They are the drops of blood that came forth from the creative organ of Ra when he went forth to divide himself. These sprang into being as Hu and Sia. They are in the bodyguard of Ra; they accompany Atum each and every day.

"I, the Living One, whose word is truth, have restored for you the Uadjat, when it had suffered extinction on the day of the combat of the two fighters, Heru and Set."

What was this combat? It was that which took place on the day when Heru fought with Set, during which Set threw filth in the face of Heru, and Heru crushed the vitality of Set. Djehuti performed the filling of the Uadjat with his own hand.

"I remove the cloud from the sky when there is a storm with thunder and lightning therein."

What is this? This storm was the raging of Ra at the thundercloud that Set sent forth against the right eye of Ra. Djehuti removed the thundercloud from the Eye of Ra, and brought back the Eye living, healthy, sound, and without defect. It is also said that the thundercloud is caused by sickness in the Eye of Ra, which weeps for its companion Eye, the Moon; at this time Djehuti cleanses the right eye of Ra.

"I behold Ra who was born yesterday from the body of the goddess Mehuret; his strength is my strength, and my strength is his strength."

Who speaks? Mehuret is the great Celestial Water; she is the image of the eye of Ra at dawn in his daily birth. Mehuret is the Uadjat of Ra.

"I, the Living One, whose word is truth, am great among the gods who are in the following of Heru. They say that I am the prince/ess who loves his/her lord."

Who are the gods in the company of Heru? They are Imset, Haapi, Daumutef, and Qebsenuf.

"Homage to you, lords of right and truth, Djatdjat, sovereign princes who appear with Asar, who do away utterly all misdeeds and offenses, and who are in the following of the goddess Hotepsekhus: grant that I may come to you.

Destroy all the faults that are within me, as you did for the Seven Spirits who are among the followers of their lord Sepa. Anpu appointed to them their places on the day when he said to them: 'Come forth.' "

Who are the lords of right and truth? They are Djehuti and Astes, the Lords of Amentet. The Djatdjat who appear with Asar are Imset, Haapi, Daumutef, and Qebsenuf. They appear in the constellation of the Thigh, in the northern sky. They banish utterly all misdeeds and offenses, they are in the following of the goddess Hotepsekhus, they are with Sobekh and his associates who dwell in the water. The goddess Hotepsekhus is the Eye of Ra. She is the flame that accompanies Asar to burn up the souls of his enemies.

"Concerning all the faults that are in me, a giver of the offerings that are made to all the gods, whose word is truth, these are the offenses that I have committed against the Lords of Eternity since I came forth from my mother's womb."

(Meditation)

Concerning the Seven Spirits: who are Imset, Haapi, Daumutef, Qebsenuf, Maa Atef Herybakef, Kheribeqef, and Heru Khenty en Ariti, Anpu did appoint them to be protectors of the body of Asar and he set them in the holy place of Asar.

And it is said that the Seven Spirits, appointed by Anpu, were: *Nedjeh-nedjeh, Aatqetqet, Nertanef besef khenti hehf, Aqher ami unnut-ef, Desher ariti ami het anes, Ubes her per em khetkhet,* and *Maa em kereh annef em hru.*

The chief of the Djatdjat who is in Naarutef is Heru, the advocate of his father. Concerning the day when Anpu said to the Seven Spirits, "Come forth," these are the words that Ra spoke to Asar. May these same words be said to me in Amentet.

"I am the Divine Soul that dwells in the Divine Twin gods."

Who is this Divine Soul? It is Asar. When he goes into Djedu, and finds there the Soul of Ra, the one god embraces the other, and two divine souls spring into being as the Divine Twin gods.

(The Henu gesture is made.)

Pert em Hru—Going Forth by Day

The true meaning of this title, given to the collection of hymns, spells, and litanies placed with the goods of the ancient tomb, is "coming into the light." For the Egyptians, the powers of the Neteru were believed to exist within reach of the individual soul, but the conflicts of material life could most certainly obscure their conscious realization. The means to preventing this were embedded in those very hymns, spells, and litanies—and possession of them was as much a guarantee of spiritual ascension as their ritual application in temple or tomb.

However the theoretical study of Egypt's religion and philosophy may satisfy our curiosity, the profound wisdom that assured these realizations is without doubt apprehended through practical experience. In this endeavor, history can be our guide, for history is the heritage of all the living. But its interpretation is not a science; it is an art. As such, each individual has the opportunity to express that art in a manner that personal experience, knowledge, and insight allow.[4]

The understanding of ancient Egyptian spirituality has been a quest sought by many through the ages. In some instances, the experimental archeologist places herself as completely as possible in the environment of the past and attempts to live as former inhabitants did, with the tools and technology of the period. Here, one is placed in the physical setting of the place. For the living history interpreter, one demonstrates the life and environment of a historical era by adopting its language, dress, customs, and beliefs. Here, the attitudes and feelings of the culture are adopted.

Re-creating the spiritual practice of the Egyptians places us in both realms and in another place as well. Here we may go to the center of the "ineffable mysteries" of which the ancients spoke, the source of our primeval origins, and the inner temple where we may come into the light of our innate wisdom.

Recitation by Djehuti, Lord of Khmennu,
Divine Scribe: May there be joy in your temple.

Figure 75—Temple Dedication

---

4. See Appendix 4: Omm Sety, A Life Well Remembered.

Suggested Program of Temple Practice

Whether one chooses a simple, uncomplicated temple practice or an elaborate, comprehensive one, all the essential components are detailed in this volume. The following protocol is the ideal guide, though modifications may be made if one is traveling, or when several practitioners form a group. The temple practice may start with a basic plan and expand as circumstances allow.

Practitioners should remember that more than any other consideration, the celestial timing for these events should be carefully chosen and recorded. Optimum results are forthcoming if this guideline is followed.

Rites

Appendix 1

CHRONOLOGY OF ANCIENT EGYPT

Period	Date	Dynasties
Prehistoric	5500 B.C.E.	
Predynastic	5500–3100	
Archaic Period	3100–2700	I–II
Old Kingdom	2700–2180	III–VI Pyramid Age
First Intermediate Period	2180–2040	VII–X
Middle Kingdom	2040–1780	XI–XII
Second Intermediate Period	1780–1570	XIII–XVII
New Kingdom	1570–1080	XVIII–XX
Late Period	1080–332	XXI–XXXI
Ptolemaic	332–30	}
		} Graeco-Roman Period
Roman	30 B.C.E.–395 C.E.	}
Byzantine	395–641 C.E.	
Islamic	641–1300	

Egyptian chronology continues to be in dispute today. This dating scheme is the conservative estimate used by most egyptologists, but the Egyptian priest Manetho, living at the time of Ptolemy II Philadelphus, places Dynasty I much earlier, at 4777 B.C.E.

Appendix 2

PLACE NAMES OF ANCIENT EGYPT

Many of the hymns and litanies in the liturgy speak of the shrines of the Neteru, in ancient cities where their sanctuaries were maintained over the ages. These regions were profoundly connected to the divine beings by virtue of their natural landscapes, which came into being when the gods made their appearances in the beginning of time. Travelers to these places find that they still possess their spiritual character today.

Ancient City	Greek Name	Modern Location
Abedju	Abydos	El Araba el Mafuna
Abu, Qerert	Elephantine	Aswan
Bakhet	Sinai	Serabit el Khadim
Behdet	Diospolis	El Bilamun
Hebyt	Iseum	Benbeit el Hagar
Djanet	Tanis	San el Hagar
Djedet, Ba Neb Djedet	Mendes	Tel el Rub'a
Djedu, Per Asar	Busiris	Abu Sir Bana
Hebennu	Hipponon	Beni Hassan
Hebet	Hibis	Kharga Oasis

Ancient City	Greek Name	Modern Location
Henen Nesut, Henensu	Herakleopolis Magna	Beni Suef
Het Sekhem	Diospolis Parva	Hiw
Iat Uabet, Per Auset	Philae	Pilak
Iat Senmit	Abaton	Biga
Ineb Hedj, Men Nefer	Memphis	Mit Rahina
Iunyt Ta Senet	Laetopolis	Esna
Iunu	Heliopolis	Misr el Gadida (NE Cairo)
Iuny	Hermonthis	Armant
Kemet	Aegyptus	Egypt
Kem Ur	Athribis	Tell Atrib
Khemenu, Khmun, Unnu	Hermopolis Magna	El Ashmunein
Kher Aha	Heliopolis (south)	El Fustat
Kush	Nubia	Sudan
Nekheb	Eileithyaspolis	El Kab
Nekhen	Hierakonpolis	Kom el Ahmar
Nubt	Ombos	Kom Ombo
Pe, Dep, Per Wadjet	Buto	Tel el Fara'in
Per Bast, Baset	Bubastis	Tel Basta, Zagazig
Per Menu	Panopolis	Akhmim
Per Rameses	Avaris	Qantir
Punt	Eritrea	Somalia
Rostau	Memphis (west)	Giza & Saqqara necropolis
Saut	Sais	Sa el Hagar
Sekhem	Letopolis	Ausim
Shet, Shedyet	Krokodilopolis	Medinet el Faiyum
Sunu	Syene	Aswan
Ta en Terert, Iunet	Tentyris	Dendera
Teb, Djeba, Mesen	Apollonopolis Magna	Edfu
Waset	Thebes	Luxor
Zauty	Lycopolis	Asyut

Appendix 3

SPIRITUAL LOCALES

These places exist in both the natural and supernatural worlds, though the Egyptians did not necessarily distinguish between the two. The natural landscape was believed to be connected to celestial and nonmaterial realms, and access to one could lead to the other.

Aakhut   The second rhythm of creation, associated with the element Fire. In this phase, light illumines the darkness of the primeval ocean. Realm of the Memphite and Esna triads of Neteru.

Akert   A common designation for the afterlife.

Ament   The fourth rhythm of creation, associated with the element Air. It is characterized by cycles of natural phenomena. Realm of the Theban, Initiatory, and Cyclic triads.

Amentet   "Western land," the realm of Asar and Shadow World of the Earth. It could be accessed through a portal between the two hills overlooking Abydos.

Ankh Taui   "Life of the Two Lands," the geodetic center of Egypt located on the west bank of the Nile at the apex of the Delta, near Memphis.

Anrut-ef   "It never sprouts," an Osirian sanctuary at Herakleopolis and a gate in the Duat north of Rostau.

Bakhu   The eastern mountains, where the Sun rises.

Djeseret   "The holy place," the tenth gateway in the Duat.

Duat   The shadow world of the Sun, comprised of two regions: *Sekhet Hetepet* and *Sekhet Iaru*. These regions were created by Ra in the first rhythm of creation, Manu. They represent the two dimensions of Solar existence: the visible sky (day hours) and the invisible sky (night hours).

Per Ur   "Great Palace," one of the names of the Sun temple at Heliopolis.

Hesert   One of the shrines of Djehuti.

Het Ka Ptah The sanctuary of Ptah at Memphis, said by ancient travelers to house a vast temple complex and industrial center.

Kebeh Set The "sanctuary of Set," located on the island of Elephantine, close to the southern border of Egypt. One of the secret caverns of the Nile god, Hapi.

Kebeh Hor The "sanctuary of Heru," situated near Heliopolis, near the Delta's geographic apex. One of the secret caverns of the Nile god, Hapi.

Maati   The celestial region of truth, where the souls of the justified reside.

Manu   "Horizon of water," the region of creation where the gods are born and return to rest cyclically.

Mesen   A chapel behind the sanctuary at the Edfu temple, called "Chamber of the Mesen," the ancestral seat of the Heru Shemsu.

Neter Khert "Divine hidden place," and one of the shadow worlds (Sky Shadow); a realm that mirrors the celestial sphere.

Per Ab   "House of the heart," one of the shrines of Djehuti.

Rostau   The ancient necropolis of the Lower Kingdom that encompassed the plain between Giza and Memphis; also a mystical locale where Asar presides.

Sekhet Hetepet "Field of peace," which came into being in the creation phase of Manu, when Ra descended to the celestial sphere. It is associated with the quiescent aspect of life, that which is becoming, in the night hours. The *Duat* is divided into two sections. *Sekhet Hetepet* is the Lunar Shadow, containing fourteen *Aats*, or regions, arranged from south to north. Each Aat possesses characteristics of the Egyptian geography that undoubtedly correspond to the fourteen Osirian shrines of antiquity and the Lunar mirror that reflects the Solar principle in the Duat.

Sekhet Iaru "Field of reeds," which came into being in the creation phase of Manu, when Ra descended to the celestial sphere. It is associated with the sentient aspect of life, that which is conscious, in the day hours. *Sekhet Iaru* contains seven *Arits,* or divisions, and twenty-one gates, also numerically corresponding to the Lunar cycle.

Sheta "Temple of the mysteries," a name given to several places in the Osirian tradition.

Urit One of the hours in the Duat symbolized as a chamber that is entered by the Solar divinity in its passage through the night sky.

Appendix 4

OMM SETY—
A LIFE WELL REMEMBERED

Tales of reincarnation and past-life memory are rarely proven. In some instances the recollection seems fanciful and speculative; in others the information may be provocative and the details unique. One of the most convincing examples of the latter in modern times is the extraordinary life of Dorothy Eady, an Englishwoman born at the turn of the twentieth century who later became known to many as Omm Sety. Portions of her life have been documented in books and on film in recent times, describing her conscious memory of a life as a priestess in ancient Egypt, which began to awaken at the age of three following a serious fall. She told the dramatic story of how it came about candidly to many people, and made no apologies for her peculiar interest in this past life or for her remarkable affinity with a well-known monarch of the 19th Dynasty, Pharoah Sety I (c. 1320–1200 B.C.E.).

I came to know Omm Sety at a dramatic time in my own life, when I made my first pilgrimage to Egypt in 1976. I had begun a temple practice in the canon of the ancient Egyptian religion and was determined to find answers to my questions about this long-forgotten spiritual work and its meaning in the present day. Books on egyptology and arcane religions did little to satisfy my confusion about what it meant and why I was doing it. I knew the solution had to exist in Egypt.

It was there that I met Omm Sety and, with her encouragement, began my own journey of awakening, just as she had decades earlier.

Dorothy Eady's Transformation

Born January 16, 1904, in London of Irish parents, Dorothy Eady was headstrong and more than a handful to her parents as an only child. After her early childhood accident (in which the attending doctor had initially pronounced her dead), the door between her past life in ancient Egypt and her present persona fully opened, and she began to regularly dream of being in an Egyptian temple. At times, she believed that she actually visited the temple at night, in her astral body.

Eventually, she discovered that the temple in her dreams really existed, at the ancient site of Abydos in Upper Egypt. As she grew up, she sought more information about this place and just about everything Egyptian, telling her parents longingly that she "wanted to go home."

She read every book and listened to every story about Egypt, and had the good fortune to be living near the British Museum. There, she befriended and learned hieroglyphs and Egyptian history from the eminent Keeper of Egyptian and Assyrian Antiquities, Ernest A. Wallis Budge, whose prolific books on Egyptian myth and magic are still in print today.

Dorothy did these things not under the tutelage of her parents or mentors, but solely on her own, and this was to be her pattern for the rest of her life. After a sporadic education that was interrupted by the First World War, she agreed to marry an Egyptian man in 1933, admittedly so that she could go to live in the world of her dreams. The match lasted only two years because, "He was ultra modern, and I was ultra ancient," she said about the split. They had one son, whom she insisted on naming Sety. Years later, she adopted the name Omm Sety, "mother of Sety," which designated her identity thereafter.

She eagerly accepted work at Giza, assisting some of the eminent egyptologists of the day in excavating and recording the extensive cemeteries and pyramid complexes of Lower Egypt.

The Two Worlds of Omm Sety

When she went to the *Per Neter* ("divine house") at Abydos, in dream/astral state, Omm Sety did not see the temple as it was in her day. Rather, she saw it as it had been thousands of years ago, replete with braziers, incense, white-robed priests, and brilliantly colored wall reliefs, finished in gold. And in those ethereal visits to her spiritual home, she saw herself moving through the corridors and chambers, going about daily life and performing the rites of a priestess of Isis, chanting the lamentations of the goddess at the funeral of her husband, Osiris, to whom the temple was dedicated.

Ancient myth told of the horrific death of the god at the hands of his brother Set, and his mystic renewal through the magic of Isis. These solemn events were celebrated at Abydos in festivals throughout the year that commemorated his death and physical reconstitution, and these observances became the prototype for the funerary tradition of ancient Egypt that lasted for millennia.

Through her dream life and visits from spirits of this past life who came to her at night, she learned that she was Bentreshyt, a young orphan girl given to the keeping of the temple as was the custom in ancient Egypt. But the more remarkable detail about her life as the young priestess was that she had caught the eye of the visiting pharaoh, Sety I, and they had broken religious law by having a physical relationship that was discovered. Nevertheless, their bond still existed, and he paid her frequent nocturnal visits throughout her present life to prove it.

Omm Sety showed a remarkable familiarity with the period in history that Sety represented, and often referred to him by his throne name, *Men Maat Ra*, "established in the light of truth."

Abydos, Abode of Ancestors

After her first pilgrimage to Abydos in 1953, she was firmly convinced that she could never live anywhere else. A few years later, she managed to get a work transfer there from the Egyptian Antiquities Department, where she held a modest job as an assistant and draftsperson.

When she set up her house, she said that all she wanted was "to live, to work, to die, and be buried here." Indeed, she arrived in 1956 and remained there until she "became an Osiris" (an ancient Egyptian term for passing over) in 1981.

Almost as soon as she arrived, her amazing knowledge of the ancient city came forth. She accurately pointed out to egyptologists the location of the temple gardens from her past-life memory, though they had not yet been excavated. She was also instrumental in the discovery of the famous wavy wall, an enclosure around the Abydos sacred precinct that emulates the primeval ocean of Egyptian myth.

Abydos was known as *Ta Ur* ("exalted land"), a time-honored place of spiritual pilgrimage and the ideal destination for burial in ancient times. Tombs from the Predynastic period (prior to 3500 B.C.E.) down to the Christian era are found here, and important records have been discovered in the area. Not far from the great cemetery was found the important Nag Hammadi scrolls, which vie with the Dead Sea scrolls as the oldest evidence of Christianity.

Humor with Reverence

Though her recollections of her Egyptian life were profound and her knowledge of ancient history quite extensive, Omm Sety possessed a wicked sense of humor about things both ancient and modern.

About sixty miles south of Abydos is Dendera (the ancient Tentyris), site of the ancient temple of the goddess Hathor. The existing temple, though a prodigious example of the Divine House of ancient times, was rebuilt in the Graeco-Roman period (approximately 300 B.C.E. to 300 C.E.), nearly 1,500 years after Sety's temple at Abydos. Omm Sety believed, as do many others scholars, that the reliefs at Dendera depict a corrupt canon of artistic representation in temple art, an inferior reflection of the flawless sacred art of former times.

And though she liked the Dendera temple's spiritual atmosphere and loved the mystic chapels on the roof that show the mutilation and resurrection of Osiris, she poked fun at the reliefs of the corpulent priests carrying the goddess' shrine up to the roof chapels. "You can almost hear them panting," she joked.

Sacred Cats

Omm Sety loved her cats, and we shared stories about our feline friends. I told her that my cat at home ate the food offerings from my temple altar, which I thought might be highly improper for spiritual work. But she was indulgent. "It doesn't matter," she said. "After all, they are sacred, too."

Her cats seem to have shared her propensity for seeing the ancient spirits that interrupted her daily life. She once had a ginger-colored male named Horemheb who liked to ride on her shoulder, and she reported an intriguing incident about this cat, who often accompanied her to the temple. "One day," she related, "he went into the chapel of Sety and let out a loud shriek. He came running out with his tail and his back puffed up."

Abruptly, she added, Horemheb then went back into the chapel and Omm Sety followed. "It was a vision of Sety that gave him the fright," she said matter-of-factly. The encounter with her soulmate was evidently a surprise to the cat, but commonplace to her.

Her last and most favored cat was named for the goddess of domestic felicity, Bastet. She had a batch of kittens on Omm Sety's bed in the spring of 1981, and they had just opened their eyes in the days before she passed over.

Rameses the Great

Omm Sety's memory of one of the great figures in ancient Egypt was quite personal. Her past-life lover's son, Rameses II, was one of the most prodigious (and prolific) monarchs of ancient times, leaving thousands of monumental works and a multitude of children (111 sons and 69 daughters are recorded in temples and tombs throughout Egypt). And though he is known in history as "the Great," his ubiquitous appearance at most of the sacred sites in Egypt has also earned him the name of "the Inevitable."

"He's a much maligned young man," she said of Sety's famous son, speaking simultaneously in her past and present personas. "But I can never think of Rameses except as a teenager. And yet when he died he was a very old man. I think he was about ninety."

She remembered young Rameses racing through the halls of his father's temple, where she served as a priestess. In the life of Bentreshyt, she would only have known Rameses to be around her age at the time. She died in her Egyptian life as a young woman, and could not have seen him in old age. Her reminiscences of him reflected that.

"Even now when I go to the temple, I can always see young Rameses coming in, rushing through the corridor—a very restless boy and rather noisy," she confided.

A Life Well Remembered

When I last saw her in March 1981, Omm Sety spoke of her difficult visit to the temple on December 8, occasioned by an ancient festival that she observed annually. It was celebrated by the Egyptians on the last ten days of their calendar year as "the great feast of Osiris," and offerings were presented at the temples and the thousands of funerary shrines in the region.

In the final year of her life, Omm Sety struggled with chronic rheumatism brought on by a broken leg, and visits to her beloved temple were severely curtailed. Nevertheless, she was determined to continue her priestess duties, and brought the traditional offering of a loaf of bread, wine, and incense to the Divine

House, though it took her two hours to make the journey. In doing so, abundance for the coming year would be ensured by the offering, as the gods would be honored and the temple's spirit would continue to function.

"Magic in ancient Egypt was a science," she noted. "It was really magic, and it worked."

I found it both strange and admirable that she contributed so much to the scholarly side of Egypt and at the same time maintained a psychospiritual connection with it, too. If anyone could walk between those two worlds, it was her. I related to that, and she certainly encouraged me to follow along those lines.

As incredible as her story may sound in its telling, those who knew her—from scholars and tourists to townspeople—regarded her with respect and affirmation. Even while she was living, she was called the "patron saint of egyptology," because of her knowledge—derived from both her practical experience living and working in Egypt—and her personal reservoir of recollection and intuition. Few separated those aspects of Omm Sety from their acquaintance with her, and even fewer questioned the validity of her beliefs because they were expressed so convincingly. It took a great deal of courage—rarely found in a woman at the early part of the twentieth century—to pursue her unfinished life at Abydos and fulfill her dedication to the temple.

After she passed away, I received a message from Bill Donovan, of the American Research Center in Egypt, an institution that had many members who worked with Omm Sety. "Ms. Eady was truly a remarkable person and she is highly respected by those in the ARCE who knew her," he commented. Afterward, many egyptologists acknowledged that her contribution to the research and writings of many in their profession was extensive.

The most accurate monument to Omm Sety's unique life is the manner in which she lived it. Ancient records left by the Egyptians show that they lived close to nature, regarding their animals and divinities with equal affection, and celebrating the simple pleasures—from enjoying freshly brewed beer to sailing on the Nile—with delight and appreciation. These things she did in this life, and she spoke of doing the very same things in the life she recalled.

For these reasons, Omm Sety accomplished something extraordinary and unique—she lived a life well remembered twice, both in the ancient and modern worlds.

—*Originally published in* FATE *magazine, January 2001.*

BIBLIOGRAPHY

I. The Legacy of Ancient Egypt

Allen, James P. *Middle Egyptian: An Introduction to the Language and Culture of Hieroglyphs*. Cambridge: Cambridge University Press, 2000.

Breasted, James Henry. *Ancient Records of Egypt (Vol. I: The First Through the Seventeenth Dynasties)*. Introduction by Peter A. Piccione. 1906. Reprint, Champaign, Ill.: University of Illinois Press, 2001.

II. Sacred Architecture

Legon, John A. "The Cubit and the Egyptian Canon of Art." *Discussions in Egyptology* 35 (1996): 61–76.

Lepsius, Richard. *The Ancient Egyptian Cubit and Its Subdivision*. Translated by J. Degreef. London: Museum Bookshop Publications, 2000.

Quirke, Stephen, et al. *The Temple in Ancient Egypt*. London: British Museum Press, 1997.

Reymond, E. A. E. *The Mythical Origin of the Egyptian Temple*. Manchester: Manchester University Press, 1969.

St. John, Michael. *Three Cubits Compared.* London: Museum Bookshop, Ltd., 2000.

Shafer, Byron E., et al. *Temples of Ancient Egypt.* Ithaca, N.Y.: Cornell University Press, 1997.

Watterson, Barbara. *The House of Horus at Edfu: Ritual in an Ancient Egyptian Temple.* Stroud, Gloucestershire: Tempus, 1998.

Weigall, Arthur. *A Guide to the Antiquities of Egypt.* 1906. Reprint, London: Bracken Books, 1996.

Wilkinson, Richard H. *The Complete Temples of Ancient Egypt.* London: Thames & Hudson, 2000.

III. Cosmic Resonance

Brady, Bernadette. *Brady's Book of Fixed Stars.* York Beach, Maine: Samuel Weiser, 1998.

Fagan, Cyril. *Astrological Origins.* St. Paul, Minn.: Llewellyn Publications, 1973.

———. *Zodiacs Old and New.* St. Paul, Minn.: Llewellyn Publications, 1950.

Lindsay, Jack. *Origins of Astrology.* New York: Barnes & Noble, 1972.

Lockyer, Sir Norman. *The Dawn of Astronomy.* Cambridge, Mass.: MIT Press, 1973.

Neugebauer, Otto, and Richard Parker. *Egyptian Astronomical Texts.* Vols. I, II, and III. Providence, R.I. and London: Brown University Press, 1960.

Parker, Richard A. *The Calendars of Ancient Egypt.* Chicago, Ill.: University of Chicago Press, 1950.

IV. Theurgy

Bell, Catherine. *Ritual: Perspectives and Dimensions.* New York: Oxford University Press, 1997.

Boylan, Patrick. *Thoth: The Hermes of Egypt.* Oxford: Oxford University Press, 1922.

Budge, E. A. Wallis. *From Fetish to God in Ancient Egypt*. New York: Dover, 1988.

Wilkinson, Richard H. *Reading Egyptian Art*. London: Thames & Hudson, 1992.

V. Liturgy

Allen, Thomas George. *The Book of the Dead or Going Forth by Day*. Chicago, Ill.: The Oriental Institute of the University of Chicago, 1974.

Budge, E. A. Wallis. *The Liturgy of Funerary Offerings*. London: Kegan Paul, Trench, Trubner & Co., Ltd., 1909.

Faulkner, Raymond O. *The Ancient Egyptian Coffin Texts*. Warminster, United Kingdom: Aris & Phillips, Vol I: 1994; Vol II: 1994; Vol III: 1996.

———. *The Ancient Egyptian Pyramid Texts*. New York: Oxford University Press (Special Edition for Sandpiper Books), 1998.

Piankoff, Alexandre, and N. Rambova, eds. *The Litany of Re*. Bollingen Series XL-4, Bollingen Foundation, New York. New York: Pantheon Books, 1964.

———. *Mythological Papyri*. Bollingen Series XL-3, Bollingen Foundation, New York. New York: Pantheon Books, 1957.

———. *The Pyramid of Unas*. Bollingen Series XL-5, Bollingen Foundation, New York. Princeton N.J.: Princeton University Press, 1968.

———. *The Shrines of Tutankhamun*. Bollingen Series XL-2, Bollingen Foundation, New York. Princeton N.J.: Princeton University Press, 1955.

———. *The Tomb of Rameses VI*. Bollingen Series XL-1, Bollingen Foundation, New York. Princeton, N.J.: Princeton University Press, 1954.

VI. Ceremony

Blackman, A. M., and H. W. Fairman. "The Significance of the Ceremony Hwt Bhsw in the Temple of Horus at Edfu." Part 1, *Journal of Egyptian Archaeology* 35 (1949): 98–112; Part 2, *JEA* 36 (1950): 63–81.

Faulkner, R. O. "An Ancient Egypt 'Book of Hours.'" *Journal of Egyptian Archaeology* 40 (1954): 34–39.

376 Bibliography

Smith, Mark. *The Liturgy of Opening the Mouth for Breathing.* Oxford: Griffith Institute, Ashmolean Museum, 1993.

Teeter, Emily. *The Presentation of Maat: Ritual and Legitimacy in Ancient Egypt.* Chicago, Ill.: The Oriental Institute, 1997.

Wilson, Epiphanius. *Egyptian Literature.* New York: The Co-Operative Publication Society, 1901.

VII. Transformation

Budge, E. A. Wallis. *The Book of Opening the Mouth.* New York: Benjamin Blom, Inc., 1972.

Roth, Ann Macy. "The *Pss-kf* and the 'Opening of the Mouth' Ceremony: A Ritual of Birth and Rebirth." *Journal of Egyptian Archaeology* 78 (1992): 113–147.

Smith, Mark. "An Abbreviated Version of the Book of Opening the Mouth for Breathing." Part 1, *Enchoria* 15 (1987): 61–91; Part 2, *Enchoria* 16 (1988): 55–76.

INDEX